CANNABIS

Jonathon Green

THUNDER'S
MOUTH
PRESS

CONTENTS

AUTHOR PREFACE

Cannabis. What a powerful trisyllable it is to be sure. All that rage, all that terror, all that proselytizing and adulation. All those prison sentences. All that hot air – from both sides of the debate. All for a weed, one of nature's earliest recorded species, which has made its home across the world.

The demonization of cannabis is as much a matter of luck, and timing, as anything more intrinsic. Its coevals alcohol and nicotine – both bearing their own drawbacks – remain legal (even if those who would deny adults the choice of their own lifestyles, injurious or otherwise, campaign hard against them). For several reasons, many of them outright racist, cannabis drew the short straw. But losing one more variety of personal recreation is of secondary importance. Until 1937 when America instituted its prohibition, cannabis was among the most widely used, and unarguably proven medicines in the Western pharmacopoeia. To outlaw so efficacious a treatment was, there is no milder word, a sin.

I smoked my first joint in 1966. I am still smoking, though less now, and in a pipe rather than mixed with tobacco. I prefer, as I have always done, hashish to marijuana. Contrary to the scare propaganda which alleges these problems, I have found cannabis neither anti-motivational, destructive of relationships, nor injurious to my memory. I have written or compiled fifty-plus books, lived with one partner for more than 25 years and I write dictionaries, a task that is particularly demanding of what one might term the 'mental filing cabinet'.

Irrespective of laws and of pieties, the contemporary reality is that cannabis is as popular and as widely used a recreational drug as ever. That situation is unlikely to change. Politicians, whose priorities are rarely those of the electorate, will fiddle. Cannabis smokers, to use the slang, will burn.

Important notice

The author and publisher cannot be held responsible for any activity which breaks the law. Any information given in this book is not intended to be taken as a replacement for medical advice. Any person with a condition requiring medical attention should consult a qualified medical practitioner.

The source of so much controversy: a cannabis joint smoulders in the smoker's mouth.

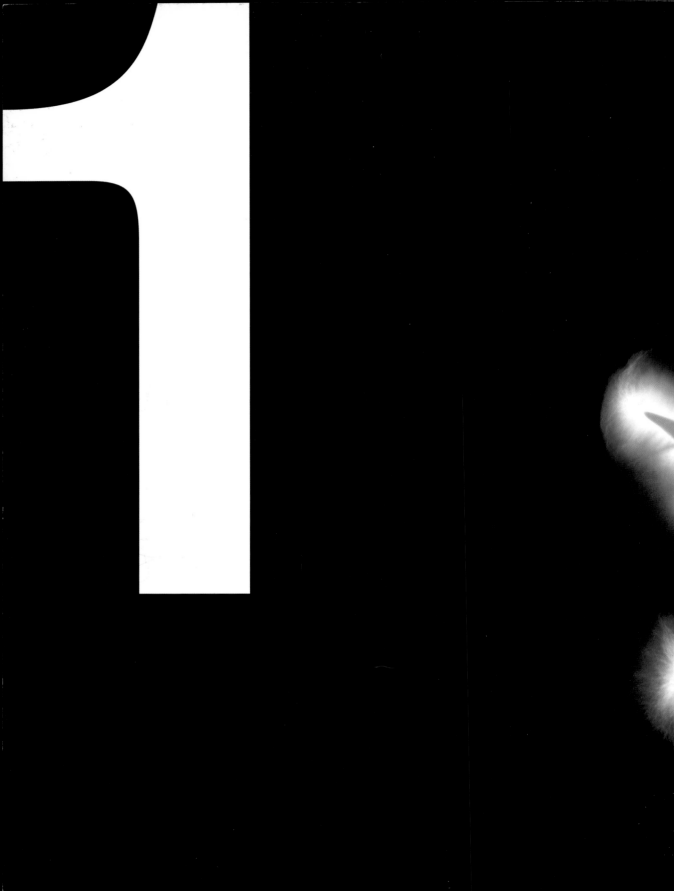

*The first plants were to be found in Asia...cannabis (used to make rope and textiles, as an intoxicant and a foodstuff) is one of the world's oldest cultivated plants...the plant spreads throughout Asia and on to Europe...*Cannabis sativa *is classified in 1753...a second species* Cannabis indica *in 1785...a third,* Cannabis ruderalis, *in 1924...a description of the plant...etymology of the name...industrial uses of hemp...cannabis as intoxicant...cannabis chemicals and their effects...*

WHAT IS CANNABIS?

Cannabis sativa (Latin for 'cultivated hemp') is one of humanity's oldest cultivated plants. Although it is known for its use in textiles and as an intoxicant, it may well have been originally planted as a foodstuff. It is related to both the nettle and the hop, and grows readily in warm and mild climates. A native of Asia, it originally grew in the temperate area that extends from the Caucasus Mountains and Caspian Sea to Eastern Asia. The oldest evidence of its existence is 6000 years old: pieces of coarse hempen cloth found at some of the earliest sites of human habitation. Other early evidence includes 3000–4000-year-old specimens found in Egypt and fabrics dug up near Ankara in Turkey dating to the eighth century BC.

Origins and species

The exact place of origin of the first cannabis plants remains unproven. Three main theories exist, attributing its emergence to China, Central Asia and South Asia. All have their proponents and all their strong possibilities. China has a plausible claim to be the site of both the earliest evidence of cannabis fibre use (rope and cloth) and the earliest written records of the plant, whether as fibre or food and, somewhat later, as a medicine or an intoxicant. The claim of Central Asia lies undoubtedly in its geographical location: ideal for the known spread of the plant, whether to China, India or Europe. Those who initiated that spread were probably the Aryans, whose invasions touched India and Persia (today's Iran). South Asia, primarily the valleys of northern India and Nepal, has also been cited, with much

The weed: cannabis is one of the world's oldest cultivated plants.

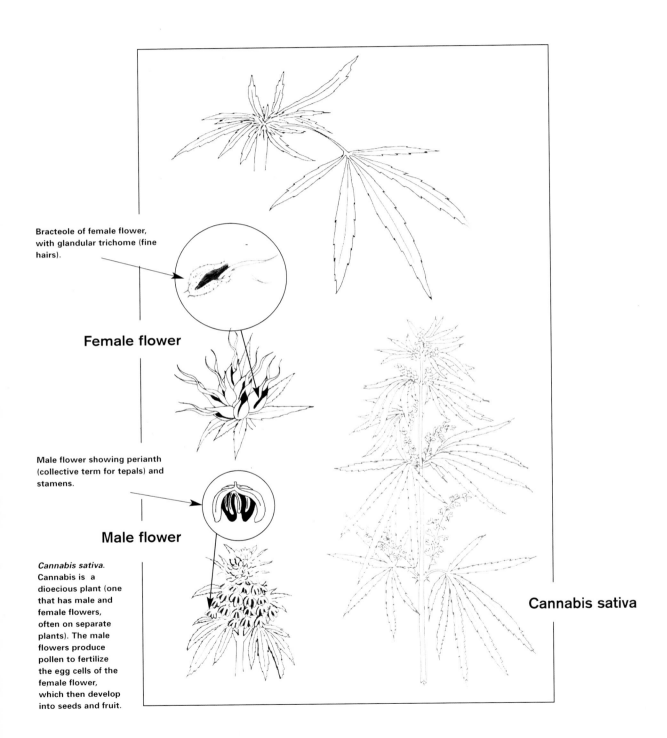

Bracteole of female flower, with glandular trichome (fine hairs).

Female flower

Male flower showing perianth (collective term for tepals) and stamens.

Male flower

Cannabis sativa. Cannabis is a dioecious plant (one that has male and female flowers, often on separate plants). The male flowers produce pollen to fertilize the egg cells of the female flower, which then develop into seeds and fruit.

Cannabis sativa

emphasis being laid on the plant's 'phenotypic diversity' – the range of differences within a single genotype or species. Such differences would typically develop over a lengthy period of cultivation. In the end, however, there is no definitive proof. Cannabis is so early a plant, that its first existence simply defies research. The author of *Hashish!*, Robert Connell Clarke, is surely right: 'Prehistoric dispersal has obscured the geographical origin of Cannabis and the exact geographical origin may never be determined. It is certain that Cannabis originated in either Central Asia or India…and that it was first cultivated in China…Central Asia may not be the origin in certainty but, at this writing, available data does not suggest persuasively any other possible origin.'

When the pioneering Swedish botanist Carolus Linnaeus (1707–1778), who set its origin in the foothills of the Himalayas in northern India (his sample, however, was grown on his own windowsill), classified *Cannabis* in 1753, he named it *Cannabis sativa* and categorized it as a monotypic species (that is, the sole specimen of its genus or group). Since then this opinion has been much debated. In 1785, the French biologist Jean Baptiste de Lamarck (1744–1825) posited and named a second species found in the East Indies: *Cannabis indica*. A third, *Cannabis ruderalis*, was named in 1924 by the Russian botanist D. E. Janischevsky, who suggested that it was peculiar to south-east Russia. At one stage, around 1930, a group of Russian students claimed that there were as many as twelve varieties. This multiplicity was rejected, as were other supposedly 'new' species, all of which would be found to be no more than spin-offs from the primary *Cannabis* genus, but the generally accepted line today is that cannabis falls into three distinct species: *C. sativa, C. indica,* and *C. ruderalis*.

The Cannabis family

Cannabis sativa is very tall, loosely branched, and the branches are remotely positioned from one another. *Cannabis indica* is low-growing and densely branched, with more compact branches and a tendency to be more conical or pyramidal in appearance. The least known is *C. ruderalis*, which is small and only slightly branched. Of the three species, *C. indica* possesses the highest 'cannabilic' content and is thus the choice of those who wish to use it as an intoxicating drug.

Cannabis is what is known as a dioecious plant, that is one that has male and female flowers, often on separate plants. The male flowers produce pollen to fertilize the egg cells of the female flower, which then develop into seeds and fruit. Harvesting takes place in two periods: the male plants are pulled in late summer, the females a little later, when their seeds have had time to ripen. Plants vary enormously in height – ranging from less than 30cm (one foot), to 75cm (30in) or so – and they can mature in anything from two to more than ten months. They are usually wind-pollinated, although bees can be attracted to the male flowers and help to deliver pollen to nearby female plants. Male plants die soon after the release of their pollen; female ones, when grown outdoors, die when the weather grows cold, although those grown indoors can last for years.

Etymology of the name cannabis

The *Oxford English Dictionary* describes the origins of the English word cannabis as coming directly from Greek *kannabis* and thence Latin *cannabis*, both of which mean hemp.

> Cannabis: 1. Common hemp, *Cannabis sativa*, a tall erect herb of the family Moraceæ having long dentate leaves on long petioles and common in central Asia and other warm regions; different regional varieties, occas. distinguished as *Cannabis americana*, *Cannabis indica* (Indian hemp), etc., are cultivated for their fibre, their intoxicating properties, or the oil obtained from their seeds....2. (Orig. *ellipt.* for *Cannabis sativa* or (esp.) *indica*.) Any of various preparations of different parts of the hemp-plant which are smoked, chewed, or drunk for their intoxicating or hallucinogenic properties and were formerly used medicinally; bhang (marijuana), ganja, and charas (hashish) are different forms of these preparations and there are many other names. (The *Oxford English Dictionary*)

But the long relationship between the plant and people, whether as one of the oldest of all cultivated crops or as an intoxicant, suggests that its linguistic roots lie a good deal further back. Indeed, as will be seen, in neither of the great classical empires did cannabis play a major role. For the word's real origins, it is necessary to look back, and look East.

In China the records of hemp date back to 2700BC, when its name was *ma*; a name that had been modified by AD1000 as *ta ma*: 'great hemp'. This is indeed old, but better linguistic clues can be found amongst the Indo-European and Semitic languages, which are found in Europe and the Middle East, where the Sanskrit roots 'an' and 'ang' recur in a variety of cannabis terms. Thus one finds Sanskrit itself has *canna*, Greek and Latin *kannabis* and *cannabis*, Persian *kanab* and Russian *konopyla* or *konop*, Gaelic *cainb*, Irish *cnáib* and Middle Breton *canap*. Linguists add that in the notional prehistoric German language, Teutonic, there are the roots *khanipiz* or *khanapiz*, and from these come the terms that link to hemp – seemingly quite different, in fact from just the same Sanskrit origin. These include Anglo-Saxon *henep*, German *henf*, Scandinavian *hamp*, Dutch *hennep*, Swedish *hampa*, Danish *hamp* and English hemp.

Back in the East one sees the 'an' root emerging in both *ganja* (from Hindi *ganjha*) and *bhang*, the name for the plant as an intoxicant in Urdu (among other Indian languages'); similarly, it appears in the Persian equivalent *bang* and Arabic *banj* and *benj*. The Portuguese, the first colonizers to reach

'Sorting and drying hemp', an aquatint by John Augustus Atkinson (1775–1831). From Volume III of *The Manners, Customs and Amusements of the Russians* (1804).

India, translated this new drug as *bangue*. (While *bhang* was generally seen as coming from Sanskrit *bhanga* 'breaking', the explorer and Orientalist Sir Richard Burton preferred the Coptic *nibanj*, a preparation of hemp. Of this, *Hobson-Jobson*, the great dictionary of the Raj, notes: 'here it is easy to recognize the Homeric *Nepenthe*' – the drug of forgetfulness; this may be so, although the *OED* opts for *ne-penthos*, 'no grief'). Despite such consistency, however, neither of the most commonly used names for the two varieties of cannabis as a drug, hashish and marijuana, seem to have these origins. Hashish is Arabic, meaning dry herb or hay, and refers to the dried resin from which it is made; marijuana is more problematic: the popular root is the jocular use of the name 'Mary Jane'; other suggestions veer between the Mexican *mariguano* or Panamanian *managuango*, both meaning intoxicant. It should be noted that here again, one can see the 'an'/'ang' root.

One last point, linking the two uses of the plant: the word 'canvas', as in sails, comes from Latin *canavasium*, 'made of cannabis' or hemp. Thus the 'official' nomenclature. For the hundreds of synonyms now ensconced in more than a century's slang, turn to the glossary on pages 234–239.

Industrial uses of hemp

Common hemp is a versatile material: the plant's trunk produces durable fibres that can be used for making rope or twine and can also be woven into cloth – both fine and rough – for making textiles from blankets, clothes and flags to boat sails. Hemp is also an unrivalled source of cellulose pulp, used for paper production and, occasionally, for money. Its seeds are rich in oil (similar to linseed oil), which is used to make paint and soap; its seeds have also been used as food, whether for humans or, more commonly, for wild birds and domestic fowl. Seedlings and seed cake are used for fish bait in a number of countries. People have planted hemp to help to control soil drift and to act as windbreak fences. Perhaps the most surprising of hemp's uses, albeit a short-lived one, was in the car body manufactured by Henry Ford from hemp-based plastic in 1941. The plastic was much lighter than steel and could withstand ten times the impact without denting. (A contemporary film shows Ford attacking it with an iron bar.) The car was even fuelled by clean-burning hemp-based ethanol fuel. Unfortunately the ban on hemp (a by-product of the 1937 Marijuana Tax Act) put an end to the project, although efforts to recreate and mass-produce such vehicles were made in 2001.

Far left: A Filipino Muslim carries Manila hemp fibres or 'abaca' for export at a warehouse in Jolo, Sulu in the southern Philippines. Abaca plants, which thrive in Sulu province, are used to make baskets, cordage, fabric and paper. It is a major source of livelihood on the island.

Overleaf: Russian peasant women harvest a legal crop of hemp, to be used for textiles and paper, 1956.

Cannabis – the intoxicant

How did the first users of cannabis discover that it was more than just a food or a source of fibre? There were no pipes, let alone 'joints' or 'blunts'. It would appear, if we agree with Robert Connell Clarke, that Neolithic man, or, more likely woman – given the possible gender divisions in hunter-gatherer tribes, found out by accident. Either, as Clarke suggests, while gathering the plants she might have accumulated the leaf-borne resin that is the basis of hand-rolled hashish – and at some time she might have licked it; or those who were already eating the plant's bracteoles (small leaves or scales growing just below the flower bud's protective tepals – see illustration on page 12) might have swallowed resin and seeds as well; or perhaps people simply gulped down whole floral clusters, without bothering to separate the seeds. Alternatively, people may have thrown the accumulated sticky resin into the fire, and then breathed in the smoke. However it happened, what matters is that intoxication ensued and was then pursued.

Cannabis as an intoxicant appears in two forms: herbal cannabis or marijuana and cannabis resin or hashish. Marijuana (slang 'grass') consists of the dried leaves and female flower heads (and sometimes small twigs). Hashish (slang 'hash') comes in the form of blocks of compressed resin, itself taken from the leaves and flower heads. Hashish, in turn, can be either hand-rolled (known typically as India's charas) or sieved (as in the best of Afghanistan hashish). The rule of thumb was once that hashish was a more potent drug than marijuana but with the advent of new varieties of marijuana, typically that grown under artificial light – such as the hydroponically cultivated 'superskunk' – that is no longer the case. If anything, the 'new' varieties of marijuana are stronger. The difference lies more in effect: hashish tends to sedate the mind, while marijuana expands it. But all this is inevitable generalization.

What kind of drug is cannabis?

As a drug *qua* drug, cannabis, if the research and allied literature and pontifications whether pro or con are to be believed, is all drugs and none of them – it stands all by itself. According to Canada's 'LeDain Commission Report' (1972) 'Cannabis has been compared to, and apparently has characteristics in common with, a wide variety of drugs including alcohol, LSD and mescaline, nitrous oxide, amphetamines, atropine, opiate

narcotics, barbiturates and the minor and major tranquilizers. Under various conditions and doses cannabis has been shown to have stimulant, sedative, analgesic and psychedelic effects. Some argue that marijuana should be classified as a sedative-hypnotic-general anesthetic like alcohol and nitrous oxide; others feel that it is a mixed stimulant-depressant; still others describe it as a mild hallucinogen especially at higher doses; many feel it should be listed in a separate category. Paradoxically, cannabis has been shown to potentiate both the stimulant effects of amphetamines and the sedative effects of barbiturates in animals. Legally, cannabis has traditionally been classified with the opiate narcotics, and while they may share some euphorogenic and analgesic properties, they are otherwise quite distinct pharmacologically.' Are there any descriptions left? And yet cannabis remains of itself, by itself.

'Toking down' on Yasgur's farm: a hippie smokes cannabis at the Woodstock Festival of 1969, held in US dairy farmer Max Yasgur's fields. Half a million 'freaks' enjoyed the three-day rock festival, featuring a roster of Sixties' superstars.

To quote once more, this time from the 1971 US report 'Marihuana and Health': 'Pharmacologically speaking, cannabis is unique and distinct from the psychotomimetics, opiates, barbiturates and amphetamines.' In the end, as LeDain, notes, it's all down to context or as the gurus of psychedelia and such hallucinogens as LSD would put it, 'set and setting'. Or, to put it another way, it ain't just what you do, it's the how, where and when that you do it. The late Allen Ginsberg (1926–1997), beat poet supreme and foremost among such gurus, has suggested that if cannabis makes one paranoid, then it is the knowledge of the prohibitory laws against it, not the nature of the drug that is responsible (see Chapter four, which outlines the history of cannabis legislation, pages 132–171).

Others have cited the drug as 'the great yea-sayer': whatever is happening when you are stoned – good or bad, ecstatic or terrifying – that is how you will feel. It is, says another pundit, no more than one more trigger: being high can just as well be brought about by meditation or even breathing exercises; if this is so, it is, says botanist Andrew Weil, no more than an 'active placebo'. And Michael Pollan, in his book *The Botany of Desire*, has noted how he found smoking cannabis in America, under the threat of the endless 'war on drugs', a far less enjoyable experience than in Amsterdam, where the pointlessness of such hysteria has long since been recognized.

Cannabis chemicals

Leaving the gurus and their undoubtedly valid point aside, the cannabis 'high' does have a pharmacological basis. Irrespective of its drug peers, or lack of them, what matters about cannabis as an intoxicant is what makes the user intoxicated, more commonly 'high' or 'stoned'. Cannabis contains a 'family' of unique carbon alkaloid chemicals, found only in the cannabis plant and known as cannabinoids.

Cannabinoids are primarily produced on the surface of the plant by small glands which are most plentiful on the flowers. Larger leaves and the surface of the stalk may contain lesser, though still substantial, quantities. They are produced in minute amounts in other parts of the plant – even the stems – and seeds may also contain small quantities of these active ingredients. If plants are grown under the right conditions, and especially in certain varieties, virtually the whole plant contains cannabinoids. That said, the real strength lies in the flowering tops. Whether male or female flowers produce more potent cannabinoids remains debatable. For many years, male flowers were considered psychotropically irrelevant but more recent experiments tend to negate such findings. On the whole, the results vary as to the strain under analysis, but it would seem that female flowers do still have the edge.

There are more than sixty cannabinoids in all. The most important, and the one that is generally responsible for the major psychological, behavioural and physiological effects, in other words the one that gets you 'high', is delta-9-tetrahydrocannabinol (THC). There are others but that's the one that counts. The levels of THC vary from plant to plant (the average THC content of resin is 2–10 per cent, whereas the average THC content of herbal marijuana is 1–5 per cent by weight) and, as the propagation of modern strains of ultra-strong cannabis makes clear, can be adjusted by breeding.

The 'bliss receptor'

In 1988 the study of cannabis, and particularly that of cannabinoids, the psychotropically 'active' part of the plant, moved dramatically forward. For the first time scientists established that there existed receptors – distinct units on a neurone (nerve cell) or other tissue that specifically recognize and respond to a chemical signal (be it from a neurotransmitter, hormone or other substance) that responds to cannabinoid stimulation.

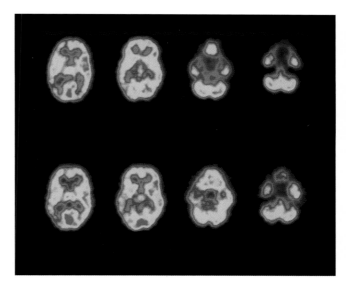

The first discovered receptor, CB-1, exists mainly within the central nervous system – the brain and spinal cord – where it is abundant, occurring in those areas that deal with body movement, coordination, learning and memory. These receptors also occur, to a much lesser extent in other body tissues. In 1992 the Israeli Dr Raphael Mechoulam made a further discovery: that the human body produces its own version of a cannabinoid – known as an endocannabinoid – that is clinically similar to those found in the cannabis plant. He named this chemical anandamide, after the Sanskrit word *ananda* meaning 'bliss'. Scientists have found high concentrations of anandamide in areas of the brain that deal with pain.

A year later the discovery of a second receptor – CB-2 – was announced. This receptor, it seems, is more widespread than CB-1; rather than being restricted to the central nervous system, CB-2 receptors are distributed all around the body. From this information, it now appeared that the human body possesses a complex network of cannabinoid receptors, which can be

Coloured PET scans of the brains of a marijuana user (bottom) and a non marijuana user (top), showing different levels of activity. The front of the brain is uppermost in these scans, which show progressively deeper slices from left to right. The active agent of cannabis, the psychoactive drug tetrahydro-cannabinol (THC), reduces brain activity in the cerebellum (lower parts of the four scans on the right). In the normal cerebellum red areas of high activity are seen, absent in the cannabis user. This absence causes a lack of coordination and poor spatial judgement.

activated by a chemical the body produces itself – anandamide. And it is this 'bliss receptor' that is at the heart of the way the body deals with pain. The receptors work by minimizing the pain signals as they travel from the nerves at the site of the injury up through the spinal cord on their journey to the brain. While research in this field is far from over, it makes one thing clear: not only do cannabinoids have pain-killing properties in themselves, but also they, and thus the *Cannabis* plant itself, could be used for an entirely new and powerful range of analgesic products.

Cannabis and its effects on the body

When cannabis is smoked – whether in a pipe (and thus usually neat) or as mixed with tobacco in a 'joint' (a word that in the drug context first applied to a pipeful of opium – the drug and implement were 'joined' together' – and latterly to a syringe full of diluted heroin), the THC is absorbed speedily into the bloodstream via the nasal passages and the lungs. The first effects are instant, the peak arriving within minutes and it can last, gradually tapering off, for up to six hours. If one eats the cannabis, typically in an Eastern confection such as *mahjoun* or in a homemade 'hash' or 'space' cake, the whole process takes longer – to start, peak and finish – but since the psychological effects on the brain last longer, the 'high' can be stronger.

But even as the effects wear off, THC remains in the bloodstream, albeit in diminished quantities, for days. It is no longer 'working' and the user is no longer 'high', but a urine test, in say a prison, will come up with bad news. On the other hand, modern medical research is starting to show that it is just this persistence that may prove that cannabis is as useful as a non-intoxicant drug with medical applications as it is enjoyable as a recreational one.

Both users and non-users – usually at opposite ends of the campaign for and against the drug – have always been keen to set out either what they have personally experienced with cannabis, or what they believe to be its effects. While the nineteenth-century's Fitzhugh Ludlow writes in praise of cannabis in the heightened manner typical of his era (see slso pages 113–115), his twentieth-century successor, the cannabis opponent Eugene Stanley intends merely to vilify the drug, their respective perceptions remain central to the opposed viewpoints on cannabis. To one side it is the drug of mystery and imagination, to the other the gateway to excess.

I stood in a large temple, whose walls were adorned with grotesque frescoes of every imaginable bird, beast, and monster, which, by some hidden law of life and motion, were forever changing, like the figures of the kaleidoscope. Now the walls bristled with hippogriffs; now, from wainscot to ceiling, toucans and maccataws [sic] swung and nodded from their perches amidst emerald palms; now Centaurs and Lapithæ clashed in ferocious tumult, while crater and cyathus were crushed beneath ringing hoof and heel. But my attention was quickly distracted from the frescoes by the sight of a most witchly congress, which filled all the chairs of that broad chamber. On the dais sat an old crone, whose commanding position first engaged my attention to her personal appearance, and, upon rather impolite scrutiny, I beheld that she was the product of an art held in pre-eminent favor among persons of her age and sex. She was knit of purple yarn!
(from 'Hasheesh and Hasheesh Eaters' by Fitzhugh Ludlow, *Harpers Magazine,* April 1858)

District Attorney Eugene Stanley's thoughts on cannabis and its effects couldn't be more different:

In many respects, the action of *Cannabis sativa* is similar to that of alcohol or morphine. Its toxic effects are ecstasy, merriment, uncontrollable laughter, self-satisfaction, bizarre ideas lacking in continuity, and its results are extreme hyperacidity, with occasional attacks of nausea and vomiting....Large doses produce excitement, delusions hallucinations, rapid flow of ideas, a high state of ecstasy, psychomotor activity with a tendency to willful damage and violence, and a temporary amnesia of all that has transpired....It is commonly used as an aphrodisiac, and its continued use leads to impotency....It is an ideal drug to quickly cut off inhibitions.'
(from 'Marihuana as a Developer of Criminals', 1936)

District Attorney Stanley, keen to condemn cannabis, lined up the usual suspects as to its effects, but even he had to acknowledge what are surely the positive experiences of 'ecstasy' and 'merriment'; other analysts come to the same conclusion, typically the authors of the contemporary *British*

Pharmaceutical Codex (1934) who stated that 'Cannabis acts chiefly on the central nervous system. It first produces excitement with hallucinations, a feeling of happiness and indifference to surroundings, this stage being followed by deep sleep. The hallucinations include inability to estimate time and space. In the East the hemp is smoked and almost immediately produces symptoms of pleasurable excitement, followed by depression and lethargy'.

The influence of set and setting

The reality of cannabis use, as underlined by the majority of the reports produced to assess it, is that, pharmacology aside, the effects of the drug are very much dependent on the individual who is smoking (or less commonly, eating) it, and the environment in which this is being done – the set and setting. The strength and/or dosage of the cannabis must obviously be taken into consideration. Aside from the psychotropic effect – 'getting high' – there are no major, let alone long-term physical effects. One's eyes may become red and one's throat dry and sore (though that soreness may occur so with any form of smoking); some people may feel sick, but many more may experience 'the munchies' – an intense hunger, usually for sweets or snack foods. All of which pass as the 'high' wears off.

The main effects, then, are less physiological than psychological. One's senses, typically as regard colour or sound (especially music) or taste, are intensified: what Michael Pollan has termed the 'italicization of experience'; like LSD in this respect, cannabis slackens off some of the filters that we use, by necessity, to allow us to deal with the vast sensory input of every sentient moment. One does not, perhaps, have the kind of visions reported by such early Western hashish-eaters as Fitzhugh Ludlow or Théophile Gautier or the writer featured in *Harper's* previously, all entering their apparently paradisiacal worlds – such memoirs can seem overblown and too ornate for our modern world – but one cannot ignore the heightening of the everyday. As Pollan has put it, with the aid of cannabis we experience 'wonder'. Senses aside, one laughs more easily and conversation seems more meaningful (even if such 'meaning', not to mention the jokes, may well tend to the absurd when considered in a colder, soberer light); one feels generally cheerful, though the inexperienced user, or one who is using cannabis far stronger than that to which they are accustomed, may suffer a degree of paranoia. Nonetheless, however bad the paranoia (and it can undoubtedly be unpleasant), the sufferer rarely loses contact with 'reality': they know they are 'stoned' and that a drug is involved; such sensibility is far from the complete disorientation that one can experience with LSD. Nor, other than in very rare cases – and it is probably that the individual is predisposed to such problems, rather than having them brought on by cannabis – do long-term mental health problems result. And like alcohol's hangover, a heavy night's smoking may produce a 'dope-over'.

Demonizing cannabis – the official line

Effects, of course, are subject to intepretation. One man's exploration of a fantastic new universe is another's homicidal insanity. Those who had actually smoked the drug, rather than campaigned so ignorantly against it, might have wondered what was under consideration at this hearing, prior to the passage of the Marijuana Tax Act of 1937.

Mr Mccormack: What are its first manifestations, a feeling of grandeur and self-exaltation, and things of that sort?

Mr Anslinger: It affects different individuals in different ways. Some individuals have a complete loss of sense of time or a sense of value. They lose their sense of place. They have an increased feeling of physical strength and power. Some people will fly into a delirious rage, and they are temporarily irresponsible and may commit violent crimes. Other people will laugh uncontrollably. It is impossible to say what the effect will be on any individual.

Mr Mccormack: Is it used by the criminal class?

Mr Anslinger: Yes, it is. It is dangerous to the mind and body, and particularly dangerous to the criminal type, because it releases all of the inhibitions.

(from the statement of Harry J. Anslinger, FBI Commissioner of Narcotics, 27 April 1937)

Harry J. Anslinger, US Commissioner of Narcotics, peddles his line on 'the narcotic problem' at the 'Attorney General Conference on Crime', Washington, D. C., 13 December, 1934.

As with any other drug that has passed into recreational use, the over-riding attitude to cannabis of governments and their law-enforcement agencies has been to vilify and indeed demonize it. Aside from the major reports commissioned to inform decisions on legislation (see pages 132–170) literally thousands of papers have been produced on the drug, but few are free from bias, driven by the needs of its vilifiers or defenders. It must also be noted that prior to the 1970s, when middle-class use of the drug expanded, it was easiest to classify its users as 'drug addicts' and dismiss them and their recreation. Ironically, those official reports commissioned from the late nineteenth century onwards tended to come out, if not in favour of cannabis, then very far from the level of knee-jerk condemnation that typifies much of the last eighty years or so's public discourse. As it turns out, the populist tone of such anti-cannabis fearmongers as Harry J. Anslinger, America's first 'drug czar', would prevail. Even today, their wilful misinformation holds disproportionate sway.

I have no wish to rehearse these arguments here, nor to oppose them with those that are set up by the drug's defenders, but would note instead, the essay on the pharmacology of marijuana, delivered at The Drug Policy Foundation's CME Seminar on 13 November 1992 by Frederick H. Meyers, MD, Professor of Pharmacology at the University of California. Despite the majority of laws and the continuing decision of the United Nations to bracket cannabis with such 'hard' drugs as heroin and cocaine, cannabis is nothing special: as his title puts it, it is in fact 'Just Another Sedative'.

In other words, for all their apparent differences, cannabis, alcohol and such tranquilizers as Valium, are in fact pharmaceutical close relatives. District Attorney Stanley was, for all his prejudice, not wholly wrong; cannabis is like alcohol, although very far from morphine. As Professor Meyers puts it 'cannabis in its several forms and essences is just another member of a large group of drugs, call them for the moment general anesthetic-sedative-hypnotics, all of which are used (and abused) at some time and in some form by some technique by some individuals to relieve anxiety, to provide surcease from memory and to cross the borders of consciousness and sometimes even of life'. Its effect, like theirs, is 'a diffuse depression of the entire central nervous system'.

The apparent differences come not from the innate pharmacology of the drugs, but from the methods of consumption. Because cannabis is primarily smoked, its effects are filtered through the way smoke takes the drug to the central nervous system. Despite the fact that the first puff of a joint can start the 'high' going, whereas it may take two or three drinks for the 'buzz' to start, the reality is that the active ingredient, THC, is in fact absorbed and metabolized far more slowly than is alcohol. Put at its simplest, the particles of THC in smoke are so tiny, that they can be absorbed fast and easily first into the bloodstream and thence to the brain. So fast, indeed, that the drug is already working before that first puff is even exhaled. The absorption of alcohol, and the onset of its effects, is a lengthier process.

But if cannabis is taken by mouth (as are alcohol and tranquillizer pills) then it is the similarities and not the differences that take pride of place. As Professor Meyers notes, his analysis is based on the hapless lab rat, but what matters is the consistency, irrespective of the drug involved.

The four stages of a 'high'

As dosage of THC (the main contributor to a cannabis 'high') is increased chemists recognize four common stages – analgesia, excitement, surgical anaesthesia and medullary paralysis.

The first – analgesia – combines a sense of relief from anxiety or a feeling of euphoria, with a slight drowsiness. Concentration, short-term memory and coordinated movement performance starts to decline (hence the advice – don't drink or smoke and drive). Judgement, too, becomes impaired – as seen, says the Professor, in the bizarre range of things that dope smokers seem to find funny.

Stage two involves excitement and is the stage most beloved of the nay-saying prohibitionists, with their tales of drug-crazed excess. Like someone using a real hallucinogen, the degree of excitement is very much determined by the social and emotional context, the 'set and setting' described earlier. A calm 'scene' may have no more effect than a slight intensification of stage one. In other, livelier situations, the signs of excitement increase. It is here that the alcohol drunk, with all its anti-social and even homicidal side-effects can take over. Ah, say cannabis' defenders, you'd never get that with

a cannabis smoker. But, responds the Professor, you would, but only were a suitable dosage achieved. Enough dope, enough craziness – but that dose is so high that it is simply not achievable. The smoker is far more likely to lapse into incoherent mutterings or a major wonderland playing out behind their eyes than evince any desire to batter their neighbour to death with a roach-filled ashtray!

One should also note that those cerebral wonderlands, while sometimes, in a non-pharmacological sense, hallucinatory, are not hallucinogenic. Alcohol and Valium, as well as cannabis, can produce this dream-like state of mind, in which 'reality' and 'fantasy' can and do merge, and in worst cases disorientate the user. But the actions of cannabis and those of LSD or MDMA (Ecstasy) on the brain are quite different.

Level three – that of surgical anaesthesia – can and has been achieved with animals; it is considered impossible, using realistic doses, with humans.

As for level four – medullary paralysis – even the poor rat has managed to stave that off. In theory, of course, it is possible. The LD50 (the lethal dosage that would cause the death of 50 per cent of the subjects) would require in excess of a monstrous 600mg/kg bodyweight of the rodent. Cannabis, in practice or rather, lab-proven theory, is susceptibile to all four of these stages.

What about the long-term effects?

Other important parallels can be seen when one considers what happens to long-term, continuous users. What is known as 'behavioural tolerance' is common to all. This can be seen in the way that a long-term user 'learns' to deal with effects. While a novice might find strong cannabis perturbing, even paranoia-inducing in externally threatening circumstances, the regular user will have come to know how to ride out the experience. A second form of tolerance, this time physiological, does exist, although it is minor and the withdrawal that follows doesn't last long – and is nothing like that from an opiate drug such as heroin. Nor, however strong the cannabis that has been smoked, does there appear to be an equivalent to the 'horrors' of the heavy drinker's *delirium tremens*.

As for 'abuse', the shibboleth that drives the 'war on drugs', it is worth mentioning once more. All drugs are 'abused', after all, 'relief of anxiety is a seductive pharmacological reward, and countless patients and non-patients are unable to resist using a little more than is prescribed, a little oftener than is necessary' (Meyers, 1992). Why cannabis remains the 'bad guy' and alcohol the tolerated offender is not a pharmacological problem. But that's the way it is and the idea of a 'responsible' use of cannabis is, as we shall see, one that most legislators, and the majority of pundits, have found until recently (and then only in a few enlightened or opportunistic quarters) almost impossible to comprehend.

The earliest archaeological evidence of hemp as textile dated 8000BC ...hemp in China and first 'recreational' use...the Greek historian Herodotus describes cannabis use by the Scythians...intoxication and ritual...tracing the origins in India...legends and religion...social customs... the history of bhang, ganga and charas...Afghanistan and hashish...the legend of the 'Assassins'...cannabis comes to Africa through Arab or Indian traders...the cult of 'dagga'...new ways of taking the drug...the story in Morocco...manufacturing kif...the practice of using cannabis as an intoxicant has not yet penetrated Europe.

A GLOBAL PHENOMENON

Whilst it is generally believed that cannabis, as one of the first plants to be cultivated, must have associations with humanity reaching back to Neolithic or later Stone Age times, records of such associations are inevitably rare. The first cultural evidence found to date originates in China, from the island of Taiwan. Here, where archaeologists have unearthed a village of some 10,000 years old, evidence of cannabis, in the form of hemp, has been found in pieces of broken pottery where strips of hemp were pressed into the wet clay as decoration. Implements, very like those later known to have been used for loosening hemp fibre from the plant's stem, were also discovered. With this weight of evidence in mind, it has been accepted that cannabis is indigenous to China, and that from there it spread across the world.

Four thousand years later, around 4000BC, came the first examples of Chinese hempen textiles, whilst hemp rope and thread appeared around 3000BC. It is possible that the first use of hemp fibre was for ropes and fishing nets; that technology would develop in clothmaking. Four of China's classic texts – the *Shih-Ching* ('Book of Odes', 900–600BC), the *Rh-Ya* (a study of shamanism, 500BC, but dealing with much earlier matters), the *Chou Li* (circa 200BC), and the *Li-Chi* ('Book of Rites', 100BC) – all cite the use of hemp. The *Li-Chi* laid down that out of respect for the dead, mourners should wear hempen-fabric clothes, a custom that was followed even until relatively recently. As ever, the initial beneficiaries of the new form of cloth were the rich; but in time everyone would dress in hempen cloth.

Hemp oil is still used for cooking in Nepal.

One of the 'five grains'

Until the year 500, hemp was also grown as a food, a 'pseudocereal', ranking amongst the 'five grains' that represented the basic Chinese diet, the others being rice, barley, millet and soy beans; hemp, however, was never as important as rice or millet. The fruits of the *Cannabis* plant were rich in triglycerides (oils) and some historians have suggested that hemp grew as a tough, sturdy weed on the nitrogen-heavy rubbish dumps where villagers deposited the remains of fish. It was from this self-seeding weed that proper cultivation would develop. (Even now it is found in Nepal being used as a source of cooking oil and of edible grain.) There have also been instances, well after mainstream hemp eating had been abandoned in favour of cereals, of wild hemp being cropped and eaten in times of famine. The seeds were ground into meal, roasted whole or cooked in a porridge. Hemp even transcended earthly life: sacrificial vessels filled with hemp seed (amongst other grains) for use in the afterlife were placed beside a corpse.

The oil from the hemp seeds, much like linseed oil, could be used for cooking, lamp fuel and lubrication, as well as a base in paint, varnish and soapmaking. After oil extraction, the residue or 'hemp cake' still contained about 10 per cent oil and 30 per cent protein, and formed a nutritious feed for domesticated animals.

Chinese names

Given the uses and extensive cultivation of the plant, there developed a number of terms to identify it. The basic name for hemp is *ma*, which is composed of two symbols that are meant to depict the plant. The part beneath and to the right of the straight lines represent hemp fibres dangling from a rack. The horizontal and vertical lines represent the home in which they were drying. It is usually amplified as *ta ma or da ma* (great hemp) but other names include *huo ma* (fire hemp), *xian ma* (line hemp) and *huang ma* (yellow hemp). Hemp seeds are *ma zi* and *huo ma ren* (fire hemp seed). The female flowers are called *ma fen* (fragrant hemp branch). The terms *da ma*, *xian ma* and *huang ma* for the plants and their products and *da ma zi* or simply *ma zi* for the fruits (or seeds) are usually applied to the fibre- and seed-producing C. *sativa* varieties. Traditional Chinese pharmacists usually use *huo ma* to describe the cleaned hemp seeds that are added to local herbal stomach remedies.

Hemp's amazing versatility

Gradually the Chinese gained expertise in their cultivation of hemp, realizing that while the male plant (now called *hsi*) provided the best fibres, the female (*chu*) provided the better seeds. Ideally a Cantonese person would be totally self-sufficient: growing rice and millet as the main crops, followed by a variety of vegetables and fruit. Then, came hemp. Soon hemp cultivation spread across the vast country and the cloth it provided was traded for food. Like the traditional division of Adam and Eve, the men 'delved', doing the actual cultivation, while the women 'span', manufacturing clothes first for their own families and then for sale. Clothes weren't the only 'garments' made from hemp, shoes were also made from the plant's tough fibres. So important would hemp become that one of the names the Chinese used for their country translates as the 'land of mulberry and hemp'.

An early eighteenth-century watercolour illustrates Chinese paper manufacture in AD100.

Inevitably so versatile a crop found its way into the country's armaments. Bows had originally been strung with bamboo fibres; when hemp string, with its far greater strength and toughness, became available bows were duly upgraded. The development led, for a while, to a 'bowstring race', with the hemp strings providing greater power than the old bamboo ones. Warlords, fighting for the possession of cannabis fields, rearmed their men with hemp bowstrings and their arrows flew further and faster – battles were won with their aid. With this in mind, large acreages were set aside purely for 'military' hemp – it would be the first crop ever to be cultivated for waging war.

Nets, rope, cloth, oil, food, shoes, paper – all these products and more ensured that cannabis was amongst China's most important crops. And in addition it was used extensively in medicine (see pages 174–178) for such

Overleaf: A South American man is shown twisting strands of hemp into rope. The paint on his chest and face symbolises scars.

illnesses as malaria, beri-beri, constipation, rheumatic pains, absent-
mindedness and 'female disorders'. It was also used, when ground into a
paste, as a sedative to relieve the pain of surgery.

The move to recreational drug use

One aspect remains to be discussed: the use of the plant as a psychotropic
drug. China is traditionally associated with opium, albeit imported there by
the British, but for a while cannabis was, as it is today elsewhere, the Chinese
drug of choice. One must assume that this knowledge came about as a
development of the 'straight' medical use: the *Pên-ts'ao Ching*, which is
dated about 2000BC and as such is the oldest pharmacopoeia known, states
that the fruits (that is, flowering tops including the seeds) of hemp, 'if taken
in excess will produce hallucinations' (the Chinese reads literally 'seeing
devils') and continues 'if taken over a long term, it makes one communicate
with spirits and lightens one's body'. The medical use persisted: during the
second century AD the surgeon Hua T'o (110–207) used a mixture of
cannabis seeds and wine to create a successful anaesthetic and thus perform
a difficult abdominal operation. Three centuries later it appeared to have

been abandoned: the physician and pharmacologist T'ao Hung Ching (452–536) stated in his *Ming-I Pieh-lu* (Records of Famous Physicians) that in recent times '*Ma fen* [hemp seed] is not much used in prescriptions'. However, it was also stated that 'Necromancers use it in combination with ginseng to set forward time in order to reveal future events' so cannabis was still in circulation, if only for the purposes of divination.

At first 'recreational' cannabis use was not approved. Taoism, with its preference for yang, the invigorating principle in nature, thought little of cannabis, which was filled with the opposite principle – yin – and thus weakened the bodies of those who ate it. This attitude was seen when a grave inscription was uncovered in which the term *ma*, meaning cannabis, was modified by an adjective, entitling it 'negative'. Yet these attitudes, typical of early Taoism, circa 600BC, would be modified over time. By the first century AD these same Taoists were suggesting that cannabis seeds be tossed into one's incense burner in the direct knowledge that they would cause hallucinations. This time, as advocated by shamans, the visions were desirable: such hallucinations, it was noted, offered a shortcut to immortality and at the same time would help the intoxicated person to see spirits. But in the event, cannabis smoking was never a major Chinese preoccupation.

Scythians and cannabis

If China is acknowledged as one probable site for the early domestication of cannabis – with its subsequent spread westward – then another is that vast tract of land stretching from the borders of China to the Black Sea, from where the plant would then spread southward and eastward. The Scythians lived around 600BC and were a nomadic Indo-European people. Whilst evidence for cannabis's origins here is vague, and some experts simply suggest that the plant emerged anywhere from China to the Balkans, the Scythians certainly have a strong case. Archaeological evidence has found that their funeral ceremonies involved the burning of hemp seed; and the use of the seeds for both rituals and intoxication was noted by the Greek historian Herodotus (fifth century BC) who stated, 'The Scythians then take this seed of hemp and, creeping under the mats [that is, small tents], they throw it on the red-hot stones; and, being so thrown, it smoulders and sends forth so much steam that no Greek vapour bath could surpass it. The Scythians howl in their joy at the vapour bath'.

The survival of ritual

That Herodotus was telling no lies was proved 2000 years later when the Russian archaeologist, Professor Sergei I. Rudenko, digging in the Pazyryk Valley of central Siberia, uncovered a burial site in which, amongst other things, were found a bronze cauldron filled with burnt hemp seeds plus some metal censers (containers in which incense is burnt) apparently designed for inhaling cannabis smoke. Rudenko suggested that on this evidence cannabis was used not only in a religious context but also for simple recreation. The Scythians were not the only contemporary tribe to use cannabis. Herodotus fails to name them, but he describes another tribe who, when they 'have parties and sit around a fire, they throw some of it [cannabis] into the flames. As it burns, it smokes like incense, and the smell of it makes them drunk, just as wine does. As more fruit is thrown on, they get more and more intoxicated until finally they jump up and start dancing and singing'.

The Scythians had been nomads and as they settled, their wandering lifestyle was inevitably eroded. For perhaps 500 years their rule had extended from China to the Ukraine, but by 200BC it had effectively disappeared. They would be replaced in time by the Sarmatians, another group of hunters and herders. But Scythian customs, certainly those regarding cannabis use, did not die. As the cannabis historian Ernest Abel has noted, 'On Christmas Eve, for instance, Benet (the Polish etymologist and historian of the early uses of hemp) notes that the people of Poland and Lithuania serve semieniatka, a soup made from hemp seeds. The Poles and Lithuanians believe that on the night before Christmas the spirits of the dead visit their families and the soup is for the souls of the dead. A similar ritual takes place in Latvia and in the Ukraine on Three Kings Day (January 6, Twelfth Night). Yet another custom carried out in deference to the dead in Western Europe was the throwing of hemp seeds onto a blazing fire during harvest time as an offering to the dead – a custom that originated with the Scythians and has seemingly been passed on from generation to generation for over 2500 years' (Abel, 1980).

Herodotus is not the only writer to note Central Asian cannabis use. Intoxicating resin is mentioned in the Zoroastrian sacred writings *Zend-Avesta* (599–500BC) and the Assyrians used cannabis as incense as early as the ninth century BC. The Greek philosopher Democritus (460–370BC) says that cannabis was drunk with wine and myrrh to produce visionary states, whilst Ephippus (460–370BC), a writer of comedies in the fourth century BC, includes cannabis in a list of delicacies. Pliny (AD23–79) speaks of the 'gelotophyllum' (literally 'laughing leaf') from Bactria (that is, Scythia).

Tracing the origins in India

India, the great subcontinent stretching from the Himalayas to the Indian Ocean, has never had any doubts as to the importance of the cannabis plant, whether in spiritual, secular or medicinal use, and records date from the earliest times. Thus, Sanskrit and Hindu names for cannabis, the antithesis of the vilifiers used in the modern West, all praise its attributes: those of healing, strength and success. Such names include *vijaya* and *jaya* 'victorious'; *trailokyavijaya* 'victorious in three worlds'; *indracana* 'Indra's food'; *virapattra* 'leaf of heroes'; *capala* 'the light hearted'; *ajaya* 'the unconquered'; *ananda* 'the joyful'; *harsini* 'the rejoicer'; *vakpradatava* 'speech giving'; *medhakaritva* 'inspiring of mental power'; and *creshadipanatva* 'a most excellent excitant'.

Stories from Indian legends

Unsurprisingly the cannabis plant has accrued many legends. The *Vedas*, four sacred books retelling the myths of the early Aryan gods worshipped by the tribes who invaded India in the latter half of the second millennium BC, recount how the god Shiva brought the cannabis plant down from the Himalayas for people's use and enjoyment. As it is written, Shiva, fulminating over some family quarrel, had gone off to sulk in the fields. There it was hot, and he was able to take shelter in the shade of a tall cannabis plant. Grateful and fascinated by the plant, Shiva ate some of its leaves. He was so refreshed that he adopted it as his favourite food, and gained one of his titles 'Lord of Bhang'.

According to the *Raja Valabha*, a seventeenth-century text dealing with the drugs used in India, the gods, in a gesture of kindness towards the human race, sent cannabis so that humans, otherwise plagued with so many miseries, might attain delight, lose fear and experience sexual desires. In a parallel story, recounted in the *Vedas*, nectar (*amrita*) dropped from heaven and cannabis sprouted from it. Yet another story, this more widely accepted, tells that it was when the gods, with the aid of demons, churned the milk

ocean to obtain *amrita*, that cannabis appeared amongst the resulting nectars. However, once the *amrita* appeared, the demons tried to seize it. The gods successfully prevented this, and in commemoration of their triumph cannabis gained a new name: *vijaya*, victory. Whichever myth one accepts, all these nectars were consecrated especially to Shiva, god of generation; devotees of Shiva pour libations of cannabis over the lingam (the phallic symbol that is worshipped as a manifestation of the god) and offer him drinks made from cannabis and datura, a powerful narcotic based on the thorn-apple. Today's bhang lassi, a drink available in many parts of India, mixes a preparation of cannabis with lassi or yoghurt.

Cannabis is also consecrated to Kali, the goddess of death. Towards the end of the Durga Puja, the main festival for her worship, it is customary to drink and offer around bowls of a cannabis preparation. Researchers for the Indian Hemp Drugs Commission (1893–1894) noted that in Madras, the worship of Kama, god of love, similarly entails cannabis, whilst in Bombay the relevant deity is Vishnu. Indeed, each region uses cannabis as a gift to the most popular form of god locally. (This tradition continues at some modern festivals where pakoras or milk drinks flavoured with cannabis are consumed). And if the gods use cannabis, then humans can benefit in 'godly' means: people believe that it gives supernatural influence and powers to the user and as such it remains popular amongst many of India's travelling religious beggars or sadhus.

These sadhus, notably those associated with the Shaivite and Shaktéya cults, in turn believe that one approaches far nearer the deity when intoxicated and that when taken in the morning, cannabis cleanses the whole body of sin. More prosaically the cannabis plant's leaves can be chewed, *á la* coca, providing a light sedative effect when circumstances preclude the preparation of the usual bhang drink.

Nor is cannabis' religious use restricted to Hindus. Tantrism, with its deep-seated fear of demons, used cannabis as a means of challenging their power. The drug has also been incorporated in the yogic sexual or meditative acts that form part of the religion. About ninety minutes prior to the meditative ritual (which may or may not include sexual intercourse) the devotee drinks a bowl of bhang, after uttering the mantra: 'Om hrim, O ambrosia-formed

Covered in ash and wearing only strands (*malas*) of Rudraksha seeds, a naked *Naga,* or holy man, smokes marijuana as part of his spiritual quest.

goddess [Kali] who has arisen from ambrosia, who showers ambrosia, bring me ambrosia again and again, bestow occult power [*siddhi*] and bring my chosen deity to my power'. He or she then waits for the drug to take effect before beginning the ceremony, with heightened senses and a feeling of one-ness with the goddess Kali.

Yet another legend states that the Buddha ate nothing but a single cannabis seed on each day of his six years of asceticism and he is sometimes depicted with what are obviously cannabis leaves in his begging bowl. So common is the mix of cannabis and religion that one might see the use of the drug as analogous with that of wine in Christian communion.

The drink of warriors

In India cannabis (usually in the form of bhang) became a necessary accompaniment to many social events, just as alcohol has in the West. If one had no bhang at a wedding, the demons would take their opportunity to render the newly-weds wretched. It was a symbol of hospitality. Hosts who failed to offer visitors a cup of bhang on their arrival were despised as mean, whilst those who went further and reviled bhang itself were doomed to suffer the eternal torments of hell. War, inevitably, was another arena for bhang where, again like alcohol, its ingestion could and did provide a dose of the necessary 'Dutch courage.' Churning milk oceans and larcenous demons aside, the drug's name *vijaya,* 'victorious' or 'unconquerable', had more practical relevance: nervous warriors would inject bhang to fortify them for the oncoming battle. A number of folk-songs cite ganja or bhang (with or without opium) as the invariable drink of heroes before performing any great feat. The epic poem of Alha and Rudal (undated, but glorifying events around 1150) contains numerous references to ganja as a drink of warriors. (In the eighth century AD, its use was encouraged by the Muslim Ismaili sect one of whose verses ran 'We've quaffed the emerald cup, the mystery we know, / Who'd dream so weak a plant such mighty power could show!').

The history of bhang

Bhang (Sanskrit *bhanga,* 'hemp'), which can also be a preparation, typically a drink, as well as a smokable drug, consists simply of the dried leaves, with the flowering tops removed when it is carefully prepared. The leaves are

exposed to sun and dew alternately (thus they both wilt and dry) and once cured they are pressed and stored. Bhang seems to be the primary literary generic for cannabis and it is thus named at the drug's first appearance as an intoxicant, in the fourth book of the *Vedas*, the *Atharvaveda* ('Science of Charms', written between 2000 and 1400BC) where bhang is cited as one of the 'five kingdoms of herbs…which release us from anxiety'.

It appears with increasing frequency as time advances. G. A. Grierson, in an appendix to the Indian Hemp Commission Report (1893–1894), lists a range of references. The first mention of bhang appears in the work of Sucruta (before the eighth century AD), where it is called an anti-phlegmatic. During

One of many Indian 'bhang' shops. This is a government-approved premises in Jaisalmer, Rajasthan.

the next four centuries the word *bhanga* is to be found in a succession of
Sanskrit dictionaries, where it means a hemp plant. Around 1050
Cakrapanidatta, a physician at the court of prince Nayapala, included the
name *indracana*, 'Indra's food' or generically the 'food of the gods', in his
Cabdacandrika, a medical vocabulary. The *Rajanighantu* of Narahari
Pandita (circa 1300) notes that the plant possesses the following qualities: (1)
katulva (acridity); (2) *kasayatra* (astringency); (3) *usnatva* (heat); (4) *tiktatva*
(pungency); (5) *vatakaphapahatva* (removing wind and phlegm); (6)
samgrahitva (astringency); (7) *vakpradatva* (speech-giving); (8) *balyatva*
(strength-giving); (9) *medhakaritva* (inspiring of mental power); (10)
cresthadipanatva (the property of a most excellent excitant).

By the sixteenth century AD, bhang had moved from religious to popular
literature. In the farce *Dhurtasamagama*, or *Rogue's Congress,* (written circa
1500), a beggar (Grierson calls him a 'jogi' or wandering holy man) faced
with the demands of an unscrupulous judge, offers some bhang as a
payment. The play continues…'The Judge (taking it pompously, and then
smelling it greedily): "Let me try what it is like (takes a pinch). Ah! I have
just now got by the merest chance some ganja which is soporific and corrects
derangements of the humours, which produces a healthy appetite, sharpens
the wits, and acts as an aphrodisiac".' At the same time there were
substantial references to the drug in a variety of medical books and materia
medica (see pages 178–182). Grierson also notes the frequency of bhang's
appearance in vernacular poetry, such as a hymn composed around 1400 by
Vidyapati Tbakur in which he calls the god Shiva *Digambara bhanga*, in
reference to his habit of consuming that drug.

The Indian Hemp Drugs Commission had no doubts as to the importance
of bhang, noting that it was so interwoven with both spiritual and secular
practices that any moves against it could lead only to serious social unrest.
In his essay 'On the Religion of Hemp', included in the Commission's
Report, J. M. Campbell summed things up thus: 'To the Hindu the hemp
plant is holy. A guardian lives in the bhang leaf…Besides as a cure for fever,
bhang has many medicinal virtues…It cures dysentery and sunstroke, clears
phlegm, quickens digestion, sharpens appetite, makes the tongue of the
lisper plain, freshens the intellect, and gives alertness to the body and gaiety
to the mind. Such are the useful and needful ends for which in his goodness

**Guatama Buddha is
reported to have
survived solely on
hemp seeds. This is
an early painting on
hemp paper of him.**

the Almighty made bhang…Bhang is the Joygiver, the Skyflier, the Heavenly-guide, the Poor Man's Heaven, the Soother of Grief…The supporting power of bhang has brought many a Hindu family safe through the miseries of famine. To forbid or even seriously to restrict the use of so holy and gracious an herb as the hemp would cause widespread suffering and annoyance and to large bands of worshipped ascetics, deep-seated anger. It would rob the people of a solace in discomfort, of a cure in sickness, of a guardian whose gracious protection saves them from the attacks of evil influences…So grand a result, so tiny a sin!'

According to R. N. and I. C. Chopra, writing in the United Nations Bulletin on Narcotics (1957), bhang is not smoked, but mixed with other ingredients to provide a form of drink or food. The basic preparation 'consists of a drink made by pounding bhang leaves with a little black pepper and sugar, and diluting with water to the desired strength. Various kinds of special beverages are prepared by the middle and well-to-do classes by the addition of almonds, sugar, iced milk, curds, etc....' Often the mix would include

'Manners and
Customs', one of
four drawings
depicting the
manufacture and
use of narcotics, by
an Amritsar artist,
circa 1870.

other psychotropic substances, such as opium, datura, tobacco, wine or sometimes nux vomica, all of which were presumed to intensify the effects.

Overall, bhang use in India seems to be analogous with that of caffeine or nicotine in the West, something that soothes and restores as much as, indeed far more than, it intoxicates. Labourers, for instance, often use it to alleviate the stresses of hard physical labour; they also believe it can stave off colds. Some suggest that the sense of well-being the drug promotes helps render such labours bearable.

Ganja and charas in India

The other two forms of cannabis, both of which are smoked, are respectively ganja and charas. Ganja (Hindi *ganjha*, 'dried hemp') has a similar potency to the Caribbean sensimilla (approximately 10 per cent THC) and is made only of the unpollinated female flowering tops to which the resin adheres. As Mia Tour notes in 'The Religious and Medical Uses of Cannabis' , 'The tops are put in heaps and trodden or manually rolled; they are then allowed to dry (and wilt) in the sun, are rolled again, dried again, until the whole mass is of the right consistency and sufficient resin has been pressed out of the tops to make the mass stick together. The rolled or Bengal type is of higher quality (and therefore preferred for medicinal use) than the trodden or Bombay type.'

One of the possible etymologies for the name charas, a variety of potent hashish (and today generic for hashish in India) comes originally from the Persian and meant 'a leather bag for pressing hemp dust'. Central Asia, specifically Yarkand (now Soch'e in today's Chinese Turkestan), was the home of the very best charas. Even the Indians, whose culture celebrated the drug, accepted that Yarkand imports licensed by the British Raj and coming in over the Kara-Kash ('Black Jade') route (crossing the Karakoram pass, 5562m (18,250ft) high) were far superior to their own supplies of hashish. The Yarkand hashish remained top quality at least until the late nineteenth century, when it is cited as the main source of imported Indian charas by the Indian Hemp Commission in its report of 1893–1894.

Charas (Persian *charas*, 'cannabis resin') is the most potent cannabis product and is almost entirely pure resin. In antiquity there existed two methods of obtaining charas. The legendary one was to send people clothed in leather

coverings to go thrashing through bushes of cannabis at the correct time of
flowering. The resin that adhered to the leather was then scraped off and
collected. Mia Tour also notes that in Nepal the runners/collectors were
apparently naked and the same scraping then ensued. (Although such tales
have persisted, there are no actual witnessed reports. They may be, as one
writer has suggested, an older equivalent of the usual dealers' scam:
providing a 'sexy' story to make one's product more alluring.) The resin was
best collected a few weeks before the monsoon began and, apparently, just
after sunrise when a fall of dew had taken place. Alternatively (and more
commonly), the flowering tops were rolled between the palms and the
adherent resin peeled off once enough had accumulated. The charas of the
Yarkand region was considered the best of all: and here there was a third
method of preparation. The flowering branches were beaten above a coarse
cotton cloth until a fine greyish-white powder was obtained, consisting of
the flowers themselves plus the superficial resin-bearing tissues of the leaves
– known as trichomes (see illustration on page 12). The Indian Hemp
Commission explained that: 'This powder was placed in the sun until an
oleaginous substance oozed out; this was then compacted and finally stored
in leather bags.' It is believed that it is the addition of these glandular
trichomes that made Yarkand charas one of a kind in potency terms.

One final point: the British, despite being rulers of India for 250 years, did
not take advantage of cannabis in any form, other than to levy taxes upon
its importers and sellers. (This policy had begun in 1790 and was
underpinned by Regulation XXXIV of 1793: 'No person shall manufacture
or vend any such drugs (bhang, ganja, charas, and other intoxicating drugs)
without a license from the collector of the zillah [local administrative
area].') Some, of course, must have experimented, although opium was
probably equally alluring. One who took both drugs, according to his
biographer Andrew Lycett, was Rudyard Kipling. 'Along with opium,
Rudyard was exploring the use of another common Indian drug, hashish.
This is the evidence of his poem "The Vision of Hamid Ali", published by
the *Calcutta Review* [in] October 1885. Set in a brothel within earshot of the
muezzins of the Mosque of Wazir Khan, it tells of Hamid Ali who, after
"Drinking the ganja, drowsy with its fumes / Above the dying chillain"
breaks into an airy Coleridge-style fantasy about the overthrow of all the
world's religions, including Christianity and his own Islam....Rudyard, as

the story-teller, is enthralled not only by the powerful effect of this drug-induced dream but also by its origins. Was it the ganja that caused Hamid Ali to blaspheme in this way? Rudyard leaves the question open, but the manner in which he poses it suggests he was not simply a disinterested observer of hashish users, but wanted an answer to an epistemological problem that concerned him personally.'

The legendary Afghanistan hashish

In the near-mythical era of unfettered travel of the 1960s and 1970s, the goal of many of those who took 'the hippie trail' to the cannabis paradises of the East, was Afghanistan. And today in the conversations of those who debate the pre-eminence of the many varieties of hashish, 'Af' or 'Afghani' tends to be ranked amongst the best.

Afghanistan has maintained one of the world's longest unbroken hashish cultures. Records are scarce, and there was no official 'kingdom' of Afghanistan until 1747, but the country's position at the heart of the earliest

A Pathan tribesman checks his marijuana crop – Afhganistan.

area of 'cannabis-consciousness' ensures that the drug played a central role in its peoples' lives. There is even a Johnny Appleseed of the drug – the semi-legendary Baba Ku from the Samarkand or Bukhara regions who travelled the country (probably around the thirteenth century, but possibly later) disseminating both spirtual teaching and herbal healing. The 'little sticky balls' that he supposedly gave out to those suffering an onset of plague are generally believed to have been cannabis resin. Baba Ku is traditionally portrayed with his water pipe of monstrous proportions – holding some forty litres of water that was cooled by the mountain streams. It is claimed that Baba Ku and the followers who flocked around him consumed some three kilos of hashish via this pipe every day. More important is his role as the founder of the country's hashish culture: before he died he gave cannabis seeds (plus gold and medicinal herbs) to ten families; it would be their task to keep up his work and propagate the crop.

The Arabs and hashish

Writing in 'An Essay on Hashish' in 1912, and repeating an age-old tale that had been first set down in the lost *Treatise on Hemp* by Hassan Mohammad ibn-Chirazi in 1260, the US writer Victor Robinson explained the 'discovery' of hashish thus: 'Haidar was a rigid monk who built a monastery on the mountains between Nishabor and Ramah. For ten years he never left his hermitage, never indulged in even a fleeting moment's pleasure. One burning summer's day when the fiery sun glared angrily upon Mother Earth as if he wished to wither up her breasts, Haidar stepped out from his cloister and walked alone to the fields. All around him lay the vegetation weary and without life, but one plant danced in the heat with joy. Haidar plucked it, partook of it, and returned to the convent a happier man. The monks who saw him immediately noticed the change in their chief. He encouraged conversations, and acted boisterously. He then led his companions to the fields, and the holy men partook of the hasheesh, and were transformed from austere ascetics into jolly good fellows. At the death of Haidar, in conformity with his desire, his disciples planted the hemp in an arbor around his tomb.' These events, it should be added, allegedly took place in 1125. Given what we know of the use of charas, that is hashish, in India, there is, perhaps sadly, no real substance in the Haidar legend – hashish had been 'invented' long since but it has become part of hashish and, in particular, Sufi mythology.

A 250 gram 'book' of high-quality Camel hashish from Afghanistan.

In reality Arabs were already well aware of the drug. The works of the second-century Roman physician Galen had been translated, including his observations on cannabis, and three centuries before Haidar's tale an Arab physician, Ibn Wahshiyah, included it in his book *On Poisons*. The mere smell of hashish, he explained, could kill: 'If it reaches the nose, a violent tickle occurs in the nose, then in the face. The face and eyes are affected by an extreme and intense burning; one does not see anything and cannot say what one wishes. One swoons, then recovers, then swoons again and recovers again. One goes on this way until he dies. A violent anxiety and fainting occurs until one succumbs, after a day, a day and a half, or more. If it is protracted, it may take two days. For these aromatics, there is no remedy. But if God wills to save him, he may be spared from death by the continuance of vomiting or by another natural reaction'.

Persian roots

The main evidence for the existence of cannabis in ancient Persia is linguistic. Like India, Persia was at one time invaded by the Aryans, and thus the Persian word for cannabis is *bhanga*, effectively identical to India's bhang. There are also religio-cultural similarities. The Persian *Zend-Avesta* written by the prophet Zoroaster is the counterpart to the *Vedas*. Researchers now think that Zoroaster may well have been a cannabis user himself and, like India's holy men, seen its intoxicating powers as an ideal means of making a closer contact with the world of spirituality. One book of the *Zend-Avesta*, the *Vendidad* or 'Law Against Demons', defines *bhanga* as Zoroaster's 'good narcotic', and recounts the story of two mortals who were transported in soul to the heavens where, upon drinking from a cup of *bhanga*, they had the highest mysteries revealed to them.

Nor is chronology the sole argument against the Haidar story. Robert Connell Clarke points out in his book *Hashish!* that if all Haidar did was teach his disciples of the psychoactive properties of cannabis leaves, he wasn't really offering them much of a 'high' – leaves alone don't have enough of the psychoactive ingredient tetrahydrocannabinol (THC) – and he certainly hadn't 'discovered' hashish. On the other hand, if, rather than eat the leaves, Haidar had taught his disciples about the hand rubbing of resin, the basis of hashish-making, the legend has a good deal more importance. Perhaps most relevant, as Clarke suggests, were Haidar's deathbed instructions: laying out methods for the planting of cannabis. From Haidar's tomb, to which disciples continued to flock, the knowledge of cannabis would spread throughout the entire Sufi community.

By the end of the thirteenth century the drug had become popularly known as 'Haidar's Lady'. Other names included *hashish al-fuqara* 'herb of the faqirs', *hadim al-aqwat* 'digester of food', *baithat al-fikr* 'rouser of thought', *sultanat al-junun* 'queen of insanity', *al-akhdar* 'the green one' and *ibnat al-qunbus* 'daughter of cannabis'. And, as set down by the thirteenth-century Egyptian botanist Ibn al-Baytar, 'the Sufis had a special way of preparing their hashish. First they baked the leaves until they were dry. Then, they rubbed them between their hands to form a paste, rolled it into a ball, and swallowed it like a pill. Others dried the leaves only slightly, toasted and husked them, mixed them with sesame and sugar, and chewed them like gum'.

The Assassins

This book is not a history, but simply an introduction to a plant and its effects, and thus the long story of Hassan-i Sabah, the twelfth-century leader of the Ismailis (whose breakaway Muslim sect stood in opposition to mainstream Shi'ite Islam) and his mountain eyrie of Alamut (literally 'eagle's nest'), from whence the famed and feared Sheikh el-Jebel or 'Old Man of the Mountains' dispatched his fierce and terrible 'Assassins' is not for these pages. The word *assassin*, however, definitely is. If one looks for the etymology of assassin in any dictionary, one will read some approximation of this: 'from Arab. hashshashin and hashishiyyin, pl. of hashshash and hashishiyy, lit. 'a hashish-eater, one addicted to hashish,' both forms being applied in Arabic to the Ismaili sectarians, who used to intoxicate themselves with hashish or hemp, when preparing to dispatch some king or public man' (*Oxford English Dictionary*). It is acknowledged and widely accepted, but is it true? And if the word is a descendant of hashish, were the assassins themselves consumers of the drug? For that one does need some history, initially that provided in the celebrated description of Hassan-i Sabah by explorer Marco Polo, who visited the fortress around 1271.

Marco Polo wrote at length of Hassan's fabulous gardens, describing them as an earthly paradise locked away from all but the select. But this was no mere playground: according to the story Hassan's garden played a major role in his recruitment of young men as killers of his enemies. Polo writes, 'Now no man was allowed to enter the Garden save those whom he intended to be his ashishin…He kept at his Court a number of the youths of the country, from twelve to twenty years of age, such as had a taste for soldiering…Then he would introduce them into his Garden…having first made them drink a certain potion which cast them into a deep sleep, and then causing them to be lifted and carried in…When therefore they awoke, and found themselves in a place so charming, they deemed that it was Paradise in very truth.' They stayed for five days, enjoying every pleasure, before being drugged once more and, when they awoke, taken before Hassan. 'The chief thereupon addressing them said: "We have the assurance of our Prophet that he who defends his Lord shall inherit Paradise, and if you show yourselves to be devoted to the obedience of my orders, that happy lot awaits you".' And, added Polo, 'So when the Old Man would have any prince slain, he would say to such a youth: "Go thou and slay So and So; and when thou returnest my Angels shall bear thee into Paradise. And shouldst thou die, nonetheless even so will I send my Angels to carry thee back into Paradise".'

It is this tale that stands at the heart of the hashish/assassin connection. There is no doubt that Hassan-i Sabbah did maintain a team of what, in modern parlance, would be called 'assassins'. But the question remains: where, if at all, does hashish fit in? One thing is immediately clear: at no time does Marco Polo even hint that the 'certain potion' was hashish. It should also be noted that the drug, whatever it might have been, seemed to be used only in the garden, to enhance its resemblance to Paradise. There does not seem to be any suggestion that the assassins would toss back a lump of hashish prior to going about their business. As Shaykh Muhammad Iqbal has noted, writing recently on the topic, 'What an illogical belief it is that if a person who has lost his control over self through [hashish] how can he vouchsafe his defence with sensible strategy', and attributes their 'valour and intrepidity' to religious faith. But the Crusaders, shocked by the intensity, some say fanaticism, of the Muslims against whom they fought had to come up with some reason. Valour alone was not enough.

Writing in his book, *The Assassins – Holy Killers of Islam* (1987), another scholar of the assassins, Edward Burman, has cast serious doubts on the link

Legend has it that Hassan-i-Sabbah had such control over his 'assassins' that he bade two of them kill themselves in front of his trembling audience.

to hashish. The garden, or some form thereof, is probably real: such gardens were an essential part of Persian noble life. (Robert Connell Clarke, in contradiction, believes that Alamut was too bleak to support any such cultivation.) But he denies the existence of drugs. 'Many scholars have argued, and demonstrated convincingly, that the attribution of the epithet "hashish eaters" or "hashish takers" is a misnomer derived from enemies of the Ismai'lis and was never used by Moslem chroniclers or sources. It was therefore used in a pejorative sense of "enemies" or "disreputable people". This sense of the term survived into modern times with the common Egyptian usage of the term *hashasheen* in the 1930s to mean simply "noisy or riotous". It is unlikely that the austere Hassan-i Sabbah indulged personally in drug taking.' Nor is there any mention of it in Alamut's own library. Instead of paradisiacal gardens and mind-altering dugs, life at the fortress was typified by 'extreme asceticism and severity'. Finally, says Burman, the concept (and practice) of assassination was hardly Hassan's invention. The use of murder as a political technique, a way-station to that extreme version of political debate known as war, had been used long since, both in the Middle East and, if one looks at the homicidal excesses of the Emperors, in Rome. The word, too, was known at least as early as 1237 when the historian Wendover wrote, in Latin, of '*Hos tam Saraceni quam Christiani Assisinos appellant*' (those Saracens, that is Muslims, whom the Christians call assassins).

Modern scholarship tends now to believe that whilst the link is spurious (at least as regards the consumption of the drug) it remains and is the product of hostility towards the Ismailis by their fellow Muslims, especially the antipathetic Sunnis. Such hostility towards Muslims as a whole was fuelled as ever by ignorance found among the Christian Crusaders. As far as mainstream Islam was concerned, Ismailis were terrorists; in their own eyes, as the cliché endlessly has it, they were freedom fighters, struggling to maintain their own security. And as far as the Crusaders were concerned, no story was bad enough. Robotic, drug-crazed psychotics did very nicely. One of the best-propagated, and one that is still used to justify the hashish link, was originated after the visit of Henry, Count of Champagne to the Syrian Ismaili territories in 1194. The Count later claimed that the Old Man of the Mountains had offered to prove his absolute power and his followers' unalloyed obedience. Calling up two fida'is he commanded them to leap from a high turret. This they did – and duly died on the rocks beneath. By the end of the thirteenth century the story was a European staple, combining brutality and sheep-like obedience in one desirable canard. This story, like Marco Polo's, makes no actual reference to a drug, but the assumption was easy – there had to be something.

At first, scholars of both East and West, despite the many names – Accini, Arsasini, Assassi, Assassini, Assessini, Assissini, Heyssessini – were lost as to the proper etymology. It was not until 1809 that the 'mystery' was solved. In a lecture entitled 'Memoirs on the Dynasty of the Assassins and the Origin of their Name', the French Arabist Silvestre de Sacy (1758–1838) stated 'Nor should there be any doubt, in my opinion, that the word hashishi, plural hashishin, is the origin of the corruption heissessini, assassini, and assissini. However, one thing remained: 'What can rightly be asked,' he added, 'is the reason why the Ismailis or Batinis were called Hashishis.'

Which brings us back to our earlier question: did Hashishin actually take hashish? And if not, why did first their fellow Muslims, and latterly Occidental enemies, and in time scholars, pick up this link? This, it would seem, is the answer: amongst Muslims the main hashish-takers were Sufis, a group who were seen as heretical by strict Islamic standards. The Ismailis were not Sufis, but it should be noted that they too called themselves *al-sufat* which meant 'the pure' or 'the sincere'. (*Sufat* is one of the roots of Sufi; the other, making a pun, is *suf*, wool, and refers to their traditionally woollen garments; this led to their unpopularity: Muhammed had supposedly dressed in cotton, Christ in wool – Sufis were accused of emulating the latter.) The theological niceties that divide the two cults are irrelevant here, but what matters is that the Ismailis, already vilified by many Muslims, had in this use of *al-sufat* given their enemies another weapon. If the Sufis proper could be condemned, justifiably, as *hashishiyya* (hashish-eaters) then it was easy enough to add in the Ismailis, who as enemies already were open to whatever forms of vilification one could muster. In fact, some experts have found, the branding of the Ismailis as *hashishiyya* was not that common, but of all the slurs aimed in their direction, this is the one, especially amongst Westerners, that has stuck. And the true etymology, assassin equated with hashishin, was extended to the slanderous assumption, assassins were stoned on hash.

Cannabis in Africa

The first evidence of any African cannabis use is found in fourteenth-century Ethiopia, to which it is presumed to have come via Arabic or possibly Indian traders. (Another theory suggests that it arrived with Javanese slaves, who themselves were imported to the Cape.) In Ethiopia it was encountered by the Bantu tribespeople, originally from North Africa, whose knowledge spread the drug to southern tribes such as the Hottentots and Bushmen. The Bantus themselves developed a dagga cult based on the belief that the holy plant had been brought to earth by gods from the 'two dog star' (Sirius).

Although the word dagga (from the Hottentot *dacha*) undoubtedly means cannabis, it is also used to name certain species of *Leonotis*, the leaf of which bears a superficial resemblance to that of the *Cannabis* plant. The name dagga is always, however, qualified when it is used in reference to *Leonotis*, thus: klipdagga, knopdagga, knoppiesdagga, red dagga, rooidagga and wildedagga.

Southern Africa

Cannabis is not an indigenous Southern African plant, nor is there evidence of it being used in textiles as hemp, with all the by-products that such use would entail. It is not a legal cash crop. There is, however, evidence of its use from the early seventeenth century and the plant, now generally known as dagga across all of Africa, has remained a popular intoxicant ever since.

Bantu tribe, Ethiopia, smoking 'dagga' or cannabis from a hole in the earth. The bantus developed a dagga cult and believed that consuming the drug would cause the soul to experience reincarnation.

The first evidence of cannabis use in what would become South Africa appeared in 1609, written up by the Portuguese Dominican missionary Joao dos Santos, who travelled in both India and Africa. His book *Ethiopia Oriental* is the best description of the Portuguese occupation of Africa at the end of the sixteenth century, when Portugal was at the zenith of her power there. His African journeys lasted until 1597, when he left for India, where he would eventually die. Dos Santos identified cannabis and told how, under the name *bangue* (a Portuguese take on bhang), it was cultivated throughout the area known as Kafaria (near today's Cape of Good Hope). The kafirs (local natives, named after the Arabic word *kefir*, meaning 'infidel') were in the habit of eating its leaves, and those that used it to excess, he said, became intoxicated as if they had drunk a large quantity of wine. He had taken the drug himself, on a visit to the chieftain Quiteve.

Further descriptions of local cannabis use came in 1658 when Jan van Riebeeck, the first governor of the Dutch colony at the Cape of Good Hope, described the use of cannabis by the Hottentots. By now the word dagga was known and understood, and van Riebeeck claimed that the locals seemed to value it more than gold, although he condemned the plant that 'drugs their brain just as opium'. He noticed that, bereft of European pockets, they carried their dagga in small pouches, pushed under the ivory rings with which they adorned their arms.

Lessons from the colonialists?

If cannabis was a novelty to the white colonialists, they soon taught the native users a new method of consuming the drug: smoking. In 1661, a Dutch surgeon and adventurer, Pieter van Meerhof whose marriage to a Hottentot girl had been the first ever cross-cultural union in South Africa, stated that the Hottentots had tried to smoke dagga but they could not master the technique. By 1705, that problem had been solved and both the Hottentots and the Bushmen, were smoking as efficiently as any white man. However, these stories may be incorrect, one more product of white fantasies of cultural superiority. The smoking habit arrived in South Africa with the very first Bantu invasions, long before the whites appeared. Dagga pipe bowls of stone or earthenware have been found in association with early Bantu settlements all over Southern Africa.

The change from chewing to smoking had one major effect: one tended to chew alone but one smoked in company – cannabis become a social drug, with individuals sharing pipes made of wood, stone, bone or pottery, any of which might be fitted to a horn filled with water. As explained in E. W. Stowe's 1910 book *The Native Races of South Africa*, the horn was filled with water, the pipe bowl filled with dagga and lit. The smoker then took three or four drags and tended to explode in fits of coughing. 'This was considered the height of ecstasy to the smoker. The process continued until the fumes of the dagga produced a kind of intoxication or delirium and the devotee commenced to recite or sing, with great rapidity and vehemence, the praises of himself or his chief during the intervals of coughing or smoking.' Being invariably poor, not all tribes could run to a bowl, so some improvisation was called for. The most basic alternative method was to dig a hole in the ground, into which the dagga, mixed with burning dung, would be placed. Tunnels were dug into the sides of the hole. Smokers would then prostrate themselves at the mouths of these tunnels and inhale the dagga smoke. It may have been basic, but it worked.

By the late eighteenth century, tobacco arrived in South Africa but compared with dagga it was considered useless. To spice it up, a measure of dagga would be added to the pipe. (Today dagga itself is boosted, in the notorious *witpyp*, ('white pipe') in which the relaxant methaqualone is added to the drug.) By now the white man was firmly ensconced, and the tribes were losing both land and freedom. Dagga was naturally frowned on by the colonialists, it was seen as an equivalent to opium, and denounced as similarly deleterious. It was also accepted that the natives loved it and many white farmers grew a dagga crop, specifically to induce Hottentots and Bushmen to work for them. (Given that other whites attacked the drug as taking the workers' minds off their labours, this seems paradoxical, but it appears to have been so.) Others, typically the missionary Hugo Hahn, were less pragmatic. Hahn, like all missionaries keen to eradicate local culture and replace it with his own superstitions, campaigned hard against cannabis, burning down any crops he could find.

He would, of course, have ignored another side to cannabis use: as a medicine. The plant has been used as a snake-bite remedy amongst the Mfengu and the Hottentot tribes. Sotho women were reported in 1906 as smoking cannabis to stupefy themselves during childbirth (there are records of a doctor in Pennsylvania, some thirty years later, asked for advice as to the efficacy of that very same technique) and the same tribe used a mixture of ground cannabis seeds with bread or mealiepap to help weaning. (In his 1957 novel *City of Spades*, Colin MacInnes' Nigerian character extols the use of a quick puff to soothe a fractious or teething baby.) In what was then Southern Rhodesia the plant was used in the treatment of malaria, blackwater fever, blood-poisoning, anthrax and dysentery.

Zulus, who named the drug *iNtsangu*, and planted some in every kraal (traditional African village), smoked for sociability using a hubble-bubble (*iGudu*) made from a cow's or, when richer, an antelope's horn. It had a reed stem inserted at an acute angle half-way down its side and a small bowl for the dagga. The explorer Alfred Bryant, writing in his book *The Zulu People*

Overleaf: Marijuana, 'the weed of wisdom' or 'tree of life' is seen by the Coptic Church as a sacrament. It is believed to have been created by God as a spiritual food for all humankind and as such is a 'fiery sacrifice to be offered to the Redeemer'. As these girls, smoking marijuana at a Coptic Church in Jamaica, make clear, taking part in this form of devotion places no restrictions on age.

As They Were Before the White Man Came (1949), gives a detailed portrait of Zulu smoking. 'The smoking horn having been filled with water (to just above the level of the stem-aperture), and the bowl with dry, rubbed-up hemp leaves (*iNtsangu*) bearing a tiny glowing ember on their top, the smoker (having first taken a sip of water and retained it in his mouth) placed the large open end of the horn to the side of his mouth and cheek (so as to close all ingress of air), and gave two or three strong draws, bringing the smoke from the hemp, through the water, and so into his mouth, where part of it found its way straight into his lungs. The consequence was a violent coughing and abundant secretion of saliva, which latter, mixed together with the water and the smoke (already filling his mouth), the smoker now discharged in the form of a bubbly foam through a small reed-like stem of the *iNgwevu* plant. As this foamy spittle passed through and out of this tube (u*Tshumo*) on to the earthen hut floor, the smoker, by means of his forefinger, drew with on the floor various designs (kraals, mazes and the rest). Whilst the one smoker was thus engaged drawing his picture, his companion would be having his pull at the horn. In a few minutes the whole smoking party would be loudly coughing, each in the interval shouting out his own or his family's praises (*iziBongo*), and all of them enwrapt in a state of consummate bliss…'

He adds that 'most Zulu men smoked hemp daily without apparent harm' but followed the usual pattern of caveats, noting that smoking 'to excess', and especially when young, 'the mental faculties became gradually and permanently blunted'. He notes the variety of effects: from irrepressible laughter to extreme moroseness and 'in still others, dangerous and criminal incitement, and even delirium'. Young warriors were especially enthusiastic smokers – a belief held for many years: the Boers, for instance, were convinced that the Zulus who fought them at the Battle of Blood River were all under dagga's influence.

Ben-Riamba, or the 'sons of hemp'

The outstanding story of African cannabis use was told in 1891 by the German explorer Herman von Wissman in his book *My Second Journey Through Equatorial Africa*. The tribe in question were the Bashilange, whose local name for cannabis was *riamba*: 'One tribe with another, one village with another, always lived at daggers drawn – then about 25 years ago [circa 1850] a hemp-smoking worship began to be established, and the effect of smoking…made itself felt. The Ben-Riamba, Sons of Hemp, found more and more followers: they began to have intercourse with each other as they became less barbarous and more civilized, and made laws'.

As he explained, the transformation in Bashilange society was nothing short of miraculous. The drug itself became a symbol of peace, friendship, magic and protection. Men were no longer allowed to carry weapons in their village; cannibalism, hitherto accepted, was banned; like latter-day hippies one greeted one's neighbours with the words 'life' or 'health'. Palm-wine, once a regular intoxicant, was banned; the smoking of cannabis became a duty. Religious ceremonies were focused on the communal smoking of the cannabis pipe (even if women were, as ever, excluded: they had to do the work, not lie around stoned). Von Wissman found himself included in the new belief: he, claimed the tribesmen, was the reincarnation of an old chief, Kassongo, who had apparently been washed white during his absence. Perhaps the strangest development was a new punishment: anyone accused of a crime, was ordered to smoke *riamba* until they either admitted the crime or passed out. Adulterers suffered similar treatment, with the amount of *riamba* to be consumed calculated on the tribal status of the errant man. Once he had passed out things became nastier: he was stripped, pepper was dropped into his eyes and a ribbon threaded through his nasal bone, to be a badge of his transgression.

The new cult did not last. This proto-hippie lifestyle had as many opponents as its later equivalents. Laws based on cannabis were too lenient; the equality of the new society was seen as unacceptable by those, the aristocracy, who had benefited from prior stratification; most important was the collapse of the tribe's status in local politics. Those other tribes, formerly subjugated, lost their respect and behaved accordingly – tributes, once vital to Bashilange prosperity, were simply ignored. And since they would no longer fight, let alone eat their enemies, they had no useful sanction.

Ernest Abel, a cannabis historian writing in 1980, continues the story: 'All these problems came to a head around 1876 when a serious rebellion against the chief broke out. The chief, his brother, and his sister were accused of having killed a man by sorcery. It was a trumped-up charge, but the accused

had to smoke dagga until they became unconscious. When finally they fell to the ground, they were attacked and stabbed by their enemies. Had it not been for the intervention of some of the other villagers, they would have been killed. Having failed in their attempt to assassinate the royal family, the leaders of the rebellion deserted the village, but they soon returned to their homes and were never punished for their crime. The end was near at hand, however, and it was not long before the anticannabis forces mustered enough support to overthrow the riamba cult'.

The utopia was over, but even then not all changes vanished. The tribe still attempted to maintain pacific rather than warlike relations with their neighbours and the legal system still involved cannabis smoking.

Hashish in North Africa

Although evidence has been found of plants that may or not have been hemp in the Pharaonic civilization there is no conclusive proof of its existence in this early period. The recorded spread of cannabis began in the eleventh century in Egypt where, in common with other nearby countries of the Middle East, hashish had arrived with immigrant Sufis (Muslim mystics). It was, as found elsewhere, something of a lower-class indulgence, but it was widely enough smoked for a variety of 'pleasure garden' to spring up: the Gardens of Cafour' a short distance from Cairo. A contemporary poem hymned the gardens' delights: 'The green plant which grows / In the garden of Cafour, / Replaces in our hearts / the effects of a wine / old and generous …The poor when they have taken / only the weight of one drachm / have a head superb above the Emirs.'

Cairo's Canton de la Timbalière

The gardens were memorialized by the physician and cannabis researcher William O'Shaughnessy in 1839 as 'the celebrated Canton de la Timbalière, or ancient pleasure grounds, in the vicinity of Cairo. This quarter, after many vicissitudes, is now a heap of ruins. In it was situated a cultivated valley named Djoneina, which we are informed was the theatre of all conceivable abominations. It was famous above all for the sale of the *hasheeha*, a drug still greedily consumed by the dregs of the populace, and from the consumption of which sprung the excesses which led to the name of 'assassin' [see page 57], being given to the Saracens in the Holy Wars.'

Man smoking sheesha pipe, Giza, Egypt, 1993.

Such pleasure, even of 'the dregs' was, as ever, anathema to the moralists of religion. The Moorish botanist Ibn al-Baytar, who was definitely no fan, wrote in his diary: 'People who use it habitually proved its pernicious effect…it enfeebles their minds by carrying them maniac affections; sometimes it even causes their death. I recall having seen a time when men of the vilest class alone dared to eat it, still they did not like the name hashishin applied to them'.

The garden was destroyed in 1251 but, the consumption of hashish was not affected; there were plenty of fields devoted to growing the drug. Farmers paid a tax, and the government seemed unworried. Writing in circa 1400, the Egyptian historian Taqi ad-Din al-Makrizi saw this resurgence as quite unedifying: cannabis had not been eradicated and 'as its consequence, general corruption of sentiments and manners ensued, modesty disappeared, every base and evil passion was openly indulged in, and nobility of external form alone remained to these infatuated beings'. (Makrizi, however, knew his cannabis, he notes elsewhere that oxymel and acids are the most powerful antidotes to the effect of this 'narcotic'; next to these, emetics, cold bathing and sleep; and he also tells of diuretic, astringent and specially aphrodisiac properties.)

In 1324 that tolerance ended. As in today's 'war on drugs' the military were enlisted against the plant, and fields were burnt throughout the country. Soon, inevitably they were sown again – equally inevitably bribes were offered and taken – and cannabis use went on as ever. In 1378 there was a new clampdown. Again the army moved in, but this time the growers threatened to fight back. There was a stand-off for several months, but the authorities had to win. This time the campaign was brutal. Towns and villages were destroyed, fields burnt, growers and sellers were executed while smokers were rounded up and had their teeth torn from their mouths. Yet once more cannabis came back. Soon it would be openly sold in bazaars and its production was maintained well into the twenty-first century.

The move to Morocco
With its early use in Egypt, the smoking of hashish spread along the whole North African littoral. By the twentieth century it had become a regular practice in Tunisia, Algeria and Morocco. In all cases the colonial rulers,

usually the French, attempted to stamp out the practice, but with no more success than there had been in Egypt. Perhaps the best known of all these is Morocco. Hashish itself would not be manufactured in Morocco until as late as 1962 (it had been available there, imported from Lebanon, since the 1930s), but kif, which was already being noticed by British travellers a century earlier, was widely used. As explained in 1897 by Timothy Coakley in his book *Keef*, 'Keef, it may be said, is a Moorish preparation of Indian Hemp, and, in its essential principle, is identical with the hashish of the Turks and the majoon of Calcutta. But whilst both hashish and majoon are used in the form of a paste or confection, prepared from the juices of the plant, keef consists of the leaves and tender parts of the plant itself These are pulverized; and the fumes of the powder, which are frequently mixed with a mild and aromatic tobacco, are then inhaled into the lungs through the medium of tiny pipes of burnt clay'.

Despite the French desire to do away with kif smoking, until independence, in 1956, it was just possible, to buy small paper-wrapped 'deals' of kif in the tobacco stalls of the souk. As the writer Paul Bowles noted, such small bundles 'lined the inside of the tiny tobacco stalls like so much wallpaper'.

Manufacturing kif
The main area of cultivation is in the Rif mountains of northern Morocco. Kif is in fact a mixture of cannabis and tobacco. The cannabis researcher Robert Connell Clarke describes the process: 'Kif is prepared for smoking by stripping the leaves from the dried female branches and carefully pulling the floral clusters from the stems. The seeds and small stems are removed and the flowers are chopped finely with a sharp knife. A small amount of black-market tobacco leaf is added in a ratio of 2:1, kif to tobacco, and the mixture is chopped again. When the blend is correctly chopped – not too coarse to make tidy hits and not so fine as to slip through the bowl during smoking – it is stored in a small goatskin pouch'. It is smoked either in a special pipe, a *sebsi*, or through a water pipe and consumed communally, passing the pipe from hand to hand. Paradoxically, it was the black-market tobacco mixed with the cannabis that was actually more dangerous – in legal terms – to the smoker. Being caught with kif itself is unlikely to bring any problems; being caught with the tobacco, which being illegally grown is in effect a form of tax-dodging, can see one sent to jail for up to six months.

An old man goes about preparing kif, the traditional way of consuming cannabis in Morocco.

Writing in his 1931 book *Phantastica* Louis Lewin explained that kif is also known as *shira* and *fasuch*, as well as *benj*, the Arabic name. All forms of the drug are 'very powerful in their action'. He suggested that its consumption was mainly a pleasure of 'the poorer classes' and that 'among the greater part of them, especially among the camel and donkey driver, the necessity for a bout of inebriety from kif appears every few days'. The middle and upper classes had supposedly abandoned the practice of smoking kif in the late nineteenth century.

Morocco – king of the world

Today, Morocco is the largest single manufacturer and exporter of hashish in the world. Although the hippies of the Sixties and Seventies generally eschewed it, preferring what were seen as the superior products of Afghanistan or Nepal, most modern smokers are likely to find themselves buying Moroccan; the vast bulk of that on sale in the coffee shops of Amsterdam, for instance, is sourced there.

The ancient Romans

Of the two great classical empires that of Greece seems to have had no use for cannabis in any form. Nor do the Romans seem to have used it as an intoxicant. They were, however, aware of its other properties, whether as hemp or in medicine. The main discussion of the plant was in *De Materia Medica* (AD 40–90), compiled by the Greek physician Dioscorides who had moved to Rome and then begun work as a military surgeon, travelling around the Empire tending the troops. His travels gave him the material for his book, which ran to five volumes, covering 600 plants and nearly 1000 drugs. The book identified each of the plants listed according to its native habitat and the names by which it was known. Any peculiar features were noted and, finally, symptoms and conditions for which the plant had proven beneficial were described. The illustrations were especially fine. While critics have suggested that his methods were less than properly scientific, and he dispensed a good deal of far from accurate folklore, what Dioscorides produced had never been done before. Translated into every language of the medieval world, it remained the standard pharmacological textbook for the next 1500 years.

Dioscorides divided cannabis into two types: 'wild' and 'tame'. His description of 'tame' cannabis was brief: 'A plant useful to human life for the twisting of well-strung ropes. It bears foul-smelling leaves resembling the ash [melia], large hollow stems, a round edible [esthiomenon] seed which when consumed in quantities extinguishes the semen; a decoction of green [cannabis], when instilled, is fit for ear-aches'. There was no reference, however, to any intoxicant properties.

Shortly afterwards, in the second century AD, cannabis was mentioned by another hugely important Roman physician, Galen (AD 129–199), whose work would influence both Western and Arabic medicine for centuries. His references to cannabis were also brief, but he noted that rich Roman gourmets liked to offer a cannabis-seed dessert, which had a beneficial effect on those who ate it. He warned, however, not to overindulge, that way lay dehydration and for men, impotence. Positive properties noted included antiflatulence and analgesia. He also noted the 'warm and toxic vapor' that overtakes one's head if the drug is taken to excess. Galen also offers his own recipe for dried seeds, chopped, sifted and mixed with water, then filtered through a clean cloth: the purpose of this decoction is unspecified; possibly it relates to the preparation of some form of analgesic. Finally, he stated that the only proper use of the seeds is for those who are trying to purify the blood through the urine.

Cannabis in European Christian writing…Papal condemnation implants a suspicion of cannabis in the West…early accounts of the 'exotic East' bring the drug to the attention of a Western audience…illustrations of the cannabis plant begin to appear…the Napoleonic army is introduced to cannabis after it invades Egypt…the drug is brought back to France…nineteenth-century intellectuals experiment with the drug in the names of science and inspiration…cannabis reaches the UK…the start of recreational use in America…the Jazz Age…the beats…the beatniks and hippies…Vietnam…Rastafarianism…the Hippie Trail.

RECREATIONAL AND INSPIRATIONAL USES

Although cannabis use had spread throughout Central and Southern Asia and come as far West as Egypt and North and South Africa, it had yet to penetrate Europe. That is not to say that certain writers and physicians were not interested. According to Ethan Russo in his essay 'Hemp and Headache' (2001), as early as the eleventh century, Hildegard von Bingen (1098–1179), abbess, musician, and herbalist wrote of cannabis in her *Physica* (1533), stating: 'Whoever has an empty brain and head pains may eat it and the head pains will be reduced. Though he who is healthy and full of brains shall not be harmed by it – he who has an empty brain shall be caused pain by indulging in hemp. A healthy head and a full brain will not be harmed.'

Cannabis and the Church

Hildegard von Bingen resisted bringing Satan into her assessment of the drug, but as an exotic product of the 'mysterious' East it was inevitable that the religiously credulous would equate hemp, as they termed it, with some strange, and as such demonic, drug. To quote the cannabis historian Ernest Abel: 'In 1484, Pope Innocent VIII issued a papal fiat condemning witchcraft and the use of hemp in the Satanic mass. In 1615, an Italian physician and demonologist, Giovanni De Ninault, listed hemp as the main ingredient in the ointments and unguents used by the Devil's followers. Hemp, along with opium, belladonna, henbane, and hemlock, the demonologists believed, were commonly used during the Witches' Sabbath. Hemp seed oil was also an ingredient in the ointments witches allegedly used to enable them to fly.

A Turkish woman reclining with a hookah of marijuana, circa1895. A hookah is an Oriental tobacco pipe designed to cool the smoke before it is drawn into the mouth.

Abel also notes that 'Jean Wier, the celebrated demonologist of the sixteenth century, was quite familiar with the exhilarating effects of hemp for sinister purposes. Hemp, he wrote, caused a loss of speech, uncontrollable laughter, and marvelous visions. Quoting Galen, he explained that it was capable of producing these effects by "virtue of affecting the brain since if one takes a large enough amount the vapors destroy the reason".'

Whilst such religious mumbo-jumbo seems absurd, it implanted in the credulous Western masses a suspicion of cannabis. Pope Innocent's condemnation of cannabis as an 'anti-sacrament' (based on the idea that it was used in a Black Mass as a substitute for the wine of an orthodox one) was vital if the Church should implant both fear and loathing in the worshipping regiments. That those condemned in Europe as witches and sorcerers, not to mention the shamans, fakirs and similar figures in other countries, all used cannabis merely 'proved' that Christianity was right. A fear of cannabis is hardly the only religious superstition to leave its malign imprint on the modern world.

Of course, as author of *Botany of Desire* Michael Pollan suggests, from the Establishment's point of view (and that meant the Church in fifteenth-century Europe, although the same tokens work for capitalism today) cannabis was a threat. As was any psychotropic drug. A faith that based its control on the illusion of deferred gratification is deeply threatened by anything that offers pleasure in the here and now. It was something that the counter-culture of the 1960s instinctively understood. Smoking cannabis provided not merely pleasure but also a political statement. 'Turn on, tune in' and – not for nothing did the climax of the slogan, command 'drop out'. That statement seems less pronounced today, even as the 'war on drugs' continues its largely impotent flailing; smokers have realized the simplest way round a foolish law is simply that – to go around it. And if we believe Michael Pollan, cannabis, amongst other demonized drugs, may be seen as a fount of knowledge, that very knowledge that had God hurl Adam and Eve from Eden. The idea that nature could provide knowledge, and tangible knowledge at that, was anathema to a Church that operated its whole system as a justification for power. So, cannabis must go. In a monotheistic world only God rules. All rivals are taboo. And so, says Pollan, 'unfolds the drug war's first battle'.

Hemp's divine powers

Hemp seems to have been especially popular as a form of divination, usually as a means of helping a young girl find herself a husband. Examples can be found in the Ukraine and in Ireland. Ukrainian girls with hemp seeds in their belts jump on a pile of hemp, crying out: 'Andrei, Andrei, / I plant the hemp seed on you. / Will God let me know / With whom I will sleep?' They then remove their blouses, fill their mouths with water to spit on the hemp seeds and run around their houses a magical three times. Dances involving hemp were also common in Eastern Europe, sometimes in connection with magically aiding the hemp crop to grow and sometimes as part of marriage feasts and other wedding celebrations

Nor was the UK immune to this line of thought: 'Carry the seed in your apron,' commands the 1685 book *Mother Bunch's Closet Newly Broke Open* 'and with your right hand throw it over your left shoulder, saying thus: "Hemp-seed I sow, hemp-seed I sow, And he that must be my true love, Come after me and mow". And at the ninth time expect to see the figure of him you are to wed, or else hear a bell'. If she was lucky a spectral form of her husband-to-be mowing with his scythe would be there behind her. If she were not so fortunate she would see a coffin behind her, signifying that she would die whilst still young and unmarried.

Da Orta's Colloquies

The next major book in which cannabis – in the form of hashish – played a role was *Colloquies on the Simples and Drugs and Materia Medica of India* Written by a Portuguese physician, Garcia da Orta (1501–1568) in 1563, it was soon translated into a variety of European languages; the English version appearing in 1577.

Garcia da Orta's parents were Spanish Jews who moved to Portugal in 1492 when Jews (and Moors) were expelled from Spain at the start of the Inquisition. In 1497 when compelled by the Portuguese authorities to choose between exile and conversion, the family nominally converted to Christianity, rather than face further exile. As a young man, da Orta studied at the Spanish universities of Salamanca and Alcala de Vide, qualifying as a physician in 1526. After working as a doctor for six years and then as a lecturer in natural philosophy at the University of Lisbon, he left Portugal in

1534 to accompany a friend to Goa. Here he remained, serving as physician
to the governors of Goa, and also to the ruler Burham Nizam Shah whose
capital was in Ahmadnagar. He spent the remaining thirty-six years of his
life in India.

Fired by a desire to elicit all the information he could about the country in
which he now lived, da Orta quizzed everyone he met about the local botany.
The result was the *Colloquies*. It takes the form of a discussion between da
Orta and a fictitious colleague – one Dr Ruano, who like his creator had
studied at Salamanca and in his erudition and wit may well have been a self-
portrait of the author in his younger days. Da Orta portrays himself as more
mature, a seasoned traveller and a dedicated accumulator of information.
'For me the testimony of an eye-witness is worth more than that of all the
physicians, and all the fathers of medicine who wrote on false information'.
And he tells Ruano, 'Do not try to frighten me with Dioscorides or Galen,
because I merely speak the truth and say what I know'. The *Colloquies* is
filled with this kind of information, including such arcana as the fights
between the cobra and the mongoose, the etiquette of chewing betel nut, the
taming of elephants and the rules of chess.

Amongst this plethora of still exotic knowledge come his studies of a
number of psychotropic substances, notably opium, datura and *bangue* (the
Portuguese spelling), the concoction made from cannabis. He resisted taking
it himself, but wrote about it with the authority of close observation:
'Bangue is a plant which greatly resembles hemp, except that the seed is a
little smaller, and not so white…The Indians eat the leaves and the seeds, so
as the more to incline themselves to the venereal act…Its juice is expressed
from the crushed leaves, and on occasion the seeds too, to which there can
be added…some nutmeg, or mace, or cloves, and sometimes also some
camphor from Borneo; others add amber and musk, and some add opium,
as do the richest and most opulent among the Moors. They acquire no
advantage for this, unless it is in the fact that they become ravished by
ecstasy, and delivered from all worries and cares, and laugh at the least little
thing. Indeed it is said that it was they who first found the use of it, when
their generals and men of war, exhausted by constant watches, having drunk
a little bhang with wine or opium, became as if inebriated, and slept as if
delivered from all cares.'

And he continued, 'Bangue…makes a man laugh foolishly and lifts him above all cares…I hear that many women take it when they want to dally and flirt with men…I've heard it said, although it may not be true, that the great captains, in ancient times, used to drink it with wine or opium so that they could get some rest from their work, banish their cares, and get to sleep'.

He also noted what would become the whole phenomenon of 'set and setting' – one's experience of bhang was bound up with one's prevailing mood: 'I myself saw a Portuguese jester…eat a slice or two of the electuary and at night he was pleasantly intoxicated, his utterance not intelligible. Then he became sad, began to shed tears, and was plunged into grief. In his case the effect was sadness and nausea…Those of my servants who took it, unbeknownst to me, said that it made them so as not to feel their work, to be very happy, and to have a craving for food. I believe that it is generally used and by such a large number of people, that there is no mystery about it'.

The book was an instant success across Europe. Cannabis joined the Western pharmacopoeia, with physicians using it to create variously euphoria, sedation, stimulation of appetite, hallucinations and aphrodisia. The *Colloquies* remained hugely influential, but no thanks to the contemporary Church. Shortly after da Orta's death his wife confessed to the Portuguese Inquisition that her husband had been secretly practising his original Jewish faith. The Church responded as one would expect: da Orta's corpse was exhumed and ritualistically burnt: Copies of the book were sought out and, when found, destroyed. Fortunately, in 1567, a Flemish botanist, Charles del'Ecluse, extracted the essential information on the characteristics and properties of the economic and medicinal plants of India and published an epitome in Latin. It is this epitome, rather than the original *Colloquies*, that was translated into Italian (1582) and French (1619) and that would ensure the book's longevity.

Travellers' tales

In 1578 another converted Portuguese Jew, Cristobal da Costa (1524–1594), published his book *On the Drugs and Medicines from the East Indies*. It describes sixty-nine plants and other sources of drugs and medicines but is little more than a facsimile of his great predecessor. The one advantage it had, however, was forty-six full-page illustrations (although the cannabis plant is not illustrated . Da Costa was, of course, interested in bangue. He noted that 'some take it to forget their worries and sleep without thoughts; others to enjoy in their sleep a variety of dreams and delusions; others become drunk and act like merry jesters; others because of love sickness'. He continued that those who wished to enjoy visions should mix it with camphor, clove, nutmeg and mace, whilst those who required something to boost their sexual potency should opt for amber, musk and sugar. No more original was the Dutchman Jan Huyghen van Linschoten, whose *Itinerario* appeared in 1596. Not content with plagiarizing da Orta, he often added his own material – material that tended to the fanciful and inaccurate. Not that this worried his readers, although it was from his mistaken assumptions that people began to believe, quite erroneously, that as far as their effects went, opium and bhang were one and the same.

After da Orta the next original work on the subject of hashish was that written by the Italian physician Prospero Alpini (1553–1617). In 1580 he had been appointed physician to the Venetian Consul in Egypt. In this position he was able to conduct extensive research, grilling the locals for botanical information. He amassed a detailed list of some fifty-seven plants and trees as yet unknown in Europe, and in 1591 published *De Medicinia Aegyptiorum (Of the Medicines of the Egyptians)*; it was followed a year later by *De plantis Aegypti liber (Of the Book of Egyptian Plants)*. Both were very popular.

Amongst Alpini's specimens was coffee; his was the first ever written description of the plant to be widely disseminated in the West. He also collected local recipes and made a cookbook of them. As for hashish, he writes that on imbibing a preparation of the cheap powdered leaves, the people were intoxicated and remained for a long time in a state of ecstasy, 'accompanied by the visions they desired'. He compared the early stage of hashish intoxication to that of alcohol, but emphasized that the visions hashish users experienced were to an important extent dependent on their intelligence and their psychological state at the time they took the drug. After his time in Egypt Prospero Alpini moved back to Italy, taking various authoritative posts and was generally regarded as the most important physician of the era.

An illustration of Indian hemp (*Cannabis sativa*), from a woodcut in *Gart der Gesundheit*, 1485.

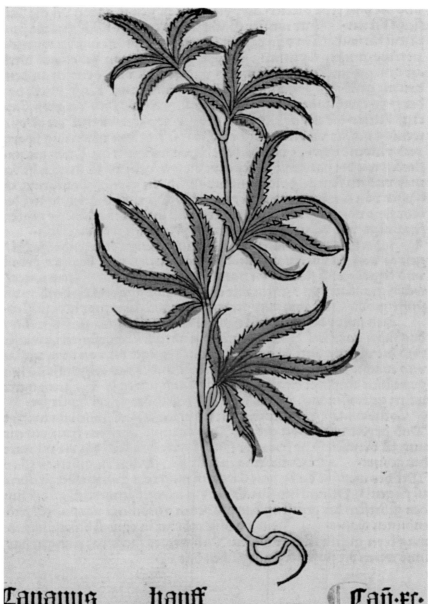

Canapus   **hanff**   **Cap·xc·**

Anapus latine·grece Canaps·arabice vero sechedenchi·
Serapio in dem buch aggregatozis in dem capitell Seche/
denchi id est canapus spricht daz diß krut werde gesetzt vnd
brenget samen vnd hait eyn langen still vnd lange este vnd eynen
starcken geroch· vñ der stam ist inwendig hoel· ¶ Paulus Canapus

Illustrating cannabis

The plant was drawn for the first time by Hendrik Adriaan van Reede tot Drakenstein (1636–1691), the Governor of Dutch territories in Malabar (today's Indian southern state of Kerala), and himself the son of a chief forester in the Netherlands. According to a paper published by the University of Kent in 2001, like da Orta before him, 'van Reede went through the same process of rejecting Arabic classification and nomenclature and European knowledge in favour of a more rigorous adherence to local system of classification'. For his information, he depended on the members of the Ezhava community of toddy-tappers, who, as noted by R. Kochar in his essay 'European Doctors in Pre-colonnial India' (1999), were 'adept both at tree climbing and plant identification'. More particularly, van Reede consulted the Vaidyars, the traditional Ayurvedic physicians with an extensive, time-tested knowledge of the medicinal value of plants. Van Reede's magnum opus, the twelve-volume *Hortus Malabaricus* (published from 1678 to 1692) described about 780 species of plants, supported by 794 illustrations. His comments on cannabis included the observation that the natives of Malabar intoxicate themselves by smoking its leaves.

The confusion of opium and bhang, initiated by van Linschoten, would recur on many occasions. In 1628, Peter Mundy, an employee of the British East India Company, wrote that bangue had the same effect as opium. In 1649 the Portuguese missionary, Fray Sebastien Manrique, told the readers of his Indian travelogue that, 'This country also produces a plant called Anfion resembling our own hemp [which is used by the people] to assist in the gratification of lust and lewdness, by increasing their sexual power... Bangue and posto [cannabis spiked with opium] have a similar effect.' In addition the natives, lacking the consolations of the Cross, appeared to worship drugs. The theme continues. In 1698, John Freyer, a physician also employed by the British East India Company, compounded the error in his *Account of East India*, suggesting that the two drugs were not merely alike but that opium was actually made from bhang. And of the two, that bhang was the more potent. It is also, again erroneously, seen as equally addictive. More interesting, and perhaps accurate, was Freyer's depiction of what he saw as an especially Indian punishment, albeit exercised only on those who were too important for simple and immediate execution. 'Upon an offence they are sent by the King's order, and committed to a place called the Post (from the punishment inflicted), where the Master of the Post is acquainted with the heinousness of the crime; which being understood, he heightens by a drink, which they first refuse, made of Bang (the juice of the intoxicating hemp), and being mingled with Dutry (the deadliest sort of Solanum or Nightshade) name [sic] Post, after a week's taking, they crave more than ever'. The upshot is death. Since the word 'post' comes from the Persian and Urdu *post*, meaning skin, rind or poppyhead, one assumes that again Freyer is confusing bhang with opium, or that the two drugs were mixed. Certainly one would not procure the required 'craving' with the non-addictive bhang.

A plethora of publications

Writer followed writer in their enthusiasm to bring home tales of the drug-ridden and exotic East. A few are worth mentioning, such as *A Geographical Account of Countries Round the Bay of Bengal* written around 1680 by the veteran sailor and writer Thomas Bowrey. He had no qualms about indulging himself in all aspects of Indian culture, including bhang, and his descriptions of his own use of the drug were very likely the first ever to be set down by an English user. Like da Orta, Bowrey recognized the importance of 'set and setting', stressing that bhang 'operates accordage to the thoughts or fancy of the Partie that drinketh thereof, in such manner that if he be merry at that instant, he shall continue soe with exceedinge great laughter for the before mentioned space of time [four to five hours], rather overymerry than otherways…and, on the contrary, if it is taken in a fearefull or melancholy posture, he shall keep great lamentation and seem to be in great anguish of spirit, takinge away all manly gesture or thought from him'.

In addition, Bowrey paints an alluring picture of a bunch of what one might term 'prototype stoners' enjoying a serious session with 'theire so admirable herbe'. Only the doublets and hose, and four centuries, seem to separate his companions from ourselves. Eight or ten of the crew went to the bazaar, where they engaged a local fakir to score them each a pint of bhang – total outlay six old pence. They then went home and locked themselves in, 'that none of us might run into the street, or any person come in to behold any of our humors thereby to laught [sic] at us'.

After a while the bhang began to take effect: 'It soon tooke its operation upon most of us, but merrily, save upon two of our number, who I suppose feared it might doe them harme not being accustomed thereto. One of them sat himselfe downe upon the floore, and wept bitterly all the afternoone, the other terrified with feare did runne his head into a great Mortavan Jarre, and continued in that posture 4 hours or more; 4 or 5 of the number lay upon the carpets (that were spread in the roome) highly complimentinge each other in high termes, each man fancyinge himselfe noe less than an emperor. One was quarrelsome and fought with one of the wooden pillars of the porch, until he had left himselfe little skin upon the knuckles of his fingers. My selfe and one more sat sweatinge for the space of 3 hours in exceedinge measure'.

In 1692 there appeared the *Amoenitatum Exoticarum Politico-Physico-Medicarum* by the German physician (not to mention historian, political scientist, diplomat, and botanist) Englebert Kaempfer (1651–1716). As fleet surgeon to the Dutch East India Company he was able to experience bhang at first hand. This was part of his tale: 'At the time of the sacrifices in honor of Vishnu, virgins pleasant to behold and richly adorned, were brought to the temple of the Brahmins. They came out in public to appease the god who rules over plenty and fine weather. To impress the spectators, these young women were previously given a preparation with a basis of hemp and datura, and when the priest saw certain symptoms, he began his invocations. The Devadassy [literally 'slave-girl of the gods' and in reality temple prostitutes – one doubts the 'virginity'] then danced, leapt about yelling, contorted their limbs, and, foaming at the mouth, their eyes ecstatic, committed all sorts of eccentricities. Finally, the priests carried the exhausted virgins into a sanctuary, gave them a potion to destroy the effect of the previous one, and then showed them again to the people in their right mind, so that the crowd of spectators might believe that the demons had fled and the idol was appeased.'

The Bard and the bud

One writer, no traveller other than in the mind, should perhaps have a brief mention. The academic Francis Thackeray has written extensively on the possibility, in which he firmly believes, that 'at least some of the 154 sonnets relate to metaphors for perceptions associated with altered states of consciousness induced by one or more hallucinogenic plants, including Cannabis sativa.' He suggests, in his article 'The Tenth Muse: Hemp as a source of inspiration for Shakespearean literature?' published by the *South*

African Journal of Science in March 2001, that cannabis provides just such an extra stimulation to creative talents, and Shakespeare was well aware of it. He has looked closely at all the sonnets and believes that Shakespeare knew all about this still relatively new source of intoxication. Amongst the potential drug references are sonnet 119: 'What potions have I drunk of siren tears / Distilled from limbecks foul as hell within... / How have mine eyes out of their spheres been fitted / In the distraction of this madding fever?'; and that to 'compounds' in sonnet 76, that is 'Why with the time do I not glance aside to new-found methods and to compounds strange?'. There are several more. It may be that Thackeray protests too much; on the other hand he may be right. Shakespeare could have read and perhaps did read the *Colloquies* (see pages 81–83) and there were other cannabis-related volumes that he could have seen. It is, if nothing else, an intriguing possibility.

Cannabis arrives in Europe

Given the antiquity of the widespread nature of cannabis in the countries of what today is termed the 'third world', it is surprising how very long it took for cannabis to cross the last boundaries, and arrive in Europe. Explorers and empire-builders had certainly encountered the drug, if only at second hand, and were happy to tax its merchants and importers. It seems hard to believe that at least a few young men, probably those who 'went native' and took local wives, were not introduced to the drug on a more intimate level. Opium, equally popular, certainly appears to have permeated the colonial ranks; then, why not cannabis? Given the trading that after all was used to justify much of the colonists' intrusions into other cultures, it seems odd that this one product was excluded from the merchants' manifests. Yet there is no evidence otherwise, and recreational consumption of cannabis, until the late eighteenth century, remained outside the Western experience. There was considerable interest in the drug, either as an exotic pleasure to be indulged by 'natives' (and the very occasional and extremely intrepid visitor) or, more commonly, as a potential addition to the Western pharmacopoeia. But recreational use: not yet.

It was, albeit indirectly, the colonial push that did the trick. In 1798 the French emperor Napoleon invaded Egypt, the first step on what he saw would be a campaign to establish a French kingdom there and in time to drive on to India. He would be expelled in 1801, his conquest a disaster and

his troops would make their way back to France. Beforehand, however, the soldiers had made a new discovery: hashish, sold to them by local dealers.

French troops, left behind after Napoleon's march to Syria, halt at Syene on their journey to upper Egypt, 1799.

In October 1800 the following orders were issued: 'Art. 1. Throughout Egypt the use of a beverage prepared by certain Moslems from hemp (hashish), as well as the smoking of the seeds of hemp, is prohibited. Habitual smokers and drinkers of this plant lose their reason and suffer from violent delirium in which they are liable to commit excesses of all kinds. Art. 2. The preparation of hashish as a beverage is prohibited throughout Egypt. The doors of those cafés and restaurants where it is supplied are to be walled up, and their proprietors imprisoned for three months. Art. 3. All bales of hashish arriving at the customs shall be confiscated and publicly burnt.'

But even so rigorous a ban had no real effect, and like the US troops who brought heroin habits home from Vietnam in the 1970s, so Napoleon's soldiers came home with samples of cannabis. The upshot would be the gradual popularization of the drug in Europe, and notably in France. But before discussing this new expansion, it is worth noting one earlier example of a French interest in the plant.

Rabelais and Pantagruelion

In 1546, writing as Alcofribas Nasier (an anagram of his own name) the physician, humanist and satirist Francois Rabelais (1494–1553) published *Tiers Livre de Pantagruel*, the further adventures, as it were, of the giant, who had first appeared in *Pantagruel* in 1533. The second book, dealing with Pantagruel's father Gargantua, had appeared in 1534. Whilst the bulk of the *Tiers Livre* satirizes and debates current events, chapters forty-nine to fifty-two deal with the herb Pantagruelion, otherwise known as hemp.

More importantly Rabelais explains how when Pantagruel was preparing his ship for a voyage, 'amongst other things, it was observed how he caused to be fraught and loaded with an herb of his called Pantagruelion, not only of the green and raw sort of it, but of the confected also'. The confected, one must assume, refers to mahjoun, or some similar cannabis-based sweetmeat. It should also be noted that Rabelais' father Antoine had farmed hemp and that Rabelais himself had translated Herodotus, who was one of the first writers to mention the use of cannabis as an intoxicant.

The Hashish Club

The original arrival of hashish – the dried leaf form of cannabis – from Egypt was followed by more regularized imports and soon one could buy it at any pharmacy. It was therefore unsurprising that the medical establishment, in the person of Dr Jacques-Joseph Moreau (1804–1884), who would come to be regarded by many as the father of clinical

psychopharmacology and psychotomimetic drug treatment, began to take an interest in its properties. Moreau was a pupil of Jean Esquirol (1772–1840), an early psychiatrist, and from him had become fascinated by the role of hallucinations and their links to mental breakdown. Moreau decided that if it were possible, through this new drug, to achieve what might be termed 'artificial insanity', it might help in working out what lay behind the real thing.

Approaching the 'dream state'

As Dr Moreau put it in his study 'Hashish and Mental Illness', 'To understand an ordinary depression it is necessary to have experienced one; to comprehend the ravings of a madman, it is necessary to have raved oneself but without losing the awareness of one's madness, without having lost the power to evaluate the psychic changes occurring in the mind'. He visualized a person as having two modes of existence: one involving communication with the external world; the other with one's inner self. Dreams linked the two and, he believed, hashish could project one directly into that 'in-between' dream state. (Just over a century later Aldous Huxley and his successors used first mescaline and then LSD for much the same experiments.)

Moreau was no hashish novice: he had toured the Arab countries during the 1830s and whilst there had tried the drug. What triggered his more immediate interest was a piece by a fellow doctor (at the hospital Bicêtre in Paris), Louis Aubert-Roche: 'Concerning Typhus and the Pestilence in the Orient'. In it Roche suggested that the reasons Egyptians appeared to suffer less from such diseases as typhus, which decimated the European population, was because they smoked cannabis. He proposed it as a remedy for a number of contagious diseases. Moreau, in turn, wondered what else the drug might do.

Thus, in 1840, Moreau swallowed some cannabis, with the intention of reporting on its intoxicating effects. What he experienced was a mixture of euphoria, hallucination and incoherence, and at the same time an extremely rapid flow of ideas. As one dose followed another he began to notice that the effects varied in direct proportion to the quantity consumed. The more one took, the nearer one approached the hallucinatory 'dream-state' that Moreau believed approximated true insanity. His own experiences led him to

A self-portrait by Horace Vernet (1789–1863) smoking 'hasheesh' dated 1835.

various conclusions, notably that insanity was not the product of brain damage (as had been believed), but of chemical changes in the nervous system that led in turn to changes in the way the brain worked.

Like any good scientist Moreau realized that experimenting on oneself, especially with a drug of which the implicit nature was to distort one's sensations and impressions, was not enough. What he needed was a group of guinea pigs whom he could observe.

Gautier's guinea pigs

In 1844, he met the French philosopher, writer and journalist Théophile Gautier (1811–1872), a man who was at the heart of the current intellectual movement Romanticism, and whose own manifestos were amongst the primary underpinnings of the movement epitomized by the slogan 'art for art's sake'. Gautier was impressed by Moreau's theories, especially perhaps his description of cannabis as 'an intellectual intoxication', preferable to the 'ignoble heavy drunkenness' of alcohol. Gautier, determined to take on the required guinea-pig role, brought with him a number of leading Parisian littérateurs: Alexandre Dumas, Gérard de Nerval, Victor Hugo, Honoré de Balzac, Ferdinand Boissard, Charles Baudelaire, Eugène Delacroix, Roger de Beauvoir (then known as 'the idol of Paris') and many others. The group, calling themselves the Club des Hachichins ('Hashish Club') would gather regularly between 1844 and 1849 at the suitably gothic Pimodan House, also known as the Hôtel Lauzun on the Left Bank. The house, more a palace, was a wonderfully decayed building, once a Parisian landmark, now decrepit but still displaying the faded glories – amongst them the gargoyle dragon that stood guard from the first floor – of a building erected in 1657.

An illustration of 'The dream of the Old Man of the Mountains' (1891): the legend of the 'Assassins' had a strong hold on nineteenth-century French imagination.

Here, ritualistically garbed in Arabic clothing, they drank strong Arabic coffee, liberally laced with the hashish, which Moreau called *dawamesk* in the Arabic manner. It looked, reported the members, like a greenish preserve and its ingredients were a mixture of hashish, cinnamon, cloves, nutmeg, pistachio, sugar, orange juice, butter and cantharides (extract of a green beetle and widely, if erroneously known as the aphrodisiac 'Spanish fly').Some of the Hachichins would write at length of their 'stoned' experiences, although not all. Dumas, for instance, who had been viewed with some asperity as overly bourgeois – he mixed after all with the royal

court – and thus insufficiently bohemian never set down his own drug-taking. However Dumas, as a novelist, appreciated the commercial potential of the exotic. Readers of his best-known novel *The Count of Monte Cristo* (published in 1844–1845 when the Club was at its height) would read a chapter headed 'Sinbad the Sailor'. On an apparently deserted island the hero Franz meets a mysterious stranger, in fact the leader of a band of smugglers, who refers to himself only as Sinbad. Sinbad, whose magnificent palace is situated beneath the island, invites him to dine. A grand meal is followed by the appearance of a servant.

'Franz lifts the lid of the cup and sees a "greenish paste". "Taste this," his host says, offering the paste, "and the boundaries of possibility disappear, the fields of infinite space open to you, you advance free in heart, free in mind, into the boundless realms of unfettered reverie.' Sinbad has some paste, and entertains Franz with the legend of the 'Old Man of the Mountains' and his Assassins. Franz knows it and exclaims, 'It is hasheesh!' He too eats some paste. The story continues and, after Franz has fallen asleep, only to wake back at ground level, and wondering whether he dreamed the whole thing, he realizes the truth: it was real and 'Sinbad' was the Old Man, Hassan-i Sabbah himself. Like an actual assassin he has been introduced to Hassan's magical garden, in this case the underground palace, drugged, indulged in pleasant experiences, and then returned to earth.'

Honoré de Balzac, author of the multi-volumed *Comédie Humaine*, was another who attended the Club but preferred not to indulge. Baudelaire, who did, recounted what happened when his old friend visited the Hôtel Lauzun for the first time. Cannabis historian Ernest Abel describes the occasion: 'Balzac doubtless thought that there is for man no greater shame, no greater suffering, than to abdicate his will. I saw him once in a drawing-room, where they were talking of the prodigious effects of hashish. He listened and asked questions with an amusing attention and vivacity. Those who knew him may guess that it must have interested him, but the idea of thinking despite himself shocked him severely. They offered him dawamesk. He examined it, sniffed at it, and returned it without touching it. The struggle between his almost childish curiosity and his repugnance to submit himself showed strikingly on his expressive face. The love of dignity won the day.' Not for ever, though. Sometime late in 1845 the great man 'cracked' and ate the magic spoonful. This time he told fellow members that he had heard celestial voices and seen visions of divine paintings. It was a one-off occasion: in the end coffee, sans hashish, was a greater inspiration for the tireless creator of the *Comédie* and he left, this time for good.

Three members, however, were dedicated memoirists: De Nerval, Baudelaire and Théophile Gautier himself.

Gautier's experiences of the magic spoonful

It is Gautier who is the best informant as regards what went on. Whilst others, such as Baudelaire, detailed their hashish experiences, with all the rococo detail they could muster, Gautier – a journalist rather than a poet – was astute enough to pander to the public fascination for such exotic get-togethers. In his essay 'Le Club des Hachichins', published in the *Revue des Deux Mondes* in 1846, he preferred to talk of the Club itself. This was not his first discussion of hashish. He had, in 1843, read the anonymous Le Hachych (its author, as printed in the 1848 reprint was Francois Lallemand) – the first book to use hashish as a plot device. Gautier quickly wrote his own piece: 'Le hashish', concentrating on the hallucinations he had experienced whilst intoxicated. Three years later came 'Le Club des Hachichins'. It is a gratifyingly 'over the top' piece of writing, conveying exactly the sort of melodramatic atmosphere such a drug, and such a place, was supposed to have. It begins:

> One December evening…I arrived in a remote quarter in the middle of Paris, a kind of solitary oasis which the river encircles in its arms on both sides as though to defend it against the encroachments of civilization. It was in an old house on the Ile St Louis, the Pimodan hotel built by Lauzun, where the strange club which I had recently joined held its monthly séance. I was attending for the first time.
>
> Though it was scarcely six o clock, the night was black. A fog, made thicker still by the nearness of the Seine, blurred all the shapes under its quilting…The pavement, inundated with rain, glistened under the street lamp as water reflects an image; a sharp dry wind carrying particles of sleet whipped into the face…None of winter's rude poetry was wanting that night.
>
> It was difficult in the clump of sombre buildings along that

Overleaf: A drawing by Jean-Martin Charot (1825–1893), produced under the influence of hashish. Hôtel de la Salpetrière, Paris.

deserted quay to distinguish the house for which I searched; nevertheless my coachman, perched high on his seat, managed to read on a marble plaque the half-worn, gilded name of the old hotel, the gathering place for the initiates.

I raised the carved knocker...and several times heard the catch grate unsuccessfully; at last, succumbing to a more vigorous pull, the rusty old bolt opened and the door of massive planks turned on its hinges.

As I entered, an old porter, roughly outlined by the flickering of a candle, appeared behind a pane of yellowish transparency, a perfect Skalken painting. The face regarded me with singular grimace, and a skinny finger stretched outwards to point my way...

(from 'Le Club des Hachichins' by Théophile Gautier, *Revue des Deux Mondes*, 1846)

After a description of the Hotel's interior, Gautier arrives in a room where 'several human shapes were stirring about a table, and as soon as the light reached me and I was recognized, a vigorous shout shook the sonorous depths of the ancient edifice. "It's he! It's he!" cried some voices together; "let's give him his due!"

His 'due', of course, is his potion of dawamesk. 'The doctor stood by the side of a buffet on which lay a platter filled with small Japanese saucers. He spooned a morsel of paste or greenish jam about as large as the thumb from a crystal vase, and placed it next to the silver spoon on each saucer. The doctor's face radiated enthusiasm; his eyes glittered, his purple cheeks were aglow, the veins in his temples stood out strongly, and he breathed heavily through dilated nostrils. "This will be deducted from your share in Paradise," he said as he handed me my portion. After each had eaten his due, coffee was served in the Arab manner, that is to say, with the coffee grounds and no sugar. Then we sat down at the table...'

There follows a banquet – Gautier provides a loving rundown of the 'large Venetian goblets, cut in milky spirals, German steins embellished with coats of arms and legends, Flemish jugs of enamel' as well as the plates, the porcelain and china. By the time the meal ends, the hashish is beginning to take effect.

His neighbours begin to appear 'somewhat strange. Their pupils became big as a screech owl's; their noses stretched into elongated proboscises; their mouths expanded like bell bottoms. Faces were shaded in supernatural light'. Meanwhile 'a deadening warmth pervaded my limbs, and dementia, like a wave which breaks foaming onto a rock, then withdraws to break again, invaded and left my brain, finally enveloping it altogether. That strange visitor, hallucination, had come to dwell within me'.

The next 3000 words delineate those hallucinations, sometimes terrifying, sometimes uplifting, sometimes hilarious and sometimes tragic. The entire experience lasted about five hours until 'The charm was broken. "Hallelujah! Time is reborn," cried childish, joyous voices. "Go look at the clock now." The hand pointed to eleven. "Monsieur's carriage is waiting below," said a servant.

Gautier took hashish 'some ten times or so' then decided to give it up. His feelings were not that he had suffered any harm, physical or mental, but that, like his friend Balzac, 'a real writer needs no other than his own natural dreams, and does not care to have his thought controlled by the influence of any agency whatever.'

Baudelaire's artificial paradise

Charles Baudelaire (1821–1867), best known for his 1857 collection of poetry *Les Fleurs du Mal* (*Flowers of Evil*) with its address to his '*hypocrite lecteur*' or hypocritical reader, was a logical person to be part of the Club. He had a reputation for debauchery and a taste for the exotic, which would surely have predisposed him to a new drug, but the truth was that he rarely, if indeed ever, indulged. He wrote on hashish, with great acuity, but it was from his studious note-taking, rather than any in-depth personal experience.

Gautier, writing an essay on the poet, noted that 'It is possible and even probable that Baudelaire did try hascheesh once or twice by way of physiological experiment, but he never made continuous use of it. Besides, he felt much repugnance for that sort of happiness, bought at the chemist's and taken away in the vest-pocket, and he compared the ecstasy it induces to that of a maniac for whom painted canvas and rough drop-scenes takes the place of real furniture and gardens balmy with the scent of genuine flowers.

He came but seldom, and merely as an observer, to the meetings in Pimodan House [Hôtel Lauzun], where our club met...' As Baudelaire put it, 'wine makes men happy and sociable; hashish isolates them. Wine exalts the will; hashish annihilates it'.

Baudelaire's best piece on hashish was published in 1860 and entitled *Les Paradis Artificiels* (*Artificial Paradises*) – a comparison of hashish and wine 'as means of expanding individuality'. For him, 'among the drugs most efficient in creating what I call the artificial ideal, leaving on one side liquors, which rapidly excite gross frenzy and lay flat all spiritual force, and the perfumes, whose excessive use, while rendering more subtle man's imagination, wear out gradually his physical forces; the two most energetic substances, the most convenient and the most handy, are hashish and opium'. A century and a half later, Baudelaire's note-taking again rings true:

At first, a certain absurd, irresistible hilarity overcomes you. The most ordinary words, the simplest ideas assume a new and bizarre aspect. This mirth is intolerable to you; but it is useless to resist. The demon has invaded you...

It sometimes happens that people completely unsuited for word-play will improvise an endless string of puns and wholly improbable idea relationships fit to outdo the ablest masters of this preposterous craft. But after a few minutes, the relation between ideas becomes so vague, and the thread of your thoughts grows so tenuous, that only your cohorts...can understand you.

Next your senses become extraordinarily keen and acute. Your sight is infinite. Your ear can discern the slightest perceptible sound, even through the shrillest of noises. The slightest ambiguities, the most inexplicable transpositions of ideas take place. In sounds there is colour; in colours there is a music...You are sitting and smoking; you believe that you are sitting in your pipe, and that your pipe is smoking you; you are exhaling yourself in bluish clouds. This fantasy goes on for an eternity. A lucid interval, and a great expenditure of effort, permit you to look at the clock. The eternity turns out to have been only a minute.

The third phase...is something beyond description. It is what the Orientals call 'kef' it is complete happiness. There is nothing

Self-portrait painted by Baudelaire while under the influence of hashish.

whirling and tumultuous about it. It is a calm and placid beatitude. Every philosophical problem is resolved. Every difficult question that presents a point of contention for theologians, and brings despair to thoughtful men, becomes clear and transparent. Every contradiction is reconciled. Man has surpassed the gods.'

(from *Les Paradis Artificiels* by Charles Baudelaire, Paris, 1860)

Unlike Gautier, Baudelaire believed that the hashish taker was likely to suffer psychological, although not physiological, problems. *Les Paradis Artificiels* concludes with a section entitled 'Morale' in which Baudelaire says that whilst hashish certainly enhances the imagination and thus creativity, it is highly dangerous to subordinate all such processes to the drug. For the creative artist to believe that they can create only when 'high' is a disaster. In the end, cannabis destroyed your personality and that was unacceptable.

De Nerval's supernaturalism

Another friend of Gautier, the poet and writer Gerard de Nerval (1808–1855), was another of the Hachichins to commit his thoughts to paper. De Nerval was an unabashed proselytizer, who saw the effect of cannabis as offering a 'new life...liberated from the conditions of space and time'. He described the state of intoxication as 'supernaturalist'. More than any of his peers, de Nerval was already very much influenced by the East. He had travelled through the Levant and it can be assumed that whilst there he encountered and indulged in hashish. Joining the Club was an excellent way of maintaining his indulgences. He had come to notice with an exemplary translation of Faust, but his hashish writing came in his 1847 story *Journey to The Orient*. In this he wrote one chapter, the tale of Caliph Hakim, devoted completely to the drug. Supposedly told to him by a Druze Sheik named Saide-Eshayrazy, it tells the story of Caliph Hakim of Egypt, who liked, as is often the way in such tales, to pay visits to his city disguised as a commoner. On one such visit he meets and befriends a young man, Yousouf, who persuades him to try hashish (or simply joins him in doing so). The Caliph duly eats the usual 'greenish paste' and as the drug begins to work, tells Yousouf that 'Hashish renders you equal to God.' This is a mistake: bystanders are appalled by the blasphemy and beat the disguised Caliph. Foolishly he refuses to abandon this idea and is thrown into an insane asylum where his claims to be the Caliph are dismissed as the ravings of a hashish-crazed psychotic. Eventually he escapes, only to find a doppelganger sitting on his throne. Worse still the real Caliph is then murdered, and the fake continues to rule in his stead. Beware hashish, de Nerval is saying: it renders illusion and reality too dangerously intertwined.

The Club des Hachichins had broken up by the middle of the nineteenth century but in strictly scientific terms it had done its work. In 1846 its instigator, Dr Moreau, published his major work on cannabis: the 439-page book *De Hachish et de l'Alienation Mentale – Études Psychologiques* (Hashish and Mental Illness – Psychological Studies).

Cannabis reaches the UK

There had been hemp in the UK since Roman times, but recreational use was effectively non-existent. The odd colonial administrator might have brought some home from the East, but opium was always more popular. Hemp had been known in Europe since the herbalist Nicholas Culpeper listed its medical uses in the seventeenth century, but other than in folk-remedies the drug had not entered mainstream use, medical or otherwise. In the nineteenth century, the work of Dr William O'Shaughnessy of Calcutta relaunched an interest in its medical uses (see pages 183–186), and as the century drew to a close, there were increasing questions over the uses of 'Indian hemp', culminating in the Indian Hemp Commission (1893–1894). But that was in India.

Nicholas Culpeper, British herbalist and astrologer (1616-1654).

The great drug of early nineteenth-century English Romantics had been opium, as epitomized in Thomas De Quincey's novel of 1821, *Confessions of an English Opium Eater*. Nor was De Quincey in a minority in that respect: the literary community threw up a number of distinguished fellow-users, many of whom, notably Samuel Taylor Coleridge and Thomas De Quincey himself, were part of a circle who focused on the Bristol physician Dr Thomas Beddoes. The circle included Shelley, Byron, Keats, Walter Scott and Branwell Brontë. Cannabis, however, did not enter their calculations, although De Quincey, an unabashed libertarian, declared publicly on his sixtieth birthday that since he had tried every drug except 'bang' (cannabis) he was about to remedy the omission.

English experimentation

Some, however, did buck the opium trend. There was no problem in acquiring whatever one wanted – under the Pharmacy Act of 1868 virtually any drug could be obtained in a pharmacy – and that included cannabis. Thus, albeit limited, there was a degree of 'recreational' cannabis use. As in France, the main users were élite or artistic groups, often coming together in such like-minded associations as the Society for Psychical Research, the Fellowship of the New Life, the Rosecrucians, the Theosophists and so on. Ostensibly focused on the occult and the paranormal, they often included experimentation with drugs in their 'researches'. In 1888 a number of Masons, Rosicrucians and others interested in changing society formed the 'Hermetic Order of the Golden Dawn', a self-proclaimed group of 'Christian cabalists', addressing its appeal to 'students of Zoro-astrianism, Egyptology, Hermetism, Mystery Schools, Orphism, Pythagoreanism ...etc.' Its leaders – the Mason William R. Woodman and Dr William Wynn Westcott, a London coroner – were relatively anonymous, but amongst their recruits were such literary stars as William Butler Yeats and his Irish nationalist lover Maud Gonne, and Aleister Crowley, the self-styled 'Great Beast' and 'Wickedest Man in the World'. Crowley, whose motto 'Do

Aleister Crowley, the self-styled 'wickedest man in the world'.

what thou wilt shall be the whole of the Law' gave him a direct line to all sorts of indulgence, wrote favourably of a drug that gave him 'a thrill...as of a new pulse of power pervading one. Psychologically, the result is that one is thrown into an absolutely perfect state of introspection. One perceives one's thoughts and nothing but one's thoughts'. The downside, 'a terrible experience', is that one may be 'swept away in the tide of relentless images' but in the end there is a simple solution: 'One simply goes off to sleep'.

The Hermetic Order of the Golden Dawn also mixed with another group called the Rhymer's Club. This group was one of the centres of 1890s 'decadent' London, much influenced by the French Symbolists, and home to such figures as poet Ernest Dowson (also an enthusiast of absinthe, not to mention 'the most degraded' of dockside prostitutes), Arthur Symons (author of *Confessions: a Study in Pathology*, in which he discussed his two years in an Italian lunatic asylum), Francis Thompson (already an opium user) and Richard le Gallienne (a friend, as was Symons, of Oscar Wilde, Aubrey Beardsley and other prominent decadents). All these tried cannabis in its hashish form and, consciously or otherwise, paralleled their French hashish-indulging peers. The practical link between London and Paris appears to have been Symons, whose own interests would help unite the two groups. His pursuit of the avant-garde led him to Symbolism, the movement to which many of the French 'hachichins' belonged, and in the pursuit of this he had actually visited the Symbolist poet Paul Verlaine, a latter-day hashish-smoker, while on a trip to Paris with the sexologist Henry Havelock Ellis. They also tried mescaline, the chief active ingredient of mescal buttons, which had been synthesized in 1896. Once again the same group of experimenters took on this new source of inner adventuring. Symons, Havelock Ellis – who was especially interested in the connections between dreams, visions and drugs – Yeats and Dowson all tried it out. Yeats professed that he would rather take hashish; Dowson, who seemed to qualify as what later commentators would call a 'multi-drug abuser', was more enthusiastic about it.

Amongst the strangest of such figures was one Count Eric Stenbock, the son of a German family who had settled in England. Stenbock was gay, enjoyed opium, cannabis and alcohol to an excessive extent and was accustomed to appear in public sporting a live snake around his neck. A literary 'groupie' rather than a littérateur in his own right, he did produce two books – *The Shadow of Death* (1893) and *Studies of Death* (1894) – but his main role was as a hanger-on around the Rhymers. Unsurprisingly he died young, the victim of either drink or opium, aged thirty-five.

Recreational use in America

Cannabis as a cash crop – that is hemp – was amongst the first plants to be farmed in the colonies of what would become America. The colonists were, apparently not especially enthusiastic, but the authorities demanded that hemp be sewn, and so it was. By the time of the Revolution in 1776, and especially in Virginia, it was a major crop. George Washington and Thomas Jefferson both farmed hemp; and whilst slavery is usually associated with cotton farming, slaves were vital to the production of hemp as well. But despite the hopeful suggestions of latter-day hippies, who put forward the idea that, if Washington and Jefferson farmed the plant, they must have appreciated its intoxicating qualities, one can take as read the fact that neither the early colonists nor their successors the early Americans, were using hemp as a drug.

Homeopaths and medics embrace cannabis

Even on a purely medicinal level, cannabis was relatively late to join the America materia medica. When at last it did come to the attention of medical experts, its main fans seem to have been homeopaths. The homeopathy journal *American Provers' Union* published the first of many reports on the effects of cannabis in 1839. Three years later the *New Homeopathic Pharmacopoeia and Posology or the Preparation of Homeopathic Medicines* (based on an original German text) informed homeopathic physicians, 'To make the homeopathic preparation of hemp,' the author explained, "we take the flowering tops of male and female plants and express the juice, and make the tincture with equal parts of alcohol; others advise only to use the flowering tops of the female plants, because these best exhale, during their flowering, a strong and intoxicating odour, whilst the male plants are completely inodorous".'

Establishment medicine was not far behind. It was first noted in a 'straight' medical text in 1843 and in 1846 Dr Amariah Brigham, the editor of the *American Journal of Insanity*, published a review of Jacques-Joseph

Moreau's use of cannabis in his studies of insanity. It was a very positive review, and Brigham went so far as to have his own supply of cannabis imported from Calcutta. This he gave to a number of his patients at the Lunatic Asylum in Utica, New York. He was fully satisfied and declared that 'From our limited experience we regard it as a very energetic remedy, and well worthy of further trial with the insane, and thank M. Moreau for having called attention to its use'.

Less respectable, but still ostensibly 'medical', was the appearance of the drug in *The Marriage Guide, of Natural History of Generation; a Private Instructor for Married Persons and Those About to Marry* (1860) penned by a quack doctor from Philadelphia – one Frederick Hollick. Cannabis, according to Hollick, was a genuine aphrodisiac (and in fairness modern users would agree that it definitely enhances love-making). For those suffering from an under-performing libido, he offered his own cannabis-based preparation, which he also marketed as a lucrative sideline and according to cannabis historian Ernest Abel, Hollick promised that 'The true aphrodisiac, as I compound it, acts upon the brain and nervous system, not as a stimulant, but as a tonic and nutritive agent, thus sustaining its power and the power of the sexual organs also...'.

Dispatched, no doubt, 'under plain cover', and only on receipt of a letter from the suffering supplicant, the stimulant represented the epitome of discretion. 'For convenience, I have it so put up, in a dry form, air and water tight, that it can be kept uninjured, for any length of time, in any climate, and under any circumstances. It can also be taken without the inconvenience of measuring, using liquids, or any other troublesome requirement, thus ensuring secrecy and facility of use, let a man be situated however he may. A gentleman can keep it in his vest pocket without any fear of detection from smell, or appearance. It will go anywhere by post, with perfect safety, and in such a form that no one through whose hands it passes would ever suspect its nature, or that it is anything peculiar!'

Given the supposed delights of marriage, this was definitely using cannabis for pleasure, though such libido enhancement was still not what one might term recreational, that is using the drug in the same way as one might take a drink with friends, mixing psychotropic effects with social intercourse. But it was around the middle of the nineteenth century that the 'recreational' aspects of cannabis did begin to be appreciated. As in France and England, one was hardly seeing the kind of mass consumption in America that would follow a century later, but once again there were certain brave souls who were first intrigued and then driven to experiment with the drug for themselves. After which, in the way of their European peers, they wrote up their experiences for a wider audience, some of whom, in their turn, decided to make their own experiments.

Just before that, in 1854, there had appeared the first 'discussions' of cannabis as a drug, although it was used for metaphorical rather than practical reasons. John Greenleaf Whittier (1807–1892) included a poem entitled 'The Hashish' in his 'Anti-Slavery Poems', but this appears to have been based, in its comments on the drug's effects, on reading and indeed hearsay rather than hands-on experience. The use of hashish is seen as an addiction and is set up in some detail in the poem's dozen verses. It begins with the predictable clichés: 'Of all that Orient lands can vaunt / Of marvels with our own competing, / The strangest is the Haschish plant, / And what will follow on its eating. / What pictures to the taster rise, / Of Dervish or of Almeh dances! / Of Eblis, or of Paradise, / Set all aglow with Houri glances!' But this eastern exotic is described only to introduce its homegrown counterpart: "the Haschish of the West." This too makes 'fools or knaves of all who eat it'. It is not a drug, however, other than in the effect on those who encounter it, an effect in its turn described in verse. And Whittier concludes: 'O potent plant! so rare a taste / Has never Turk or Gentoo gotten; / The hempen Haschish of the East / Is powerless to our Western Cotton!'.

Bayard Taylor's hashish intoxications

John Greenleaf Whittier wrote of cannabis as a metaphor; the next man to focus on the drug did so to explain just that: it was a drug, and one to be experienced. Bayard Taylor (1825–1878) was something of a polymath and one of America's best-known literary figures. He wrote novels, translated such foreign classics as those of Faust, wrote lyrics for music, worked as a war correspondent and had been Secretary to the American legation to Russia and US ambassador to Germany. For all this, the quantity of his writing was considered to have far outweighed its quality and the critics, one of whom noted that Taylor had 'traveled more and seen less than any man living' were less than sympathetic. The public, as ever less scrupulous, were more enthusiastic. Thus, Taylor's success.

Taylor's beloved wife had died in 1851 and in an attempt to cheer himself up, he set off to the Middle and Far East. The trip led to two books, *A Journey to Central Africa* (1854) and *The Land of the Saracens; or, Pictures of Palestine, Asia Minor, Sicily, and Spain* (1855). It was in the latter that Taylor introduced his readers to hashish. Taylor's first experience of the drug had been in Egypt, where he had taken a mild dose, been intoxicated for thirty minutes and returned to 'normality'. But 'curiosity, instead of being satisfied, only prompted me the more to throw myself, for once, wholly under its influence'. Thus, whilst staying in Damascus, 'that insatiable curiosity which leads me to prefer the acquisition of all lawful knowledge through the channels of my own personal experience, rather than in less satisfactory and less laborious ways, induced me to make a trial of the celebrated Hasheesh –

American writer Bayard Taylor, an engraving by J. C. Buttre, circa 1865.

that remarkable drug which supplies the luxurious Syrian with dreams more alluring and more gorgeous than the Chinese extracts from his opium pipe'.

Along with some friends, Taylor swallowed a teaspoon of hashish paste and waited for developments. When, after an hour, nothing had happened, Taylor suggested that they take an extra half-teaspoon. So they did. This time there was no disappointment. 'The sense of limitation – of the confinement of our senses within the bounds of our own flesh and blood – instantly fell away. The walls of my frame were burst outward and tumbled into ruin; and, without thinking what form I wore – losing sight even of all idea of form – I felt that I existed throughout a vast extent of space. The blood, pulsed from my heart, sped through uncounted leagues before it reached my extremities; the air drawn into my lungs expanded into seas of limpid ether, and the arch of my skull was broader than the vault of heaven.'

112

Such emotions were enough and he would have been happy to call a halt, but Taylor couldn't switch off the experience: 'the Spirit (demon, shall I not rather say?) of Hasheesh had entire possession of me. I was cast upon the flood of his illusions, and drifted helplessly whithersoever they might choose to bear me'. From thereon he runs through the full spectrum of hashish intoxication: hysterical laughter; a feeling of omnipotence; and a series of grotesque and frightening visions from which, however he tries, there seems to be no respite. Above all was the all-embracing intensification of his senses: 'I reveled in a sensuous elysium, which was perfect, because no sense was left ungratified. But beyond all, my mind was filled with a boundless feeling of triumph. My journey was that of a conqueror – not of a conqueror who subdues his race, either by Love or by Will, for I forgot that Man existed – but one victorious over the grandest as well as the subtlest forces of Nature. The spirits of Light, Color, Odor, Sound, and Motion were my slaves; and, having these, I was master of the universe'. Finally, after several hours, he falls asleep. On waking he still feels stoned and not until he has slept a further thirty hours does he return to full reality.

It was, he concludes, frightening but worthwhile. 'Fearful as my rash experiment proved to me, I did not regret having made it. It revealed to me depths of rapture and of suffering which my natural faculties never could have sounded. It has taught me the majesty of human reason and of human will, even in the weakest, and the awful peril of tampering with that which assails their integrity.'

Fitzhugh Ludlow – the Hasheesh Eater

In 1856 *Putnam's Magazine* (which two years earlier had printed a version of Taylor's 'Vision') published 'The Apocalypse of Hasheesh' by Fitzhugh Ludlow (1836–1870). Ludlow had written student songs at college but this piece was his first adult publication. It served as a dry run for his book *The Hasheesh Eater*, published in 1857. He wrote widely and in a number of magazines in his brief lifetime, and further drug-related writing focused on opium, notably the 1867 article 'What Shall They Do to be Saved?'. This, too, was later developed into a book.

Ludlow died at thirty-four, but he had already discovered cannabis (in the shop of a friend, an apothecary) at the age of sixteen. Five years later came

Aubrey Beardsley's title page to Fitzhugh Ludlow's book *The Hashish Eater* (1857).

his essay and book on the drug. An admirer of De Quincey, the name 'The Hasheesh Eater' was a conscious homage and he acknowledged in his introduction 'that, if the succeeding pages are read at all, it will be by those who have already learned to love De Quincey'. A further influence was Bayard Taylor, whose piece he had read. As a fellow reporter on cannabis there are certain similarities, but the difference was that Ludlow was taking his drug at home. Before starting out he taught himself what he could via the description of the 'Extract of Hemp' in The Dispensatory of the United States. That done he set off for two years of experimentation. The fruit of those two years was *The Hasheesh Eater*.

The Hasheesh Eater is a substantial volume and it has come to be regarded as one of the classics of drug-taking literature. By modern standards it is somewhat overblown, as evinced by its chapter headings – The Shadow of Bacchus, the Shadow of Thanatos, and the Shadow of Shame; Nimium – The Amreeta Cup of Unveiling; Then Seeva Opened on the Accursed One His Eye of Anger; The Hell of Waters and the Hell of Treachery; and the like – but it is an unrivalled exposition for its time. Like every sophisticated analyst Ludlow noted the drug's essential effects: the heightened senses, depersonalization, hallucinations, altered time perceptions, anxiety and panic. He experienced synaesthesia, 'the interchanging of the senses...the hashish eater knows what it is...to smell colours, to see sounds, and, much more frequently, to see feelings'. Then there was uncontrollable laughter, the rapid flow of ideas, the feeling of unquenchable thirst, the 'awakening of perception which magnifies the smallest sensation till it occupies immense boundaries'. He was also aware of the effect the circumstances of taking the drug have on the experience one has. 'At two different times, when body and mind are apparently in precisely analogous states, when all circumstances, exterior and interior, do not differ tangibly in the smallest respect, the same dose of the same preparations of hasheesh will frequently produce diametrically opposite effects.' One's personality was also vital: 'Upon persons of the highest nervous and sanguine temperaments hasheesh has the strongest effect; on those of the bilious occasionally almost as powerful a one; while lymphatic constitutions are scarcely influenced at all except in some physical manner, such as vertigo, nausea, coma, or muscular rigidity'. The 1856 magazine article, initially by 'Anonymous' was essentially a taster for what was to come: 'The tendency of the hasheesh-hallucination is almost always toward the supernatural or the sublimest forms of the natural. As the millennial Christ, I have put an end to all the jars of the world; by a word I have bound all humanity in eternal ligaments of brotherhood; from the depths of the grand intrude forest I have called the tiger, and with bloodless jaws he came mildly forth to fawn upon his king, a partaker in the universal amnesty. As Wagner's Rienzi hurling fiery invective against the usurpations of Colonna, I have seen the broad space below the tribune grow populous with a multitude of intense faces, and within myself felt a sense of towering into sublimity, with the consciousness that it was my eloquence which swayed that great host with a storm of indignation, like the sirocco passing over reeds. Or, uplifted mightily by an irresistible impulse, I have risen through the ethereal infinitudes till I stood on the very cope of heaven, with the spheres below me...But, if I found the supernatural an element of happiness, I also found it many times an agent of most bitter pain. If I once exulted in the thought that I was the millennial Christ, so, also, through a long agony, have I felt myself the crucified.'

'In all these experiences,' he declared, 'research and not indulgence was my object, so that I never became victim of any habit in the prosecution of my headlong investigations. When the circuit of all the accessible tests was completed, I ceased experimenting...'. But this was somewhat disingenuous. In the end Ludlow came to believe himself psychologically dependent on the drug. He gave it up, with a degree of difficulty, and turned instead to writing about its effects in print, claiming that given his own experiences with cannabis, it was necessary to expound upon the drug, both its positive and negative sides, just as De Quincey had with opium.

The doomsayers

Not everyone was as fascinated, nor as positive about hashish as Taylor or Ludlow. In 1871 Reverend Jonathan Townley Crane wrote *Arts of Intoxication*, a negative appraisal. Paraphrasing Taylor's experiences he carefully renders them absurd and Taylor himself is dismissed as 'silly' for even thinking of using the drug. 'Thus ended an experiment which came near costing life. It illustrates in an exaggerated from the whole process of inebriation, the dreamy, senseless pleasures of the first effect, and the horror, the wretchedness, which so soon buries in darkness and woe the memory of the previous fleeting enjoyment.' As for Ludlow, 'A few years ago a student of Union College, New York, became addicted to the poison, and, after his escape from the enemy, recorded his experience in a volume entitled *The Hasheesh Eater*'. Crane's verdict: 'The hemp intoxicant is a hateful poison. He who trifles with it sports on the brink of a gulf tossing with lurid fires and haunted with all shapes of evil'. And he concludes with this warning: 'I will here add that the manufacturers of patent medicines here at home are using this abominable intoxicant in the preparation of their wares. This is no random assertion. Let the reader govern himself accordingly'.

The American poet Thomas B. Aldrich (1836–1907) was also less than enthusiastic. His 1874 poem 'Hascheesh' tells first of the wondrous visions the drug produced, but then…horrors! Vile creatures assail him, terror has him in its grip. 'Away, vile drug!' he cries, 'I will avoid thy spell. / Honey of Paradise, black dew of Hell!'

Cannabis catches on

Doomsayers aside, cannabis went from strength to strength. In a two-part piece in the *Boston Medical and Surgical Journal*, published in the same years as Ludlow's book (1857), the physician John Bell declared that 'The various periodicals of this country have abounded, during the last few years, with accounts of the Haschisch; every experimenter giving the history of the effects it has had upon himself'. He then joined them. Whilst he had seen specimens imported from Damascus (analysis revealed some 25 per cent opium content, presumably enhancing the visionary aspect) he took his hashish via a popular remedy that was based on cannabis, Tilden's Extract, advertised as being 'used with success in hysteria, chorea, gout, neuralgia, acute and sub-acute rheumatism, tetanus, hydrophobia and the like'.

And while he 'had taken the drug with great scepticism as to its reputed action, or at any rate with the opinion that it was grossly exaggerated', the real experience put an end to that. 'From scepticism, to the fullest belief of all I had read on the subject, was but a step.' He had read Moreau, and his own experiences seemed to bear out the Frenchman's equation of hashish with the 'dream state' of insanity. Added Bell, 'in functional diseases of the brain, it certainly gives promise of possessing powers more directly useful than any other specific drug of the materia medica.' His final conclusion was upbeat: 'Any one who, under the influence of Cannabis Indica, has seen what the human mind is capable of becoming, cannot but feel a lively interest in those who are suffering under mental alienation; he cannot but look with hope to it, as a means of more fully comprehending what is the most distressing of finite calamities, and he cannot but think that a substance, the action of which is so powerful and unique, will be found, when fully understood, to possess valuable therapeutic virtues'.

John Bell's assessment of cannabis' popularity was born out elsewhere. In *The Seven Sisters of Sleep* (1860), a study of the seven most popular narcotic plants of the Victorian era – tobacco, opium, cannabis, betel nut, coca, datura and fly agaric – the English naturalist, mycologist (and eccentric) Mordecai Cubitt Cooke informed the public that 'Young America is beginning to use the "bang" so popular among the Hindoos, though in a rather different manner, for young Johnathon must in some sort be an original. It is not a "drink", but a mixture of bruised hemp tops and the powder of the betel, rolled up like a quid of tobacco. It turns the lips and gums of a deep red, and if indulged in largely, produces violent intoxication. Lager beer and schnaps will give way for "bang" and red lips, instead of red noses become the style'.

From our perspective perhaps the most unlikely of the drug's proselytizers was Louisa May Alcott (1832–1888), best known as the author of the less than obviously drug-infused homily *Little Women*. In 1869 she published, anonymously, a short story entitled 'Perilous Play'. It opens with a young woman, Belle Daventry, exclaiming, 'If someone does not propose a new and interesting amusement, I shall die of ennui!'. Fortunately, help is at hand. One of the party, Dr Meredith, produces 'a little box of tortoiseshell and gold' in which repose half a dozen 'bon-bons'. 'Why, what are they?' she

Louisa May Alcott, an unlikely exponent of the drug, wrote about it in her short story 'Perilous Play' in 1869.

asked, looking at him askance. 'Hashish; did you never hear of it?' 'Oh, yes; it's that Indian stuff which brings one fantastic visions, isn't it? I've always wanted to see and taste it, and now I will,' cried Belle, nibbling at one of the bean-shaped comfits with its green heart. A companion cautions her but Belle is adamant. And the doctor assures her all will be well: 'A heavenly dreaminess comes over one, in which they move as if on air. Everything is calm and lovely to them: no pain, no care, no fear of anything, and while it lasts one feels like an angel half asleep'.

The story focuses on the hashish-embellished affections of another girl, Rose, and her admirer Mr Done. A kiss is snatched, a storm endured, intimacies shared and, in the finale, a happy ending. 'He stretched his hand to her with his heart in his face, and she gave him hers with a look of tender submission, as he said ardently, "Heaven bless hashish, if its dreams end like this!".' Not quite the home life of the saccharine March sisters (from *Little Women*), although they might have agreed with those women's temperance societies who, in the 1890s, promoted the recreational use of hashish in place of alcohol: liquor led to wife-beating, hashish did not.

Less literary, but very popular, and surely indicative of the ubiquity of the drug, was the new Hasheesh Candy, marketed from the 1860s by the Gunjah Wallah Company of New York. 'The Arabian Gunje of Enchantment confectionized,' they promised. 'A most pleasurable and harmless stimulant – Cures Nervousness, Weakness, Melancholy, &c. Inspires all classes with new life and energy. A complete mental and physical invigorator...Beware of imitations...' The candy sold well for forty years.

'Secret dissipations in hasheesh hell'

In his book *Low Life* (1991), the story of New York's nineteenth-century underworld, Luc Sante devotes much space to opium, a drug that seemed to permeate society, but makes no mention of hashish. Cannabis, at least until the new century, seems to have been something of a middle-class diversion. Thus when, by the 1870s, the drug was sufficiently well known to appear, suitably embellished, in the pages of mass-market magazines, its users were invariably bourgeois. The 'Secret Dissipation of New York Belles: Interior of a Hasheesh Hell...' in the *Illustrated Police News* (1876) is typical: the illustration shows five young women, elegantly dressed, and languishing on divans.

Similarly there was little genuine 'low life' on display when in 1883 *Harper's New Monthly Magazine* ran its piece 'A Hashish House in New York, The Curious Adventures of an Individual Who Indulged in a Few Pipefuls of the Narcotic Hemp'. (Initially anonymous, the author is generally assumed to have been the then leading physician, H. H. Kane, who published several books on the growing 'drug menace' in the United States, such as 1881's *Opium Smoking in America*.)

Kane's interest is piqued by a friend who, commenting on his interest in opium, notes this alternative intoxicant and tells him, 'there is a large community of hashish smokers in this city who are daily forced to indulge their morbid appetites, and I can take you to a house up-town where hemp is used in every conceivable form, and where the lights, sounds, odors, and surroundings are all arranged so as to intensify and enhance the effects of this wonderful narcotic'.

'Ladies who smoke':
New York women
experimenting with
a new diversion,
from the *Illustrated*
Police News, 1876.

The next night finds the pair making their way to the hashish house, somewhere north of 42nd Street. As might be expected, the 'setting' is as important as the drug itself, and those who visit are first arrayed in suitably oriental clothes: 'First a long plush gown, quilted with silk down the front, and irregularly ornamented in bead and braid with designs of serpents, flowers, crescents, and stars, was slipped on over the head. Next a tasselled smoking-cap was donned, and the feet incased in noiseless list slippers'. The house itself was exotically luxurious: the writer said that he was expecting something out of the *Arabian Nights*, but this exceeded it.

'All about the sides of the spacious apartment, upon the floor, were mattresses covered with different-colored cloth, and edged with heavy golden fringe. Upon them were carelessly strewn rugs and mats of Persian and Turkish handicraft, and soft pillows in heaps. Above the level of these divans there ran, all about the room, a series of huge mirrors framed with gilded serpents intercoiled, effectually shutting off the windows. The effect was magnificent. There seemed to be twenty rooms instead of one, and everywhere could be seen the flame-tongued and fiery-eyed dragons slowly revolving, giving to all the appearance of a magnificent kaleidoscope in which the harmonious colours were ever blending and constantly presenting new combinations.' Interior decoration takes a good few paragraphs.

Kane is especially interested in the habitués: he notes that the 'clients seem to divide 50:50 between Americans and foreigners…all the visitors, both male and female, are of the better classes and absolute secrecy is the rule. The house has been opened about two years, I believe, and the number of regular habitués is daily on the increase'. And he asks, recalling those dissipated belles, 'Are there many ladies of good social standing who come here?' 'Very many. Not the cream of the demi-monde, understand me, but ladies. Why, there must be at least six hundred in this city alone who are habitués. Smokers from different cities, Boston, Philadelphia, Chicago, and especially New Orleans, tell me that each city has its hemp retreat, but none so elegant as this.'

The experience that follows is more *Arabian Nights*, with the author's visions and fantasies offering up a checklist of the required clichés. Unlike more academic experimenters he makes no analysis of the drug's effects, merely records the exotic dreams. Then it's over and he leaves: 'The dirty streets, the tinkling car-horse bell…and the drizzling rain were more grateful by far than the odors, sounds, sights, sweet though they were, that I had just left. Truly it was the cradle of dreams rocking placidly in the very heart of a great city, translated from Bagdad to Gotham'.

All good sensational stuff, there would be much, much more in the century to come. The truth was that cannabis, against which there were as yet no laws, was available as and when you required it, *One Thousand and One Nights* backdrop or not. For instance, the 1876 Centennial Exposition in Philadelphia featured a fashionable Turkish Hashish Exposition that was enjoyed by a great many attendees, and at that same exposition some US pharmacists stocked up with supplies – in case any visitors fancied a puff as they toured the show.

The modern world

It may appal those who pursue the 'war on drugs' and similar campaigns, but however vilified, however outlawed, however sensationalized, cannabis is undeniably one of the great consumer success stories of the last century. A drug that, in the West at least was in recreational terms no more than the amusement of a few intellectual dilettantes, and otherwise experienced only at the behest of the medical prescription or across the pharmacist's counter, is today a worldwide winner. Pinned firmly to an accelerating and ever-widening sense of 'youth revolution', its popularity has increased unchecked. And if the world's Establishments remain almost without exception pitted against its popularity, those who are less easily propagandized, have simply voted, as it were, with their rolling papers and their pipes. The concept that bad laws need only be observed in their dismissal has rarely been so well illustrated.

Music makers and 'dope smokers'

The expanding status of this once exotic drug developed, like much of today's 'youth culture' in the world of black America. While the immigrant workers crossing from Mexico to the US brought with them a taste for marijuana, the 'cultural' exposure of cannabis was far more of a black phenomenon. The black (and in time white) musicians of the 1920s were smoking, and their lyrics reflected it, with references to 'muggles', 'reefer',

..s, images of
.. had entered
..ss as Hollywood often
..mic effect – from the
.. movie *Reefer*
..Chong and Chevvy
..n industry produced
..Brenda Blethyn, about
..lear her debts by
..illa in Cornwall in

'gage' and 'weed', not to mention 'the viper', 'the dope smoker'. A decade on and smoking was sufficiently widespread for the core of today's cannabis slang to be in place: 'lighting up', 'getting high', a 'joint'. Hugely popular musicians such as Louis Armstrong or Cab Calloway made no bones about their smoking preferences – how could the fans, black and increasingly white too, not pick up on the new amusement.

Unlike the swinging Sixties, when the supposedly unfettered young rockers tended to resist direct references to their pleasures, these early cannabis devotees and musicians were unashamed, making many a direct reference to cannabis in their lyrics. Song titles such as 'Reefer Man' (Don Redman and His Orchestra, 1932); 'Texas Tea Party' (Benny Goodman and His Orchestra, 1933), 'Light Up,' (Buster Bailey's Rhythm Busters, 1938), 'Jack, I'm Mellow,' (Trixie Smith, 1938), and 'Sweet Marijuana Brown,' (Barney Biggard Sextet, 1945). The problems of Harry J. Anslinger's new laws (see pages 140–149) were reflected in 'The G-Man Got the T-Man,' (Cee Pee Johnson and Band, 1945) while such as 'Wacky Dust' (Ella Fitzgerald, 1938) and 'Who Put the Benzedrine in Mrs. Murphy's Ovaltine?' (Harry 'The Hipster' Gibson, 1944) showed that in the drug world, cannabis was one among many.

Cab Calloway singing 'Reefer Man'.

Milton 'Mezz' Mezzrow, went further: a white musician-cum-dope dealer, his marijuana stocks were so prized among his creative peers that as he put it in his memoir, *Really the Blues* (1946), mezz meant 'the tea' and mezzroll 'the kind of fat, well-packed and clean cigarette I used to roll.' The singer Rosetta Howard (and the Harlem Hamfats) brought it all together in the words of the song 'If You're a Viper', explaining, 'Dreamed about a reefer five foot long / The mighty mezz but not too strong, / You'll be high but not for long / If you're a viper.'

From beatniks to hippies

If the take-up of cannabis among whites was still marginal in the 1930s – for all Anslinger's hysterical campaigning, and the legislation he pushed through

– in the decades that followed it exploded. The beats – Jack Kerouac, Allen Ginsberg, Neal Cassady – loved both jazz and its preferred intoxicant, even if their friend William Burroughs continued to opt for the jazzman's harder alternative, heroin. As beat, a creation of the later Forties, developed into beatnik (coined in 1958), so the bandwagon rolled, and on jumped an ever-widening constituency of the young and, at least in theory, rebellious. The 'drugged cigarette' as the tabloids put it, was as essential a part of the beatnik uniform as the black clothes, sandals, beards, leotards and so on. In one more decade beatniks transformed into hippies and the spread of cannabis went with them. If there had been hundreds of young, white smokers in 1950, then there were thousands ten years on and tens of thousands by 1970.

Beat poet Allen Ginsberg leads a group of pro-cannabis demonstrators in New York City's Greenwich Village.

A worldwide cannabis explosion

Nor was the cannabis explosion limited to the US. As the youth movement gathered steam, cannabis use went with it – whether to the UK, always the first to imitate her American cousins, or on to the countries of continental Europe. It may seem unlikely today, when for millions of young people smoking cannabis is as unexceptional as their grandparents' scotch or gin, but Sixties' cannabis was not merely recreational, it came with built-in political cred. As is often the case, the canabis smokers had not declared the war, it was those, following in Anslinger's footsteps who were determined to perpetuate it. Thus cannabis, along with such ephemera as long hair and such serious matters as the war in Vietnam, became one more interface of counter-cultural strife. The police with their heavy-handed raids on a variety of leading rock stars, not to mention thousands of less-celebrated youngsters, merely exacerbated the divide. Meanwhile, the activists campaigned for legalization, governments set up commisions – and just like the parallel enquiries into that contemporary source of moral outrage, pornography, they tended to minimize the hysteria and opt for individual

choice: the governments dismissed results that failed to amplify their control-besotted agenda.

The Seventies and Rastafarianism

One other factor – the same, but also different – should not be overlooked. The same in that once again one is looking at black use of cannabis; different in that for the UK at least, the users were not musicians and similar cultural nay-sayers, they were simply immigrants, Jamaicans mainly, who had been brought to the country in the Fifties. Not every Jamaican smoked 'charge', but if you were young and white in the Fifties or early Sixties, and you knew nowhere else to find it, then the black clubs of West London's Notting Hill were where you went. A decade on, the West Indian connection was even more important. The rise of reggae, and its prime apostle Bob Marley, with his profession of Rastafarianism, boasting ganja (cannabis) as not merely a pleasure but a sacrament, ensured that from the Seventies, the drug gained an ever-more-important role. Hippies may not have espoused every aspect of the spiritual aspect of ganja use in Rastafarianism, but the idea of the weed as something sacred fitted well into at least one strain of hippie preoccupation.

Following the hippie trail

It was that preoccupation, a heightened spirtuality, often aided or inspired by cannabis use, that created another important stimulus to the drug's popularity. The phenomenon of the 'hippie trail', a journey from country to country that in its shortest version took in the Balearic Islands – Ibiza or Formantera, or the kif-capital of Morocco (see pages 72–74), and in its more extended version went, via the Eastern Mediterranean, to Iraq, Iran, Afghanistan and Nepal, and ultimately to India; (some would go even further, via Burma and Thailand, eventually to wartorn Vietnam). Few of those countries are so easily permeable today, even though the cannabis is doubtless still available.

Back then, the hippie trail was considered to be a rite of passage, not dissimilar to, albeit somewhat longer than, one's first LSD experience: a 'long strange trip', to quote those psychedelic minstrels, The Grateful Dead. There were many reasons to go East, not least the age-old fascination with travel that had taken Westerners in that direction for centuries, but

Previous page: The sacramental herb – a Rastafarian smoking marijuana, Jamaica.

An American soldier in Vietnam smoking a pipe of marijuana.

The Grateful Dead posing beneath the sign for San Francisco's Haight Ashbury district – dope central, USA.

there was no denying the primary lure: cheap, high-grade drugs. Why wait for the cannabis to turn up at home when one could set off and get it oneself and have some interesting adventures on the way?

And there were plenty of drugs to be had in the East: foremost among them was hashish, of the highest quality and at minimal cost, but there was also morphine, heroin, and a variety of 'uppers' and 'downers'. North Africa provided more of the same, only here it was kif rather than charas, while those, a minority, who chose South America for their enlightenment, found the added bonus of cocaine. Vietnam and Thailand offered marijuana. On the whole one consumed what one bought, but there were inevitably those – usually the least overtly 'hippie' in style – who planned to bring or send home a supply. It was probably not the most sensible of plans, especially as the decade proceeded and European customs started tightening up their controls, but for a while it worked, helped, undoubtedly, by the remarkable permeability of local borders.

Recent trends

In the event, neither mossy-backed governments nor optimistic activism changed much. The laws stayed on the books, the young continued to smoke. And in purely legal terms, so, with a few egregious examples – the Netherlands, the first and still the most liberal – have things remained. Practically, however, the story has moved on. The last thirty years have witnessed an inexorable expansion of the cannabis community. The politics may have long since vanished – today's young smokers are, after all, the children of those counter-cultural strivers – but the popularity of the drug has never been greater. The gap between pious government pronouncements and practical cannabis use merely grows. To their credit, many police forces, notably those in the UK, have realized that their hard-pressed and overstretched officers have better things to do than implement this particular law. And it was undoubtedly pressure from such officers that led to the decision, in mid-2002, to downgrade cannabis in the UK from a class II to a class III drug, thus rendering its simple possession (outside certain caveats) as no longer an imprisonable offence. However, in fairness too, it is rumoured though at the time of writing yet unlegislated, that in England at least, mere possession of the drug is due for effective decriminalization.

The recent story of cannabis is as much as anything a story of a generation ageing, but staying with the beliefs and knowledge of its youth. Once the drug moved out, quite literally, of the ghetto and into first counter-cultural and then mainstream youth society, it was inevitable that personal experience would put paid to political calculations. However, the government and its selected teams of experts would play the bogeyman, dope smokers were not going mad, turning homicidal nor plunging willynilly into narcotic addiction. They grew older and grew up, and their preoccupations changed, but what they had discovered about cannabis remained, and would be passed on. There will be exceptions, there always are, but for the millions-strong majority cannabis is no different, as a drug (rather than in its effects), to alcohol. It simply happened, for what history shows were racist, rather than pharmacological reasons, to have drawn the legislative short straw. The chapter that follows illustrates how such legislation came about.

Worries about 'native' indulgence encourage the British to produce a report on cannabis...the Indian Hemp Commission (1893–1894)...the drug is readily available in the UK...cannabis legislation begins in the US in 1914...Harry J. Anslinger becomes America's first drug czar...the Marijuana Tax Act of 1937...cannabis is demonized...the situation in the UK...1967, the 'summer of love', sees an unprecedented attack on cannabis...the Wootton report, 1969, is rejected by the UK government...the situation in the Netherlands...the Hulsman Committee and the Baan Committee...international drug laws.

LEGISLATION AND CONTROL

The authority must display its power. The legislator must legislate. The agents of such authorities and legislators – the police – must act to make the legal theories practice. There is, and always was, something about the phrase 'recreational drug use' that seems almost from its inception to have overexcited the 'powers that be' both in Europe, especially the UK, and in North America. It is perhaps paradoxical to find that if there was in these countries any period of drug use that might be termed a 'golden age', it was the nineteenth century, one usually dismissed as 'Victorian', with all the pejorative stereotypes that that eponym brings. It was, for a brief period, possible to buy opium, cannabis and other now supposedly 'dangerous' drugs in any pharmacy. Adults could choose and, having chosen, experience the consequences. They were not, as in opium addiction, always pleasant, but one's choice was one's own. Nanny remained in her place – the nursery, where her particular skills applied: she had yet to move into the corridors of power. By the end of the century, unfortunately, things had changed.

An anti-marijuana book cover: The author notes that 'This young artist has been completely freed from this horrible habit which so long held him in its grip...
accepted Christ as his personal Saviour, and it was he who... pictured for me his conception of "The God Moloch of Marihuana"'.

India – legislating the locals

Although it was in American magazines that the first inklings of the demonization of cannabis could be found, the first country to set up a commission, and that done produce a report into the drug, was the UK. Not that this commission, as its name explains, was dealing with home consumption. The Indian Hemp Drugs Commission (1893–1894) dealt with that 'jewel in the crown' India, where cannabis was and had been for many centuries central to everyday life.

Cannabis was, of course, seen as a 'native' indulgence. In the recreational sphere a number of colonial administrators undoubtedly dabbled in 'un-English' amusements 'on station' but their drug, like that of their contemporaries at home, was more likely to be opium. Nor did those who did dabble bring the habit home: cannabis was not addictive, it could be dropped as one mounted the gangplank for England. 'Bhang', as it was known, was merely another piece of Oriental exoticism, best-suited to the 'natives'. But just as it was sometimes confused in its effects with opium, so too did it enter the frame when, for the first time in 1891, worries began to emerge about that poppy-based pleasure.

Establishing the Indian Hemp Drugs Commission

In that year a member of Parliament Mark Steward, who had already showed himself a campaigner against the opium trade, asked a three-part question about the prevalence of 'ganja' in parts of India. For Steward ganja was even more harmful than opium: was the Secretary of State for India aware, for instance, that the lunatic asylums of Bengal 'are filled with ganja smokers'? Did he also know that in Lower Burma, where the drug had been outlawed, legislation had been of enormous benefit to the people? And, finally, would he consider extending the ban throughout India? In all cases the answers were 'yes', but agreement did not guarantee action. A year later Steward received a detailed response from the Viceroy's Office in India, referring back to a survey carried out in 1873 and underlining the essential pragmatism of the authorities – at least as far as the Empire was concerned. It was noted that India-wide prohibition would prove impossible and that, in any case, 'it does not appear…to be specifically proved that hemp incites to crime more than other drugs and spirits'. It was also noted that the profits from taxing ganja were substantial.

In March 1893 the cannabis 'problem' was addressed once more, this time by William Caine, MP for Bradford East, who requested the Under-Secretary of State for India 'to create a commission of experts to enquire into and report on the cultivation and trade in all preparations of hemp drugs in Bengal, the effects of that consumption on society, and on the moral condition of the people, and desirability of prohibiting its growth and sale'. The result of his question was the creation of the Indian Hemp Drugs Commission – a dedicated committee for the study of cannabis use in India.

The Commission began work in August 1893 and by April 1894 they had interviewed 800 witnesses and assembled 3000 pages of evidence (making seven volumes in all, plus a confidential extra volume on hemp use in the Indian Army's native troops). Particularly fascinating was the substantial essay by J. M. Campbell, the Collector of Land Revenue and Customs and Opium in Bombay, on the 'religion of hemp'. He wrote at length on the importance of the drug to Hindu culture (see pages 43–52) and his findings were backed up by his fellow official, the magistrate G. A. Grierson, laying out the lengthy list of literary references to the drug in both Sanskrit and Hindi writings. Like the rest of the report, their opinions are refreshingly free of moralizing.

A finding of 'no harmful effects'

The report was released in early 1895 – and promptly vanished into the files. It concluded: 'In regard to the moral effects of the drugs, the Commission are of the opinion that their moderate use produces no moral injury whatever. There is no adequate ground for believing that it injuriously affects the character of the consumer. Excessive consumption…indicates and intensifies moral weakness or depravity. Manifest excess leads directly to loss of self-respect, and thus to moral degradation. In respect to his relations with society, however, even the excessive consumer of hemp drugs is ordinarily inoffensive. His excesses may indeed bring him to degraded poverty which may lead him to dishonest practices; and occasionally, but apparently very rarely indeed, excessive indulgence in hemp drugs may lead to violent crime. But for all practical purposes it may be laid down that there is little or no connection between the use of hemp drugs and crime'.

Its main recommendation, that 'the long-term consumption of cannabis in moderate doses has no harmful effects' was noted, but then who in England qualified as a user of any duration, let alone 'long-term'. The mystics and decadents could go take their own paths to hell; the majority of the country was untainted and in any case an upcoming general election concentrated the political mind elsewhere. Cannabis really wasn't that important. The Commission's report, the basic material of which remains as germane today as on the day of its publication, was shelved, gathering dust until disinterred in 1967 for Baroness Wooton's report (see pages 152–155) and nor would it be read by any of those debating the drug in the US until around the same time. The drug remained available in the UK.

Early Days in America

Cannabis legislation in America did not begin until after 1914, when the passage of the Harrison Narcotic Act, a piece of anti-drug legislation that posed as a tax measure, effectively prohibited both the opiates (namely, heroin, opium and morphine) and cocaine. Cannabis had not been mentioned, but the simple fact of passing some drug legislation ensured that its time was certain to come. The public was prepared: the publicity that surrounded the Harrison Act had ensured that the mass-perception of the drug addict was negative. The 'dope fiend' was de facto a criminal; it helped that opium at least had a strong Chinese connection; cannabis would be similarly affected by race: it was seen either as a Mexican or, by the Twenties, as an African-American perversion.

The jazz drummer, Gene Krupa, was one of many famous showbiz personalities who were busted for cannabis possession.

It is this identification of cannabis, generally in the form of marijuana, with the Mexican population, which had hugely increased over the last twenty years, that is found in all of the sixteen western states who legislated against the drug prior to 1930. Such racism naturally helped the laws pass unchallenged: the majority white population simply didn't care; if the Mexicans and their beloved 'killer weed' had to be kept under control, who would worry. Thus one saw anti-cannabis legislation in Utah (where the dominant Mormons were terrified of any form of intoxicant), New Mexico, Texas and others. Bills were passed without opposition and with only nugatory press coverage.

On the other side of the country, on the East Coast, there were no Mexicans to blame, but marijuana faced a ban there too. This time the reason was substitution – the Harrison Narcotics Act had banned opiates; users would, it was believed, move to a drug that they could obtain: marijuana. That, therefore, must also be banned. The usual hysterical stories were peddled, legislators were mustered, and in 1927 marijuana, classified (despite a complete lack of medical evidence) as 'a "habit-forming drug", was duly banned in New York state.

The Panama Canal Zone Report

In 1929 America was presented with her first ever report into the effects of cannabis. It was carried out by the US Army, which had found that a major culture of cannabis smoking amongst soldiers stationed in the Canal Zone of Panama had developed. A panel of civilian and military experts was convened. After an exhaustive study, with many witnesses, they delivered their verdict: 'there is no evidence that Marihuana as grown and used [in the Canal Zone] is a 'habit-forming' drug [...] or that it has any appreciable deleterious influence on the individual using it'. Thus, they recommended that 'no steps be taken by the Canal Zone authorities to prevent the sale or use of Marihuana'.

This was not, of course, what those who backed prohibition wished to hear. More to their taste was a completely contradictory piece of research: a New Orleans physician – one Dr Fossier – published his study, which stated that marijuana was a highly dangerous drug with habit-forming properties. It had no empirical backup, merely the doctor's opinion, and the piece went unremarked until the New Orleans District Attorney Eugene Stanley read it, used it and made it the basis for his own article: 'Marihuana as a Developer of Criminals'. Stanley claimed that the drug's main effect was to suppress any inhibitions and negate the restraints of conscience. It was thus the perfect criminal drug. 'At the present time the underworld has been quick to realize the value of this drug in subjugating the will of human derelicts to that of a master mind. Its use sweeps away all restraint, and to its influence may be attributed many of our present day crimes. It has been the experience of the Police and Prosecuting Officials in the South that immediately before the commission of many crimes the use of marihuana cigarettes has been indulged in by criminals so as to relieve themselves from the natural restraint which might deter them from the commission of criminal acts, and to give them the false courage necessary to commit the contemplated crime.' That his conclusions were effectively spurious was irrelevant. The courts loved them and they were recycled, often embellished with ever more lurid addenda, as the campaign against cannabis intensified.

Medical opinion is divided

All through the 1930s the debate over cannabis continued much as it continues to do today. In 1933 the *Journal of the American Medical Association* stated unequivocally that 'cannabis, at the height of its action, usually produces hallucinations, with or without euphoria, and that these are followed by a deep sleep. Its most marked after-effect is the liability to the establishment of a craving for the drug, the habitual use of which undermines the intellectual qualities and the social value of the victim and leads to general physical deterioration. It is stated that smokers nearly always become imbecile in time'. A year later Dr Walter Bromberg, a senior psychiatrist at New York's Bellevue Hospital, who based his results on examining some 2216 Bellevue inmates (all convicted of felonies), reported that marijuana was not a habit-forming drug and was far less responsible for crime than other drugs such as alcohol. He added that marijuana users tend to be passive in comparison to users of alcohol and that the hemp drugs should lead to crime only in cases of use by already psychopathic types.

The move towards criminalization

In 1932, against the background of such discussion, came the Uniform Narcotic Drug Act. This attempt to improve upon the Harrison Act, by creating uniform laws that could be applied by every US state, did not prioritize cannabis, but it was included as another 'habit-forming drug' in an optional provision. There was no scientific study to back up this provision, and the impetus for its inclusion seems to have come from the Federal Bureau of Narcotics. Not that the Feebs would be satisfied. Five years later, amidst far greater publicity, would come America's first real assault on cannabis: the Marijuana Tax Act.

Anti-cannabis crusader – Harry J. Anslinger

Of all those who pitted themselves against the 'evil weed' none was so dedicated as the prototype US 'drugs czar' Harry J. Anslinger, Commissioner of Narcotics from 1930–1962. His efforts have made a lasting impression on legislation on cannabis and are widely diffused. Anslinger, best known for his proselytizing of the Marijuana Tax Act of 1937, had joined law enforcement when still at school in Altoona, Pennsylvania, where he had taken a holiday job with the railroad police. It was then that he began a lifetime's campaigning against drugs when a friend allegedly died from smoking opium. An unsatisfactory spell with the US War Department in 1917 led to overseas duties with the Foreign Service until in 1926, after battling a fleet of Bahamas rum-runners, he was recruited to the Treasury Department's Prohibition Unit. Three years later, he became Assistant Commissioner of Prohibition.

Anslinger was a devoted hard-liner. Even as Prohibition waned he was calling for tougher penalties, demanding punishments not merely for sellers, but for buyers too. First offenders were to face six months in jail and a $100 fine; further drinking upped the jail sentence to two to five years and the fine to a possible $50,000. His wish-list remained unachieved, and when Prohibition was wound up in 1933 Anslinger already had a new job: as Commissioner of the US government's Bureau of Narcotics. His main target was narcotics addiction, and his credo was simple: hit the addicts and the dealers hard, with 'strong laws, good enforcement, [and] stiff sentences'.

Despite its forthcoming elevation to the commissioner's *bête noire*, marijuana (by far the main variety of cannabis available in the US) was relatively marginal in 1930. As a homegrown product it had been excluded from the Harrison Narcotic Act of 1914 so there was no federal law with which to prosecute its sellers and users. More pragmatically Anslinger was aware of the extent of marijuana smoking – and the Bureau simply didn't yet have the manpower for the fight. Ironically it would be these problems, in the face of which the Bureau was indeed faltering, that would prioritize marijuana and make it Anslinger's primary target.

Building a case against marijuana

In the traditional manner of government agencies who need funding that might not otherwise appear, Anslinger needed to manufacture a *cause célèbre* that would justify his access to a vast budget. There had always been a trickle of scare stories in the US press that featured marijuana and Anslinger determined to use the drug, hitherto of minor interest, to get his funds. He opened his expanding files: the result was a flood of pieces variously entitled: 'Youth Gone Loco' (*Christian Century*), 'Uncle Sam Fights a New Drug Menace – Marihuana' (*Popular Science Monthly*), 'Sex Crazing Drug Menace' (*Physical Culture*), 'Tea for a Viper' (*New Yorker*) and 'Exposing the Marihuana Drug Evil in Swing Bands' (*Radio Stars*).

Perhaps the classic was Anslinger's own contribution, 'Marihuana: Assassin of Youth' published in *American Magazine* in 1937: 'The sprawled body of a young girl lay crushed on the sidewalk the other day after a plunge from the fifth story of a Chicago apartment house. Everyone called it suicide but actually it was murder. The killer was a narcotic known to America as marihuana, and to history as hashish. It is a narcotic used in the form of cigarettes, comparatively new to the United States and as dangerous as a coiled rattlesnake'. Another anecdote told how 'An entire family was murdered by a youthful addict in Florida. When officers arrived at the home they found the youth staggering about in a human slaughterhouse. With an ax he had killed his father, his mother, two brothers, and a sister. He seemed to be in a daze. "I've had a terrible dream," he said. "People tried to hack off my arms!" "Who were they?" an officer asked. "I don't know. Maybe one was my uncle. They slashed me with knives and I saw blood dripping from an ax!" The officers knew him ordinarily as a sane, rather quiet young man; now he was pitifully crazed. They sought the reason. The boy said he had been in the habit of smoking something which youthful friends called "muggles:" a childish name for marijuana'.

The outlawing of cannabis

That Anslinger was sincere in his personal terror of marijuana must be taken as so; that he was honest in his promotion of the drug as a 'killer' and a 'menace' is perhaps otherwise. Like any bureaucrat with a budget to maintain, his alliance of his own prejudices with the predictable 'economies' of truth was perhaps inevitable. And his efforts paid off. In spring 1937, persuaded by his propagandizing, the US Treasury finally capitulated, agreeing to hold hearings before creating a bill that would add marijuana to America's outlawed intoxicants. Anslinger was principal witness for the prosecution. Armed with a library of carefully chosen horror stories, he made his gruesome case. As he put it, 'If the hideous monster Frankenstein came face to face with the monster marijuana he would drop dead of fright'.

There were no actual experts, whether on crime or pharmacology. The bulk of his stories quoted newspapers – the very same articles that had been written originally with the Bureau's own files as their only source. Expert opinions and substantial reports of marijuana's effects did exist, of course – that they all ran contradictory to Anslinger's doom-saying assured that they remained carefully uncited. Anslinger even set himself up as a medical

In the fifties bohemians experimented with recreational cannabis, by the sixties it's use would balloon throughout the middle class youth of the world.

New York Mayor Fiorello LaGuardia, whose 1944 report declared that marijuana 'does not lead to addiction'.

witness, his primary 'evidence' the legend of the Assassins (see pages 57–59). When it came to challenging Anslinger, the main pressure groups turned out to be the nation's manufacturers of paint and varnish (both of which employed hemp oil) and of birdseed. In both cases their special interests made their particular use of marijuana exempt from prosecution.

There was one other major source of dissent: the American Medical Association, who complained that no doctor had been consulted and that this supposedly important bill had been effectively prepared in secret. This opposition was not, however, a sign of any great liberalism. (An American Medical Association essay had recently cited the drug as a cause of sex crimes and insanity.) Doctors had been much inconvenienced, whether as prescribers or indeed addicts, by the passing of the Harrison Narcotics Act; they wanted no more of what they saw was interference with their freedom to prescribe as they wished. In the event their pleas failed. Congress disliked the American Medical Association, which had recently fought to block the inclusion of health insurance in the Social Security Act. Their plaint against Anslinger was tossed aside.

The Marijuana Tax Act became law on 3 August 1937. Nominally it did no more than place a small tax of $1 on all shipments of marijuana, but alongside this came a vast range of bureaucratic restrictions that ensured that virtually no-one would be allowed to use the plant, including prescribing doctors. Cannabis, as we shall see, had been one of the most popular and important medicinal drugs available to Americans. Now, virtually overnight, it had been withdrawn. The corresponding police powers, ensuring suppression, were placed in the hands of the bill's progenitor, Harry J. Anslinger. And, the bill passed almost without opposition. There was effectively no debate in either the House of Representatives or the House of Senate. Official records offer merely:

Mr Snell: What is the bill?
Mr Rayburn: It has something to do with something that is called marihuana. I believe it is a narcotic of some kind.
(taken from The Congressional Record, June 10, 1937)

The LaGuardia Report

The line between legislation and the conclusions offered by scientific research was drawn once more in 1944 when a new report appeared: 'The Marihuana Problem in the City of New York, prepared by the New York Academy of Medicine, and published by the City of New York'. Best known as The LaGuardia Committee Report, it had begun life in 1938 when New York's Mayor Fiorello LaGuardia gathered a team of scientists to study the medical, social and psychological aspects of marijuana use in the city. The committee contained two interns, three psychiatrists, two pharmacologists, one public health expert, the Commissioners of Correction, Health and Hospitals and the Director of the Psychiatry Division. As much as anything it was a response to the steady propagandizing of the Bureau of Narcotics, which inevitably characterized New York, with its substantial black population, as a hotbed of drugged depravity.

In his introduction to the Report, LaGuardia set out his own stall, explaining his appointments and noting that his own interest in marijuana stretched back to the Panama Canal Zone Report of 1925 which 'emphasized the relative harmlessness of the drug and the fact that it played a very little role, if any, in problems of delinquency and crime in the Canal Zone'. Now, with this new report he was 'glad that the sociological, psychological, and medical ills commonly attributed to marihuana have been found to be exaggerated insofar as the City of New York is concerned'. However, he saw no reason to decriminalize the drug, or at

Marijuana Girl

SHE TRADED HER BODY FOR DRUGS— AND KICKS!

N. R. DeMexico

8328
35¢
K

NEVER WAS THERE SO OUTSPOKEN A NOVEL AS THIS...TELLING THE PLAIN, UNCENSORED TRUTH ABOUT TEEN-AGE ADDICTS — AND THEIR DESPERATE SEARCH FOR THRILLS!

A GLIMPSE INTO THE LIVES OF OUR LOST GENERATION

Reefer Club

by Luke Roberts

35¢

The girl was the slave of marijuana—yet was

Long before scantily clad 'hippie chicks' tossed aside their tie-dyes for the leering tabloids, and 'swingers', it was assumed, toked deep as a prelude to their suburban orgies, cannabis meant sex. Or more precisely the kind of sex – cleavage, lingerie – that buyers of pulp fiction had always wanted. Thus these titles, and many, many more. The truth was, of course, that past the cover not that much happened. Unlike the first-hand heroin reminiscences of such writers as William Burroughs the pulp hacks tended to swallow the prohibitionist line, and tout it accordingly.

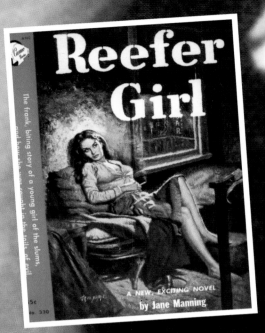

Reefer Girl

The frank, biting story of a young girl of the slums, and how she was caught in the toils of evil

25c
No. 330

A NEW, EXCITING NOVEL
by Jane Manning

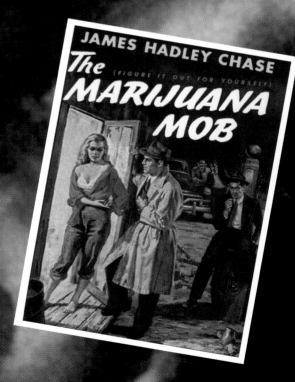

JAMES HADLEY CHASE

The MARIJUANA MOB

(FIGURE IT OUT FOR YOURSELF)

least not unless further research (which he promised) indicated such a course. He hoped that cannabis might prove an aid in helping narcotics addicts.

The research is dismissed

Research began in 1940, and focused on a group of seventy-seven prisoners, who were long-term cannabis users. The results were first published in the scientific press in 1942, where they initially received good reviews. Acknowledging that New York's main users were African or Latin Americans, the report stated that 'the practice of smoking marihuana does not lead to addiction in the medical sense of the word', and that 'the use of marihuana does not lead to morphine or heroin or cocaine addiction'. It found that there was no 'Mr Big' behind the selling of the drug; smoking was not widespread amongst schoolchildren and nor did marijuana create criminals: 'Juvenile delinquency is not associated with the practice of smoking marihuana'. The researchers also declared that 'the publicity concerning the catastrophic effects of marihuana smoking in New York City is unfounded'.

Sensing an attack on the power of his own deliberate and destructive misinformation Anslinger came out fighting. He accused the researchers of 'immorality' and bombarded the media with counterinformation. As ever, ignorance prevailed and the report was largely dismissed as nonsense.

Anslinger was still in power in 1961, when he and his acolytes, received another important boost for their anti-cannabis campaign. That year saw the passing of the Single Convention on Narcotic Drugs, created under the auspices of the United Nations and its medical arm the World Health Organization. It focused on opium, cocaine and cannabis with the intention of setting down laws under which the medical use of these drugs could be properly administered and the recreational use stamped out. The concept of a 'war on drugs' still lay decades in the future; but the principle was in place.

The impact on the UK

In the history of 'recreational' drug consumption in the United Kingdom cannabis had, until the 1960s, been something of a 'poor relation'. It lacked the romantic miasma of opium, the deadly potential of heroin or the class-connotations of cocaine. It neither made you go faster, like amphetamines, nor slowed life down like barbiturates. Hashish (but not marijuana) had had its brief moment in the late nineteenth century, both as a drug of pleasure and as one of medicinal use, but that had faded very fast. Its incorporation into the pharmacopoeia of illegal drugs had, compared with the campaigning against cocaine and opiates, been something of an afterthought. At the international conference of 1925, which saw it placed off-limits, the British delegate had not even agreed to vote for its outlawry, merely not to vote against. Such headlines as did focus on 'evil drugs' for the next fifty years did not see cannabis as a prime target. Even in the 1950s, when it gradually pushed its way forward and as statistics show, began to provide the police and courts with more action that did its rivals, it remained basically a black people's indulgence, with a few white bohemians and jazz musicians joining in.

There were, of course, a few stories. They focused, as ever, on the 'alien-ness' of drugs, in this case 'reefers' or 'doped cigarettes'. Those who penned the tabloid articles (not that the quality press were offering anything different, other than in vocabulary), with their references to 'the same old sickening crowd of under-sized aliens, blue about the chin and greasy' or 'coloured pedlars' with 'the brains of children' whose 'perverted satisfaction [is] "lighting up" a white girl', were infinitely more pernicious pedlars themselves, of xenophobia and racism, and of gross misinformation. Thanks to the deliberate distortions of the US police and media – carried across the Atlantic as yet another cultural import – cannabis was positioned as far worse than the drugs of genuine addiction. By the time it came to mounting a proper debate on the drug such prejudices would have been locked into the mass mind. Despite mounds of contradictory evidence, they have yet to abate.

'A butterfly on a wheel'

In common with all European countries, the UK had followed international law and had outlawed cannabis since the 1920s; the most recent legislation had been the Dangerous Drugs Act of 1951. As late as the early 1960s it was still very much a minority taste: a low-yield hallucinogen that gave a private pleasure and represented nothing else. The authorities were singularly unworried; cannabis was simply not that important. Indeed, it hardly impinged on the popular mind. As the report of the Interdepartmental Committee on Drug Addiction (better known as the Brain Committee) stated in 1961 neither use nor 'trafficking' in such drugs was especially widespread, a fact the Committee was happy to attribute to public opinion: 'The cause for this seems to lie largely in social attitudes, to the observance of the law in general and to the taking of dangerous drugs in particular'. Such an attitude was, of course, 'coupled with the systematic enforcement of the Dangerous Drugs Act 1951'. It should be added that whilst 'enforcement' may indeed have been 'systematic', the country still had very few dedicated 'drug squads'.

All that changed in 1967. If it remains memorialized as the 'summer of love', it was also the summer of an unprecedented assault on cannabis – and a fight back. The Beatles and the Rolling Stones were raided, arrested and tried for possession; the august *Times* came out in favour of Mick Jagger (although not of cannabis, which was never mentioned in the celebrated editorial 'Who Breaks a Butterfly on a Wheel?') and a month later allowed pro-cannabis activists to occupy its pages with an advertisement signed by the radical great and good and demanding that: '1. The government should

Butterflies on a wheel: Mick Jagger and girlfriend Marianne Faithfull leave court after he is found guilty of possession of cannabis, 18 December, 1969.

permit and encourage research into all aspects of cannabis use, including its medical applications; 2. Allowing the smoking of cannabis on private premises should no longer constitute an offence; 3. Cannabis should be taken off the dangerous drugs list and controlled, rather than prohibited, by a new ad hoc instrument; 4. Possession of cannabis should either be legally permitted or at most considered a misdemeanour punishable by a fine of not more than £10 for a first offence and not more than £25 for any subsequent offence; 5. All persons now imprisoned for possession of cannabis or for allowing cannabis to be smoked on private premises should have their sentences commuted'. Hyde Park witnessed hippies *en fête* in the 'legalize pot' rally and the country's first ever drug-aid centre, Release, was founded.

Paul McCartney is arrested in Japan after being found in possession of cannabis, 16 January 1980.

The Wooton Report

All this was followed by the country's first attempt to assess the position of cannabis: the then Home Secretary Roy Jenkins, already responsible for the passage of major liberal legislation regarding homosexuality, the death penalty and abortion, established a Commission to report on the drug. It was headed by Baroness Wooton, a social scientist of great repute, a Governor of the BBC, a magistrate and a veteran of several other Commissions. Her fellow members included psychiatrists, a senior policeman, a pharmacologist and a sociologist. All were eminently respectable; whatever fantasies might be spun in a hostile House of Commons, these were neither lobbyists nor liberals. If anything, it would emerge, their stance had begun as generally anti-cannabis. (One member had apparently dismissed the need to consult any witnesses: the Committee's sole task was 'to stop the spread of this filthy habit'.) It would be to their great credit that they listened to their witnesses and decided to change their minds accordingly.

Witnesses were interviewed in some of the seventeen sessions that ran from April to July 1968. And if the Committee may be presumed to have no more than an academic knowledge of cannabis, some of those who appeared before it were rather better versed. Amongst them were 'anti-psychiatrist' R. D. Laing and his colleague Joseph Berke, Dr Sam Hutt (gynaecologist and prescriber of 'legal cannabis' – cannabis tincture under licence from the government), the current editor of the 'underground' paper *IT* and Steve Abrams, whose SOMA (Society of Mental Awareness) organization was the country's primary campaigner for legalization.

The printed Report was finished by Christmas 1968 and delivered on 7 January, 1969. It was a relatively concise document, running to only thirty-two pages. Aside from explaining its own procedure (in which it noted the importance of *The Times* ad and acknowledged current 'protests' against official drug policy), and running down the background and history of the drug and its controls, it quoted from the witnesses and from relevant statistics to outline the current situation in the UK. It dealt at length with the various popular fallacies and found that cannabis did not lead to violence, nor did it automatically create a vast constituency of junkies. It pointed out that a populist, contemporary assessment of a drug was nothing to go by: at one time or another tea and coffee, not to mention alcohol and tobacco, had all been excoriated in much the same terms as cannabis was now. Its most important conclusion came in paragraph 29: 'Having reviewed all the material available to us we find ourselves in agreement with the conclusion reached by the Indian Hemp Drugs Commission appointed by the Government of India (1893–1894) and the New York Mayor's Committee on Marihuana (1944), that the long-term consumption of cannabis in 'moderate' doses has no harmful effects.'

Equally vital was this passage: 'The evidence before us shows that: An increasing number of people, mainly young, in all classes of society are experimenting with this drug, and substantial numbers use it regularly for social pleasure. There is no evidence that this activity is causing violent crime or aggressive anti-social behaviour, or is producing in otherwise normal people conditions of dependence or psychosis, requiring medical treatment. The experience of many other countries is that once it is established cannabis-smoking tends to spread. In some parts of Western society where interest in mood-altering drugs is growing, there are indications that it may become a functional equivalent of alcohol. In spite of the threat of severe penalties and considerable effort at enforcement the use of cannabis in the United Kingdom does not appear to be diminishing. There is a body of opinion that criticizes the present legislative treatment of cannabis on the grounds that it exaggerates the dangers of the drug, and needlessly interferes with civil liberty'.

The Wooton Report urged that the current controversy over cannabis should be cleared up and accepted that until this was done, 'in the interest of public health' it was necessary to maintain restrictions. There was no alternative to the criminal law, but if the law was to be changed, the realities of cannabis use should be taken into account. They called for proper research into all types of cannabis use, but noted that 'the present legal position is unhelpful [to such research]'. Whilst the Committee had no authority to recommend changes in law it did state that the current situation, in which no distinction was made between cannabis and the opiates was 'quite inappropriate' and that 'the present penalties for possession and supply are altogether too high'.

The triumph of ignorance

The Wooton Report arrived in the House of Commons on 23 January 1969 when the new Home Secretary, James Callaghan, made an initial statement on it. A debate was scheduled for the following Monday, 27 January, but even in his brief report to the House, Callaghan, a former lobbyist for the Police Federation, was a very different man from the urbane, sophisticated and most importantly liberal Roy Jenkins (a man whose supposed creation of a 'permissive society' Callaghan, ostensibly a loyal colleague, had already been at pains to condemn publicly); he made it clear that Wooton was not to his taste. For a while, it was rumoured, he had even considered suppressing the Report – so antagonistic was it to his preconceptions – but eventually he gave in. Various members had threatened to resign and Steve Abrams, head of SOMA and pro-legalization campaigner had even considered publishing a pirate edition.

The debate merely underlined Callaghan's position, with some speakers congratulating him on his steadfast opposition to any change, and others taking the opportunity to air yet again their invincible ignorance of the topic as they parroted the worst populist fantasies. Callaghan's own speech merely drummed home what listeners soon realized was inevitable: Wooton, so sensible, so balanced, so rational, had been all in vain. Ignorance had triumphed. Unlike the reforms of the abortion law, or that of homosexuality, skillfully guided through the Commons by a sympathetic Home Secretary, there would be no hope for cannabis. After smearing Baroness Wooton and her colleagues as a 'cannabis lobby' and implying, quite against the facts, that they had called for full legalization, he declared triumphantly, '[The pro-cannabis lobby] is another aspect of the so-called permissive society, and I am glad that my decision has enabled the house to call a halt in the advancing tide of so-called permissiveness'. Wooton would reply via the press, but the harm had been done; as Callaghan himself, railing at smears directed against himself, would one day note elsewhere, 'A lie can be half way round the world before the truth has got its boots on'.

For her part Baroness Wooton remained positive. Writing in the *Sunday Times* she concluded with this optimistic line, 'There is no doubt that we are going to antagonize a great body of opinion who regard pot as a "beastly menace". We'd never get anywhere if we didn't make proposals that antagonized a lot of people. I'm old enough to have made what are considered outrageous proposals fairly often and lived to see them become accepted commonplaces'. Alas for the Baroness and those who backed her Report, it was not to be. She died in 1988, aged 91: her Report, which for many people was the most important (and certainly the most public) work she ever did, was not even mentioned in her obituaries.

Changing legislation

The letter of the law, however, may point in one direction, its daily practise may take a singularly different path. In his 1993 article 'Hashish Fudge' Steve Abrams suggested that whilst Callaghan may have talked the talk, he never really walked the walk. He stresses that for all 'his posturing the Home Secretary did not refuse to implement the Wooton Report. He merely refused to legislate unilaterally and immediately on cannabis at a time when new comprehensive legislation was being planned'. That legislation – the Misuse of Drugs Act 1971 – generated by Labour but enacted, thanks to their surprise defeat in 1970, by a Conservative government 'did' cut the maximum penalty for summary conviction for possession by fifty per cent.

More importantly, the then Lord Chief Justice suggested to a 1973 Conference of the Magistrates Association that they should treat cannabis users 'with becoming moderation. Set aside your prejudice, if you have one, and reserve the sentence of imprisonment for suitably flagrant cases of large scale trafficking'. Such advice may not have created the scare headlines usually reserved for drugs, but it pointed the way forward. By 1977 further legislation (that year's Criminal Justice Act) cut the basic penalty by half again: now it was just three months (even less than the Report's original suggestion of four). By the dawn of the eighties simple possession of small amounts of cannabis was effectively unpunished. In mid-2002 the British government took what appeared a major step when it downgraded cannabis from a class B drug (along with the likes of MDMA) to a class C one (similar to steroids). But while this removed the fear of arrest from the country's estimated 2.5 million smokers, it doubled the sentence for dealers to a maximum 14 years (the equivalent of narcotics) and there was no mention of relaxing restrictions on medical use. The reality of the move was simple pragmatism: cannabis smoking had long been a given; the police had better things to do than chase a bunch of latter-day hippies. Real legalization, rather than this unresolved fudge remains, predictably, out of the question

Reports tend towards the liberal

Country after country set up their commissions for reports – LeDain ('The Report of the Canadian Government Commission of Inquiry into the Non-Medical Use of Drugs') in Canada in 1970, the National Commission on Marihuana and Drug Abuse in the US, set up by President Nixon in 1973, Australia's 1971 Marriott Committee (the Senate Select Committee on Drug Trafficking and Drug Abuse), and in 1977 another Australian effort, the Baume Committee (the Senate Standing Committee on Social Welfare). Further US research came in 1982 with 'An Analysis of Marijuana Policy' by the National Research Council of the National Academy of Science. Britain too has returned to investigation, with the reports offered by the House of Lords in 1998 and the Runciman Committee, backed by the Police Federation in 2000. In almost all cases the tone of these reports tends to liberality, and rigorous scientific analysis; a softening up of certain parts of the law, usually as regards personal possession of small amounts, is advocated, but the bottom line is: keep it banned.

The Netherlands – the way forward?

Perhaps the most cannabis-friendly nation in the world is the Netherlands. Like the UK, the response of the Dutch government to the unmissable increase in cannabis smoking of the Sixties was to establish a committee of research. In fact, there were two: the Hulsman Committee and the Baan Committee. The Hulsman Committee, under the auspices of the National Federation of Mental Health Organizations, aimed to set up a drug policy commission of which the broadly defined task was 'to clarify factors that are associated with the use of drugs, to give insight into the phenomenon as a whole, and to suggest proposals for a rational policy…'. The second was a state committee, headed by Pieter Baan, a Chief Inspector of Mental Health; its brief was 'to investigate causes of increasing drug use, how to confront irresponsible use of drugs, and to propose a treatment system for those who developed dependence on these drugs'.

A tourist relaxing with a joint in one of Amsterdam's many 'cafés'.

Radical viewpoints

Hulsman reported in 1970. In the context of the time some of its techniques and suggestions were revolutionary. The idea that drugs need not be demonized but used in a limited and controlled way was quite new. The idea, as one witness pointed out, that the State's assessment of what was socially 'good' or 'bad' merely represented what the current holders of state power happened to believe, and not some over-riding philosophical given, could have come from a contemporary 'underground' press. According to Peter Cohen in his paper about the two Dutch committees (to which this section is indebted for its information), Hulsman's recommendations ran as follows:

> Use of cannabis and the possession of small quantities be taken out of criminal law straight away. Production and distribution should for the time being remain within criminal law but as a misdemeanor.
>
> Use and possession of other drugs will remain in the sphere of criminal law, as a misdemeanor, but in the long run has to be liberated completely.
>
> Those who run into difficulties with their drug use should have adequate treatment institutions at their disposal.
>
> An interesting detail of the proposals for the short term is that production of non cannabis drugs has to remain within criminal law as an offense. The background of this conclusion is not provided. It likely reflects the perspective of the Commission on gradual long term decriminalization of all drug use.
>
> (from 'The case of the two Dutch drug policy commissions. An exercise in harm reduction 1968–1976' by Peter Cohen, 1994)

As Cohen adds, Hulsman's proposals were (and remain) 'a useful, rationally argued and humane blueprint of general drug policy principles'.

The Baan Commission was equally positive. It saw no point in stigmatizing drugs, an integral part of youth's subculture, since that meant stigmatizing young people as a whole. It concentrated on cannabis, determined to end what one commentator termed 'this mess of youngsters going to prison for a few grams of hash'. As Cohen explains 'The report describes the use of cannabis products as relatively benign and the health risks as relatively limited. If sometimes unusual behavior of cannabis consuming youth is

The controversial edition *Life Magazine*, which questioned whether cannabis should be legalized.

LIFE

MARIJUANA

At least 12 million Americans
have now tried it

Are penalties too severe?

Should it be legalized?

President Nixon enlists Elvis as a special guest in America's 'War against Drugs', 21 December 1970. 'The King' preferred barbiturates to marijuana.

seen, this is more considered a result of specific subcultural norms and ideologies, than of pharmacology. But, cannabis use when driving or when operating machines in factories, is "not responsible". "Consumption without risks for the individual or society can only take place during recreation"'. Drugs were to be assessed on their pharmacology: a 'ladder' should be created defining risks, some of which would be acceptable, others not. Treatment of the drug should be based strictly on its risk potential.

The two Commissions between them resulted in today's liberal attitudes to cannabis in the Netherlands, but as Cohen notes, the conditions for this to happen there were favourable and much augmented by the fact that such attitudes as those expressed in the reports were very much mainstream views at the time. Even the Establishment no longer saw any point in imprisoning otherwise blameless young people for those 'few grams of hash'.

In 1976, the majority of the two Commissions' recommendations were also included in the remodelled Opium Act, the Netherland's primary means of drug control. Today, as anyone who has visited the Netherlands, and notably Amsterdam with its 'coffee shops' (where cannabis can be smoked freely without the slightest problem) will see, the drug has been pretty much 'normalized'. Indeed, it is far more unsettling after experiencing such an enlightened, and utterly unsensational attitude to cannabis, to return to less 'civilized' countries and to have to realign one's behaviour to far more punitive attitudes.

The International drug laws

Although the laws that currently govern the growth, trafficking and consumption on an international level of cannabis all stem from the United Nations, its predecessor body (the League of Nations, which existed between the First and the Second World Wars) had its own earlier part to play. And in its mixture of misread propaganda, national self-interest and a wilful refusal to consider scientifically proven evidence, it set the pattern for every cannabis-related law that has followed.

The first international law

The International Opium Conference opened in Geneva in November 1924. It was the third such conference of the century and the most important. Its aim was to deal with what was judged to be a worldwide opium 'problem'. It was accepted that the drug's analgesic properties were such that some had to be produced: what was important was that no-one should be permitted to take the drug purely for enjoyment.

The first international conference, proposed by US President Theodore Roosevelt, convened in Shanghai in 1908 and discussed possible measures of control. As a result, in 1912, at a second conference in The Hague, a Convention was concluded with the intention of controlling the manufacture, trade, export and import of the drug and in due course to suppress the non-medical use of opium, morphine, cocaine and any derivatives thereof. The advent and duration of the First World War put paid to all such plans, but with the formation of the League of Nations in 1920 it was declared that the Convention should be re-established and that all members were to be obliged to implement its aims. To that end an Opium Advisory Committee was established consisting of the representatives of the eight states particularly interested in opium production. (At a later stage

they were joined by a representative of Germany.) The Committee believed that most 'abuse' stemmed from overproduction of drugs aimed for medical use; its aim was therefore to register and supervise manufacture, imports and exports and to seize illicitly imported narcotic drugs.

In 1923 the Committee expanded its interests: hashish was to be included in its controls. The reasons for this were far from simple. Politics and profits were the justification, not health. The pressure to include cannabis came primarily from Egypt, which was highly dependent on its cotton exports and thus severely threatened by mass-cultivation of hemp. Cannabis was thus portrayed, with little difficulty and less truth, as a dangerous drug, as much a 'narcotic' as any opiate. The Egyptians claimed that their population suffered from a plague of hashish psychosis and despite the relatively recent and quite contradictory information provided by the Indian Hemp Drug Commission, delegates chose to believe them. (It would later emerge that if such an epidemic existed, it was due to the habit of Egyptian doctors, unwilling to make any proper diagnostic efforts, to assign all mental problems to 'hashish'; but that revelation would be far too late.) Nor, whilst the Committee was still deliberating in 1925, was the slightest attention paid to the Panama Canal Zone Report (see page 139), which came out that year and which similarly dismissed much of the allegations regarding 'narcotic' cannabis. It was not what the League wished to hear.

The third International Opium Conference at Geneva in 1924 dealt exclusively with the opium-smoking problem in Asia at its first session. A range of prohibitory decisions were duly laid down. Another conference held in 1925 dealt exclusively with medicinal opium, morphine and its derivatives, cocaine and ecgonine (a cocaine derivative) and aimed to fulfil the whole of the Committee's brief, with hashish extracts and tinctures, now classified, however incorrectly, as narcotics. All these drugs were brought under the provisions of the Convention. To its credit the UK abstained, but three years later (with the passage of the Dangerous Drugs Act 1928, which banned cannabis along with heroin, opium and cocaine, except for medicinal use) duly kow-towed to the international illusion.

Previous page:
Mexican federal
police destroying a
field of marijuana in
Mazatlan province
(Mexico's biggest
marijuana producer),
13 March 1995.

The International Narcotics Control Board

Whilst each and every country (in the case of the US each state as well as the federal government) has their own individual version of legislation as regards cannabis, all these laws are broadly responsible to three international treaties: most importantly the Single Convention on Narcotic Drugs 1961, plus its amendments by the 1972 Protocol that followed the Convention on Psychotropic Substances of 1971 and the 1988 UN Convention against Illicit Traffic in Narcotic Drugs and Psychotropic Substances (also known as the Vienna Convention).

The Single Convention consolidated a number of previous Conventions on narcotic drugs and amalgamated some of the monitoring organizations to create the International Narcotics Control Board. It was signed by seventy-three countries, including such cannabis producers as Afghanistan, Morocco and Mexico. As of mid 2002 that list had increased to 178 signatories. The 'narcotic' drugs are divided into four 'schedules': Schedule I contains the major opioids, as well as cocaine and cannabis. Schedule II contains less powerful drugs such as codeine, and Schedule III a variety of preparations based on codeine or opium. Schedule IV respecifies drugs that are regarded as having particularly dangerous properties: cannabis, as well as opiate drugs such as heroin, is listed.

The bracketing of cannabis and the opiates, let alone cocaine, flies in the face of all proven scientific knowledge. It is therefore impossible not to assume that the schedules are based as much on political motivation as on scientific pragmatism. Given that the purpose of the Convention was to tie up a number of prior such documents, this is hardly surprising. It should also be noted that the Convention's medical advisor, the World Health Organization, is one of those bodies most adamantly against the drug. The effect has been, as presumably intended, to confirm cannabis' demonization.

Those who believe the Convention and its amendments are thus accepting that cannabis is to be branded as both intrinsically dangerous and capable of causing harm to society. It has also made it considerably harder for an individual country to defy this overarching convention. When agitation for change has emerged, governments have often pleaded this inability or refusal to break ranks. Although the resolutions that justify the passing of the Convention talk nobly of 'the deplorable social and economic conditions in which certain individuals and certain groups are living predispose them to

A pro-cannabis demonstration in Melbourne, Australia, 1999.

drug addiction' and recognize the need to 'do everything in their power to combat the spread of the illicit use of drugs' and 'develop leisure and other activities conducive to the sound physical and psychological health of young people' the end result is a purely legislative document.

It is, in short, a worldwide charter for the prohibition of recreational drug use and a sanction for any nation to impose criminal prosecutions against their users. Nonetheless, this is by no means an unarguable position and despite all the tough talking, and the determination of some countries to follow it to what they interpret as the letter, the action to take is not mandatory. In reality, special measures of control can be imposed if, in the opinion of the relevant country, they are 'necessary' or 'appropriate'. And whilst the Single Convention demands that parties criminalize all activities relating to importing and dealing, the question of criminalizing personal possession and consumption remains discretionary. (Use is never specifically covered in the Convention and it is possible to read all its citings of 'possession' as implying 'possession with intent to sell'.) Different countries take a different line. Australia's Williams Royal Commission, for instance, took the line that removing any prohibitions would negate the over-riding spirit of the Convention. So, too, did Canada's Le Dain Commission. The Netherlands, however, have assessed the situation otherwise, and acted, as the world knows, accordingly. It must be presumed that the down-grading in 2002 of cannabis in Britain from a class B to a class C drug (as detailed in the Misuse of Drugs Act 1971), a move that will effectively decriminalize personal possession/consumption, takes this broader-minded view as well. However the simultaneous decision to double the potential sentence for trafficking, shows that the precise letter of the law still has its effect. Yet for all that, trafficking (importing and dealing) remains beyond any discussion – quite what 'dealing' is remains debatable. Some would suggest, this means 'when profit is involved', but life, let alone cannabis sales, is not that simple. There is, after all, a vast abyss between an international criminal 'firm', bringing in thousands of kilos, and one friend buying a few ounces for distribution among a closed circle.

Open to ideas of diversity

The International Narcotics Control Board, set up to administer the Convention, is itself relatively tolerant of potential diversity. Individual nations, they accept, do have the right to take the view that they are not forced to establish such activities as criminal offences under law. The only activities for which criminal punishments are mandatory relate to cultivation, purchase or possession for the purpose of illicit trafficking. Mere possession and personal use do not come into the equation.

Revising the Conventions

The Single Convention has been reinforced on two occasions since 1961: The Convention on Psychotropic Substances (1971) and the UN Convention against Illicit Traffic in Narcotic Drugs and Psychotropic Substances (the Vienna Convention, 1988). The first of these is essentially an expansion of the original Convention. It bulks out its predecessor by stating 'If a Party or the World Health Organization has information relating to a substance not yet under international control which in its opinion may require the addition of that substance to any of the Schedules of this Convention, it shall notify the Secretary-General and furnish him with the information in support of that notification.' The transfer of a substance from one schedule to another is also covered. As far as the former is concerned, the only area it impinges

Overleaf: 'Times with dope and no money are better than times with money and no dope.' Cartoonist Gilbert Shelton's stoners supreme, the Fabulous Furry Freak Bros.

upon cannabis is that of its psychoactive principle, tetrahydrocannabinol. If such a substance is reported, the WHO is to subject it to analysis. Then if, 'the World Health Organization finds: (a) That the substance has the capacity to produce (i) (1) A state of dependence, and (2) Central nervous system stimulation or depression, resulting in hallucinations or disturbances in motor function or thinking or behaviour or perception or mood, or (ii) Similar abuse and similar ill effects as a substance in Schedule I, II, III or IV, and (b) That there is sufficient evidence that the substance is being or is likely to be abused so as to constitute a public health and social problem warranting the placing of the substance under international control' the substance will duly fall under the original Single Convention and all its stated prohibitions.

The way forward – international co-operation

In 1987 at the International Conference on Drug Abuse and Illicit Traffic in Narcotic Drugs and Psychotropic Substances there was a perceptible split between 'producer' countries and 'user' ones. The former argued that the major problem was in the consumption of drugs amongst the end-user states and that drug-using nations were equally as responsible as the producers for controlling the problem. The latter demanded that it was primarily up to the drug-producing nations to control not merely their own producers, but the traffic over and beyond their borders. The upshot took in both sides, calling for greater co-operation between nations in fighting trafficking, and proposing greater mutual aid in such matters as extradition, legal assistance and transfer of proceedings.

As far as the criminalizing of recreational drugs is concerned, the Convention sought to fill in the loopholes of 1961. 'Subject to its constitutional principles and the basic concepts of its legal system, each Party shall adopt such measures as may be necessary to establish as a criminal offence under its domestic law, when committed intentionally, the possession, purchase or cultivation of narcotic drugs or psychotropic substances for personal consumption contrary to the provisions of the 1961 Convention, the 1961 Convention as amended or the 1971 Convention.'

However, 'The Parties may provide, either as an alternative to conviction or punishment, or in addition to conviction or punishment of an offence established in accordance with paragraph 2 of this article, measures for the treatment, education, aftercare, rehabilitation or social reintegration of the offender'. The specifics of what exactly provides an 'alternative' are open to suggestion, and implementation. The International Narcotics Control Board interprets this statement as requiring that possession, purchase or cultivation for personal use all must be covered by criminal statutes. However, it immediately modifies this demand, adding that, 'None of the conventions requires a party to convict or punish drug abusers who commit such offences even when they have been established as punishable offences. The party may choose to deal with drug abusers through alternative non-penal measures involving treatment, education, after-care, rehabilitation or social reintegration'. Other commentators see the Vienna Convention as no more than a trafficking convention. Thus, as far as use and possession are concerned, a country may choose not to retain or introduce criminal offences for those activities if such an approach does not fit in with matters such as 'the basic concepts of its legal system'. It is this loophole that has presumably justified Dutch semi-legislation, and the 2002 British amendment to the drugs laws.

New York Mayor Michael Bloomberg testifies for an ad promoting the legalization of marijuana, created by the National Organization for the Reform of Marijuana Laws (NORML).

Finding out more

For a detailed reference of the laws dealing with cannabis applied in some 143 countries, go to the website of the United Nations Office for Drug Control and Crime Prevention at:

http://www.undcp.org/adhoc/legal_library/undcp/legal_library/index-countries.html

The first recorded medical uses of cannabis in China...cannabis becomes an essential part of global pharmacopoeia...cannabis used in India by both Ayurvedic and Unani Tibbi systems, taken orally, applied externally for a broad range of illnesses and complaints...cannabis as a 'cure-all'...in the West, early herbalists include hemp...1830s and 1840s cannabis is used as medicine throughout the US, UK and France...by the end of the Second World War cannabis is outlawed in the US and also slips out of British medicine...recent attempt to bring back medical cannabis...positive effects for some AIDS, cancer and MS patients...

CANNABIS – THE MEDICINE

As they were first in the cultivation of cannabis and the use of hemp for textiles, so too were the Chinese first to appreciate the medicinal properties of this plant. In the early stages, this was far from sophisticated, nor was it apparently very successful. As part of his armoury in the constant fight against demons (seen as the creators of human diseases) a Chinese shaman might approach his 'patient' clasping a handful of cannabis stalks, into which had been carved figures resembling snakes. With these he would strike the bed around the patient – and hopefully 'drive out' the demon. (A similar method was used by Japanese Shinto priests who preferred a short, unadorned wand bound with undyed hemp fibres. The theory being that the pure white fibres would overcome the 'darkness' of the demon.) As in much 'magic' medicine, what happened next was in the hands of the sufferer. If the illness were psychosomatic – 'all in the head' – there was a good chance that he or she might recover; otherwise, given the absence of necessary medicine, there was very little chance. The shaman, however, was not blamed for any inevitable demise.

Cannabis, one of the most widely used, and widely proven medicines in existence.

Shamanic medicine, fortunately for its subjects, was gradually declining by the third millennium BC, when the emperor Shen Nung (who was also a herbalist) produced the herbal pharmacopoeia *Pên-ts'ao Ching*. (However, although this body of work dates from 2700BC, the only surviving version appeared in the first century AD. The anonymous author claims he found it and was simply reproducing it; sceptics believe he may have been the

original writer. Either way it became a standard text.) This herbal pharmacopoeia is, amongst other things, the oldest record of medical cannabis use in China, and it recommended hemp (*ma*) for absent-mindedness and rheumatic pains, constipation, disorders of the female reproductive tract, malaria and beri-beri. According to legend, Shen Nung had a transparent abdomen, and for the sake of hands-on research consumed as many as seventy different plants (some versions of the tale specify 'poisons') per day so he could watch their effects and discover their various qualities. In this way he identified the hundreds of different medicines that were then written up in the *Pên-ts'ao*. The basis of these recommendations lay in the Oriental system of yin and yang. As written in the *Pên-ts'ao*, *ma fen*, the flowering tops of female cannabis plants, contain the greatest amount of yin energy, the receptive female dynamic. Illnesses such as those listed above were seen as demonstrating a loss of yin; thus *ma fen* was to be administered as a booster. Too much *ma fen*, warned the emperor, could cause one to see demons – that is go mad – but, on the other hand, regular, moderate dosage promoted the ability to communicate with

Cannabis grown indoors under carefully controlled lighting conditions to produce the highest THC content.

spirits. In time Shen Nung would be sanctified as the 'father of Chinese medicine' and until the Maoist Cultural Revolution (1966–1976), Chinese pharmacies would offer discounts, on the first and fifteenth of every month, in his honour.

A diverse range of uses

The *Pên-ts'ao* proved merely a beginning; the list of possible uses of cannabis in early Chinese medicine is impressive. In the second century AD the herbalist Hua T'o (190–265) recommended *ma yo*, a mixture of cannabis resin and wine (otherwise known as *ma fei san*, or 'bubbling-drug medicine'), as an analgesic during surgery. Most people at that time relied on acupuncture as the first resort, but if that failed the next line of treatment was surgery. According to records, *ma yo* was hugely successful, making it possible for a number of complex operations. Without causing the slightest pain, Hua T'o was able to perform organ grafts, resectioning of intestines, laparotomies (incisions into the loin) and thoracotomies (incisions into the chest). However, modern commentators are less sure: whilst cannabis does have some anaesthetic properties, they would hardly be sufficient for complete unconsciousness; more likely, the patient might become slightly drowsy, but it was the sheer acute pain of the knife's first cut that actually knocked them out.

Chinese doctors used every part of the plant; mainly the seeds but also the oil, stalks, roots as well as leaves and flowers. Of the many diseases considered susceptible to the drug's curative powers were constipation, diarrhoea and continuous vomiting, intense thirst and 'flux' (which last pair were both treated with an 'infusion of hemp'). There is some evidence that diabetes was also treated with cannabis. The drug was administered in pills (made after boiling down the seeds with water) and in various 'porridge'-style pastes, which could be applied externally to treat a variety of skin diseases, for ulcers, wounds, skin eruptions and even for hair loss. Hair loss and incipient greyness could also be treated with a mixture of cannabis oil and fresh leaf juice.

Chinese medicine also treated other diseases including rheumatism and leprosy (using a mixture of cannabis and a powdered form of Burmese chaulmoogra seeds). Cannabis' painkilling properties were not only utilized in operations, but also in quelling labour pains. Chinese practitioners would also administer cannabis to stop the haemorrhage that could follow childbirth as well as for the more regular 'menstrual disorders'. It was sometimes used as a diuretic and was supposed to help the evacuation of small kidney stones. The use of *ma fen* gradually died out, but it lasted until the fifth century when it was still being recommended as useful in the treatment of 'waste diseases and injuries'. There were also claims that it 'clears blood and cools temperature, it relieves fluxes; it undoes rheumatism; [and] it discharges pus'.

Indian medicinal practices

Whilst there is some dispute over quite what they were, there is no doubt that cannabis was used in India in very early medical applications. People believed it could quicken the mind, prolong life, improve judgement, lower fevers, induce sleep and cure dysentery. Given that it also had known psychotropic properties, it was seen as even more efficacious than those medicines that lacked such 'extras'.

The two main systems of medicine in India are the Ayurvedic (the 'Veda of Long Life' and categorized as 'scholarly' as opposed to 'folk' medicine) and, after the Muslim invasions of the ninth century, Unani Tibbi (Arabic for Greek medicine), which was the name given by the Hindus to this imported Arabian system of medicine with its concepts of the humours and their effects on bodily functions.

Ayurvedic physicians see cannabis as 'pittala', a term approximately equal to 'choleric', as used in medieval European medicine. Choler, or 'yellow bile,' is one of three humours in Ayurvedic medicine. Pitta rules the activating, heating and metabolic functions and has its main seat in the liver. A pittala drug will increase heat generally and will usually activate the liver specifically. Thus therapeutic use is mainly for conditions where heat or dryness are felt to be needed. As explained by Mia Tour writing in the *Journal of Psychoactive Drugs* (January–March, 1981): 'Cannabis increases the 'gastric fire' (i.e., digestion and, therefore, appetite), the 'generative fire,'…If one accepts that what was meant here was 'mucus', then this classification is quite correct for cannabis acts both as an expectorant and suppresses the production of mucus'.

Early eighteenth-century depiction of an Ayurvedic physician in India.

The first major work to lay out the uses of cannabis in medicine was the Ayurvedic treatise of Sushruta Samhita (generally known as the *Sushruta*), written in 600BC. The book describes over 120 surgical instruments, 300 surgical procedures and 760 vegetable-based medicines. Surgery was divided into eight categories. Like Shen Nung before him, Sushruta Samhita has since been extolled as his country's 'father of medicine'. Within the *Sushrita*, cannabis is cited as an anti-phlegmatic and a cure for leprosy.

Although Ayurvedic medicine, founded around 1000BC, long predates the Greek/Arabic system, originated by Hippocrates around 400BC, it would appear that it was not until the introduction of Unani Tibbi into India that cannabis joined that country's pharmacopoeia. Thereafter use of cannabis (and opium) was common practice and potions containing cannabis became as popular in Muslim India as they already were in Arabia and Persia.

A cure for all ills?

Irrespective of date, however, is the wide range of uses that both Ayurvedic and Unani Tibbi medicine offered an Indian patient. Indeed, whether taken orally or, as fresh leaves, applied externally, cannabis was used for pretty much everything as this article on Indian medicinal practices testifies:

> The prime uses were for the nervous system, the gastrointestinal tract and as an aphrodisiac. It was commonly employed for many other functional or organic troubles in the genital and urinary systems, both of women and men. Cannabis was as much a panacea for respiratory disturbances, especially those involving oversecretion of mucus, pain or frequent coughing (in other words, almost all), as for gastric malfunction. Further, it was used for a wide variety of infectious diseases, so much so that it has been referred to as the "penicillin of Ayurvedic medicine" (Indian Hemp Drugs Commission 1894). As an antirheumatic...it may have been only the analgesic properties that were active or it may have had some effect on the rheumatism itself, which is now widely accepted as being one of the autoimmune class of diseases. Some cannabis constituents have been shown to be antihistaminic, like the corticosteroids used to palliate autoimmune diseases. Use as a vermifuge and skin remedy were among its other common applications; it was used against the

venom of poisonous fish bites and scorpion stings; it was used even against leprosy…

Because of its sedative action, cannabis was taken as an insomnia remedy, often in the form of majum (Lamarck 1783). It was considered as effective as opium (Dastur n.d.). The analgesic properties of cannabis ensured its application against a wide variety of painful conditions. Cannabis was used for neuralgia, especially common forms, sciatica and facial neuralgia, as it was for migraine headaches, headaches in general and the terrible headaches which accompany malaria. It was used to relieve the pain of any inflammation or inflammatory disease. It was held to be such an effective anodyne that it was used as a liniment to relieve the pains of broken bones…Topical anesthesia and even general anesthesia were said to be achieved with cannabis. Cannabis was applied to every conceivable sort of spasm or convulsion, from simple stomach cramps, to tetanus, epilepsy and rabies. For infant convulsions extract would sometimes be mixed with belladonna…Charas calmed whooping cough, ganja being substituted when it was unavailable. Similarly, in dysentery cannabis' value may have been due to antispasmodic as well as antidiarrheic and perhaps antibiotic effects. An odd dosage route would sometimes be employed in this case: ganja smoke was blown into the rectum . The same method was used for strangulated hernias. Cannabis was even used in "brain fever," where its febrifuge and anodyne qualities would have been as useful as the antispasmodic ones.

…It calmed coughs, as in whooping cough, bronchitis, asthma and so on, while at the same time it decreased pain. Its expectorant and antihistaminic qualities were other factors greatly contributing to its usefulness for inflammatory respiratory ailments. Evidence of some antibiotic and even antiviral activity implies that applications in infectious diseases were justified…Cannabis was used to check excessive salivation…Cases of lack of appetite, indigestion, colic, nausea and insufficient weight gain were all treated with bhang drinks of various kinds or often with majum. The drinks were almost always made with either milk or ghee (Indian Hemp Drugs Commission 1894), thus obtaining the full complement of fat-soluble as well as water-soluble substances. Very intriguingly,

cannabis is reported as an antidiabetic...Cannabis' spasmolytic
action may have been the reason for its usefulness in
jaundice...Indian herbals specify cannabis as a means of controlling
diarrhea almost without exception. Not only simple diarrhea was
meant here, but also that which was a symptom of diseases as severe
as cholera...It was also applied externally on painful hemorrhoids
[and] fresh leaf poultices were even employed for pain of a prolapsed
anus (Indian Hemp Drugs Commission 1894)...The major effect of
cannabis on the urinary system noticed by the Indians was that of
diuresis [which] combined with cannabis' sedative and anti-
inflammatory action results in a remedy well-suited to the treatment
of cystitis and urethritis...Cannabis was often applied to diseases
and problems of the genital and reproductive systems...It was said to
"check the discharge" in gonorrhea.'

Cannabis was used extensively for a variety of reproductive
disorders. Poultices of fresh leaves were applied in orchitis and other
swellings of the testicles, including hydrocele...Likewise in labor this
combination of qualities enabled cannabis to give nearly or
completely painless childbirth...It was taken against uterine
hemorrhage as well as during labor. Cannabis was commonly given
for incontinence of sperm and was believed by the Moslem doctors
to give control over ejaculation. Obviously, a plant considered to be
such a good aphrodisiac was standard in remedies for impotence.
Since cannabis is effective against gram-positive bacteria, but loses its
potency in blood serum...dysentery and erysipelas could be
influenced by it, as well as local infection. Fresh leaf powder was
sprinkled into wounds and sores. It was used externally against eye
and ear infections...Fresh juice was likewise used as a vermifuge both
internally and externally for ear and eye worms...Applied to the
head it rid one of lice and dandruff...Unlike other intoxicating
drugs, except coca leaves, cannabis was widely used by poor people
to give them endurance while they worked...This contrasts strangely
both with the "amotivational syndrome" cannabis is supposed to
induce and with one's usual idea of an intoxicant...Finally, cannabis
was put to a number of unclassifiable uses, including diseases of the
spleen and heart.

(from the *Journal of Psychoactive Drugs*, vol.13 (1) Jan–March 1981)

It is, undeniably, a phenomenal list. Few drugs, then or later, can have been regarded as so literal a 'cure-all'.

Western medicine

Basing their knowledge on the Greek and Roman physicians Dioscorides and Galen, medieval herbalists in the West had recommended 'bastard hempe' (that is that growing as a weed, rather than the 'manured' variety used in textiles) as a cure for 'nodes and wennes and other hard tumors'. Other uses included treatment of coughs, jaundice, venerial disease and bed-wetting. Too much, however, was dangerous: it 'drieth up... the seeds of generation' in men 'and the milke of women's breasts'. Perhaps the most interesting use was that suggested to anglers, thus giving it the sixteenth-century nickname – 'angler's weed'. It seemed that a good method of persuading earthworms to appear from their underground homes was to pour hemp-based liquid into their holes. The worms would emerge, ready to be used as bait.

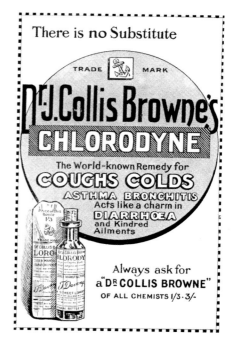

In 1693 English painter and author William Salmon (1664–1713) wrote that the seeds, leaves, and juice of cannabis, plus essence and decoctions were all widely available in pharmacists' shops. But there were many nay-sayers. It was suggested that these same pharmacists were rendered epileptic by the negative effects of simply stocking the seeds; botanist William Turner (circa 1508–1568), author of the herbal *Ortus sanitatis de herbis et plantis* (1517) quotes an earlier author called Simeon Sethy (or Sethi) who wrote that: 'hemp sede if it be taken out of mesure taketh mens wittes from them'. And added, in what surely must be a reference to psychoactive rather than medicinal properties, that the powder of the dried leaves makes men 'drunk'.

William O'Shaughnessy

As in France and America, the 1830s and 1840s were to prove the 'great leap forward' for the medical use of cannabis in the UK. In 1839 William O'Shaughnessy (1809–1889), Assistant Surgeon and Professor of Chemistry

An advertisement for for the many Western patent medicines that employed cannabis.

at the Medical College of Calcutta published a paper entitled 'On the Preparations of the Indian Hemp, or Gunjah (*Cannabis indica*); their Effects on the Animal System in Health, and their Utility in the Treatment of Tetanus and other Convulsive Diseases'. This paper, which mixed a brief background of the drug with a number of case histories, effectively brought cannabis to Western medicine. His positive response to the drug was widely influential, and until the mid-twentieth century, when American pressure managed to bulldoze a world too exhausted by war to argue, cannabis would be one of the leading drugs in the pharmacopoeia.

'A preparation of hemp'

Born in Ireland, O'Shaughnessy arrived in India in 1833 where he combined work for the East India Company with his teaching at the medical college in Calcutta and it was from here that he published his epochal paper. However, in that same year he was starting what would become a lifelong interest – the electric telegraph – and another essay on that topic appeared at much the same time. In the event O'Shaughnessy would abandon medicine and concentrate on this new means of communication, being largely responsible for its spread throughout India. He was knighted for his efforts in 1856, retired in 1861 and died in 1889.

O'Shaughnessy's study of cannabis was relatively short, but it covered a good deal of ground and, whether or not he knew it, would serve to launch a hugely effective new drug into the Western world. 'In the subsequent article,' he wrote, 'I first endeavour to present an adequate view of what has been recorded of the early history, the popular uses and employment in medicine of this powerful and valuable substance. I then proceed to notice several experiments which I have instituted on animals, with the view to ascertain its effects on the healthy system; and, lastly, I submit an abstract of the clinical details of the treatment of several patients afflicted with hydrophobia [rabies], tetanus, and other convulsive disorders, in which a preparation of Hemp was employed with results which seem to me to warrant our anticipating from its more extensive and impartial use no inconsiderable addition to the resources of the physician.'

All this he did, moving from the 'botanical characters', 'chemical properties [and] production' to 'popular uses', 'historical details' and 'medical properties'. He offered an overview of previous writings – as he noted, primarily out of the East – on the drug both as an intoxicant and as a medicine. He noted that cannabis remained effectively absent from the European materia medica. He dealt with bhang and the confection mahjoun (and supplied a recipe for both) and recorded the smoking of 'gunjah'. He noted Sushruta Samhita and the Arabic writer Taqi ad-Din al-Makrizi (see page 72), who wrote extensively on the drug and its history. Finally come his case histories.

O'Shaughnessy's case histories

The first of O'Shaughnessy's studies were on animals: a 'middling sized dog' who consumed 'ten grains of Nepalese churrus [charas]' and a smaller one who had one drachm of mahjoun. In both cases the dogs displayed what he termed 'drunkenness', but recovered completely. A variety of other animals were similarly dosed. In all cases they suffered no harm, although he did note that there was 'one remarkable result. – That while carnivorous animals, and fish, dogs, cats, swine, vultures, crows, and adjutants [a gigantic species of stork], invariably and speedily exhibited the intoxicating influence of the drug, the graminivorous, such as the horse, deer, monkey, goat, sheep, and cow, experienced but trivial effects from any dose we administered'.

O'Shaughnessy's next case studies involved humans, treating sufferers of variously rheumatism, hydrophobia, cholera, tetanus and infantile convulsions. Case histories vary as to detail, but the general results were positive and the doctor wrote that in the case of the rheumatics many enjoyed 'an alleviation of pain in most – remarkable increase of appetite in all – unequivocal aphrodisia, and great mental cheerfulness. In no one case did these effects proceed to delirium, or was there any tendency to quarrelling'. The results were beneficial in all the illnesses he treated.

His conclusions bore out what he had already determined from his reading, that: 'There was sufficient to show that Hemp possessed in small doses an extraordinary power of stimulating the digestive organs, exciting the cerebral system, of acting also on the generative apparatus. Larger doses, again, were shewn by the historical statements to induce insensibility, or to act as a powerful sedative. The influence of the drug in allaying pain was equally manifest in all the memoirs referred to. As to the evil sequelae so unanimously dwelt on by all writers; these did not appear to me so numerous, so immediate, or so formidable, as many which may be clearly traced to over-indulgence in other powerful stimulants, or narcotics, viz. alcohol, opium, or tobacco'.

Cannabis enters the pharmacopoeia

O'Shaughnessy returned to England in 1842, bringing with him a consignment of cannabis. This he gave to the pharmacist Peter Squire who created a form of tincture – cannabis dissolved in alcohol – which was marketed successfully as Squire's Extract. According to the *Journal of the Chemical Society's Transactions*, quoted in *Squire's Companion* (a booklet that described and puffed the company's products), 'the important constituent is a resin. The active principle is stated to be a red oil, Cannabinol, which is liable to become oxidised and inert. Its medicinal properties are sedative, anodyne, hypnotic and antispasmodic. It has been used with success in migraine and delirium, neuralgia. pain of the last stages of phthisis and in acute mania: also in menorrhagia and dysmenorrhoea [excessive or long-continued menstruation]'. The medical journal the *Lancet* added that it 'does not produce constipation or loss of appetite: on the contrary it restores the appetite which had been lost by chronic opium or chloral drinking'. As with cannabis in India, the extract was seen as a cure-all and, while it lasted, doctors prescribed it for a wide range of ailments.

It was the first of many successors, patent medicines such as Chlorodyne; Dr Brown's Sedative Tablets; One Day Cough Syrup (with added morphine); Syrup Tolou; Syrup Lobelia; Corn Collodium and Australia's Dr Poppy's Wonder Elixir 'with Cannabis Extract: the one bottle cure for coughs and colds'. Sold by some of the world's leading drug companies – Eli Lilly, Squibb (whose 'nerve tonic' tablets came plain or chocolate-coated), Parke-Davis, Smith Brothers and Tildens – cannabis extract was one of America's three most regularly prescribed drugs.

It was inevitable that O'Shaughnessy's paper would receive American attention. In 1843 Professor Robley Dunglison of the Jefferson Medical College of Philadelphia wrote a response: 'New Remedies: Pharmaceutically and Therapeutically Considered'. After reiterating O'Shaughnessy's historical and medical overview, he noted his positive case histories and concluded that, 'With such strong evidence in its favour, it is certainly important, that Indian hemp should be subjected to a full and fair trial; and even admitting that it may fall short of the character given of it by Dr. O'Shaughnessy, it can scarcely fail to be an important addition to our Materia Medica'. So it was, and by 1854 cannabis was was listed in the United States Dispensatory (albeit with a warning that large doses were dangerous and that it was a powerful 'narcotic'). As in the UK, it was widely and enthusiastically prescribed.

Ever-increasing potential

With cannabis acknowledged as a useful medicine, it continued to be the subject of experiments. In 1860 Dr R. R. Meens reported the findings of the Committee on Cannabis Indica to the Ohio State Medical Society. He noted its applications and rated it as a sedative comparable to, although not as powerful as opium. He noted the effectiveness of cannabis in stimulating the appetite. In 1887 another physician, H. A. Hare, would come up with similar conclusions, adding that the drug could subdue restlessness and anxiety and distract a patient's mind in terminal illness. He also recommended it as an anaesthetic for dentistry.

Three years later the British doctor J. R. Reynolds, who prescribed cannabis to Queen Victoria for menstrual pains, added senile insomnia to the list of cannabis-sensitive illnesses, noting that one of its utilities was that unlike opium, to which the patient became tolerant, the dose never needed to be increased. He further recommended it for epilepsy, depression, asthma and various types of neuralgia, especially migraine. He saw cannabis as 'one of the most valuable medicines we possess'. Migraine was at the heart of some more recommendations, offered in 1891 by Dr J. B. Mattison, who called hemp 'a

A small ad boasts of the efficacy of 'Indian cigarettes of cannabis' in treating asthma.

drug that has a special value in some morbid conditions and the intrinsic merit and safety of which entitles it to a place it once held in therapeutics'. He, too, increased the list of potential uses: it could help recovering drug addicts (this had already been noted in 1889 by E. A. Birch), and help treat gastric ulcers. Above all, although here he echoed his predecessors, it was the best possible treatment for 'that opprobrium of the healing art – migraine'. Not only did it lessen the pain, it even prevented the attacks.

By the turn of the century cannabis prescribing was in decline. The natural drug was falling foul of scientific progress, which was coming up with an increasing pharmacy of synthetics, such as aspirin, chloral hydrate and barbiturates, all of which (whether or not some have been discredited since) were chemically more stable than cannabis, and therefore considered more reliable in treatment. The invention and resultant popularity of the hypodermic syringe also accelerated cannabis' decline. Because it wasn't soluble in water, it couldn't rival those products (typically the opiates) that were and that could therefore be injected.

The *US Pharmacopeia* would continue to list cannabis until 1941. But whereas up to the 1930s it was seen as a positive, useful medicine, in 1936, under the bombardment of the Federal Bureau of Narcotics' negative campaign, the experts capitulated to ignorance and propaganda and it was downgraded. Now it was simply 'a narcotic poison, producing a mild delirium. Used in sedative mixtures but of doubtful value. Also employed to color corn remedies'. The 1942 edition omitted it entirely.

Parke Davis were one of the major American pharmaceutical companies selling cannabis extract.

The American Medical Association, which quite literally knew better, proved remarkably supine. The fate of their representative, W. C. Woodward, the one dissenting witness to the congressional hearings that preceded the Marijuana Tax Act (1937), was probably influential. Unimpressed by the propaganda, Woodward did his best to point out a variety of inconsistencies; his interlocutors, demanding only that 'The medical profession should be doing its utmost to aid in the suppression of this curse that is eating the very vitals of the nation', had not the slightest interest. In the end he was silenced and effectively thrown out, with the caution: 'You are not cooperative in this. If you want to advise us on legislation you ought to come here with some constructive proposals rather than criticisms, rather than trying to throw obstacles in the way of something that the Federal Government is trying to do'. As usual, the specious plea of the 'greater good' had worked. There would be no more 'criticisms' of the move to supress cannabis.

By the end of the Second World War cannabis had been outlawed and the cannabis crusader – Harry J. Anslinger – and his cohorts had not merely deprived recreational users of a pleasant amusement, but ensured that many ill people, whose symptoms might otherwise have been contained, were condemned to pain and ultimately to death. The Marijuana Tax Act, ostensibly aimed only at non-medical use, made the drug so hard to obtain, that its use as a medicine was effectively destroyed as well. It remains confined on Schedule I of the Controlled Substances Act as a drug that 'has a high potential for abuse, lacks an accepted medical use, and is unsafe for use under medical supervision'.

How Western medicine changed

Ignorance, fortunately, is not impenetrable, even though it tends to prove remarkably determined. Five millennia of cannabis medicine had been thrown away at the behest of the drug czar Harry J. Anslinger, but he had barely relinquished his role as the drug's chief prosecutor, when a widening knowledge of the drug, fuelled by its increasing popularity in the later Sixties amongst America's and then the world's youth, began to challenge the status quo. That the medical properties of cannabis had been banished did not make them any the less real. As more and more people experienced the drug, found it harmless and began to read up on its background, the idea that something useful had been thrown away gathered momentum.

Given the thousands of years of successful use, even if the West had only shared wholeheartedly in them for a century, it seems bizarre that a range of 'Establishments', most notably those in America, are so determined to keep cannabis in its pariah status. Like the UK's recent plan to begin prescribing heroin to addicts – which is, of course, no beginning: the system was successfully carried out until 1971 when it was banned, at which time the country had 1000 addicts; since then the total has escalated to 500,000 – there is a distinct sense of reinventing the wheel. The irony is that despite the proven efficacy of this particular wheel, so many vested interests seem desperate to do without such a basic piece of technology. There is what can only be termed a 'wilful blindness' and even those who, to their credit, are proving by their research that cannabis does indeed have a role to play in mainstream medicine, find themselves forgetting that in their overall discoveries they are simply telling us what we have always known.

The DEA's efforts against cannabis

It is perhaps fitting that it is in the US, where the destruction of medical cannabis was so assiduously pursued, that the first attempts to overturn that policy were instigated. As noted, the increased smoking of cannabis led to greater interest in the drug's non-intoxicatory properties. In 1972 the National Organization for the Reform of Marijuana Laws petitioned the Bureau of Narcotics and Dangerous Drugs (now known as the Drug Enforcement Administration (DEA)) to reclassify marijuana as a Schedule II drug, thus allowing its legal prescription. As time passed, with no response, more and more organizations joined the campaign, notably many involved with a new illness, AIDS. Finally, in 1986, the DEA agreed to hold hearings. The named parties were the National Organization for the Reform of Marijuana Laws, the Alliance for Cannabis Therapeutics, the Cannabis Corporation of America and Carl Olsen in favour of rescheduling; against stood the DEA, the Parents for a Drug Free Youth and the International Association of Chiefs of Police. The parties agreed beforehand to contest only two questions: whether cannabis had a currently accepted medical use and whether there was a lack of accepted safety for its use under medical supervision. They prepared exhibits and called witnesses, and copies of their testimonies and the exhibits were exchanged beforehand. Each side was allowed to object to the evidence of the other side, and the DEA's own administrative law judge, Francis L. Young, ruled which evidence should be excluded. Scores of experts offered their own testimony, and subjected themselves to cross-examination; the hearings generated thousands of pages of documentation. Final oral arguments were held in 1988, and Judge Young prepared his report.

The report 'accepted as fact' that cannabis had a medical use. It lists many examples of individual doctors', hospitals' and patients' use of cannabis in the treatment of chemotherapy-induced nausea, glaucoma and multiple sclerosis.

It established as fact that cannabis is 'far safer than many foods we commonly consume' and that 'in its natural form it is one of the safest therapeutically active substances known to man. By any measure of rational analysis marijuana can be safely used within a supervised routine of medical care'.

Yet, as the succession of ignored commissions and their reports into the drug should have given notice, even a judicial decision was as nothing compared with the stubborn prejudices of a governmental body. The DEA administrator John Lawn heard Judge Young's recommendation – and simply ignored it. The whole idea of 'medical marijuana', declared Lawn, was no more than a 'dangerous and cruel hoax'. In March 1991 the plaintiffs took their case to the District of Columbia Court of Appeals, which unanimously ordered the DEA to re-examine its position. Their rejection of 'medical marijuana' was illogical and it seemed that, whatever evidence was submitted, the DEA was determined to reject it. So it was. The court had tossed the case back, but it had not gone so far as to acknowledge the idea that cannabis did have therapeutic properties. This was enough for the DEA to maintain its stance. In March 1992 Lawn announced that he had binned the Young report for good. The use of cannabis for medicine remains a criminal offence.

There was, at least in America, a back door: the legal Compassionate Investigational New Drug. Under this programme it was possible for individual patients, typically those with AIDS, to obtain and use cannabis without fear of prosecution. Once again, whilst many states were happy to implement such a compromise, the federal government remained adamant. Apparently even this would 'send the wrong message' to the young. As more than one critic has asked: is allowing people to die in pain because of government obduracy, especially when so much evidence points in the opposite direction, a 'positive' message? The Compassionate IND programme was never widespread, at the most there were thirty-four such patients, and in March 1992 it came to an end: federal opposition had won. A residue of eight patients was allowed to continue, but that was that.

Fighting the pro-cannabis researchers
The cavalier attitude of the DEA to health can be seen in another example. The DEA and other agencies funded studies at the Medical College of

Virginia looking for evidence that cannabis causes health problems. Instead of finding problems, the researchers made a breakthrough when they discovered in 1975 that cannabis showed powerful anti-tumour activity against both benign and malignant tumours. The DEA quickly de-funded the studies and prohibited any future research into cannabis and its anti-tumour properties.

Yet if the law remains unbending, many patients, and their physicians, simply ignore it. If a doctor knows that a patient with AIDS, cancer or multiple sclerosis can benefit from smoking cannabis, they are often happy to say nothing to stop them. Given that the government, for what appears increasingly to be reasons of no more than pride, refuses to acknowledge reality, then why should responsible physicians acknowledge a bad law. As Lester Grinspoon and John Bakalar (In 'Marihuana as Medicine: A Plea for Reconsideration', *Journal of the American Medical Association*, June 1995) have pointed out, 'Physicians and patients in increasing numbers continue to relearn through personal experience the lessons of the 19th century. Many people know that marihuana is now being used illegally for the nausea and vomiting induced by chemotherapy. Some know that it lowers intraocular pressure in glaucoma. Patients have found it useful as an anticonvulsant, as a muscle relaxant in spastic disorders, and as an appetite stimulant in the wasting syndrome of human immunodeficiency virus infection. It is also being used to relieve phantom limb pain, menstrual cramps, and other types of chronic pain, including...migraine. Polls and voter referenda have repeatedly indicated that the vast majority of Americans think marihuana should be medically available'.

And they added, 'Advocates of medical use of marihuana are sometimes charged with using medicine as a wedge to open a way for "recreational" use. The accusation is false as applied to its target, but expresses in a distorted form a truth about some opponents of medical marihuana; they will not admit that it can be a safe and effective medicine largely because they are stubbornly committed to exaggerating its dangers when used for non-medical purposes'.

Perhaps the most important, and considered by its opponents the most sedulously ignored, aspect of cannabis as a drug is its innate safety. It has

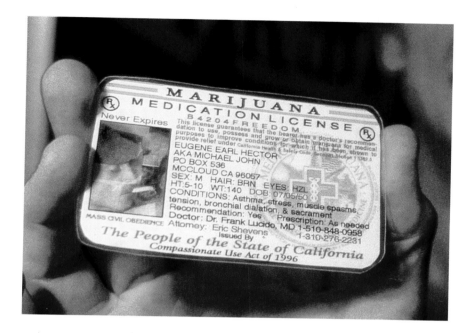

little effect on major physiological functions and there is no known case of a lethal overdose; on the basis of animal models, the ratio of lethal to effective dose is estimated as 40,000 to 1. The average, indeed well above average cannabis user simply doesn't encounter such amounts, even over a lifetime. The main problem, which even its defenders must acknowledge, is the fact that cannabis is usually smoked. Cannabis smoke is even more saturated with tars and other dangerous matter than tobacco smoke. The difference however, is that far less cannabis smoke is ever ingested than that of cigarettes. And in medical use this figure is even lower. In addition, there are simple ways – typically filtering the smoke through a water pipe – that will improve the situation even further. As Grinspoon and Bakalar conclude, echoing the old smoker's axiom: 'At present, the greatest danger in medical use of marihuana is its illegality, which imposes much anxiety and expense on suffering people, forces them to bargain with illicit drug dealers, and exposes them to the threat of criminal prosecution'.

In a further paradox, a number of US states have challenged the federal refusal to change by passing laws that effectively remove state-level criminal penalties for growing and/or possessing medical cannabis. These states

include California, Hawaii, Maine, Nevada, Oregon, and Washington. Ten states, plus the District of Columbia, have symbolic medical cannabis laws – laws that support medical cannabis but do not provide patients with legal protection under state law. Nor is the government, thanks to a law suit in September 2000, able to bar doctors (whom it threatened with being struck off) from recommending, although not actually prescribing, cannabis. However, as long as the federal statutes remain in place, users, however justified, still face prosecution. In total, thirty-five states have passed legislation acknowledging cannabis' medical value.

The UK – caution above all

Nothing similar, even at a symbolic level, exists in the UK. But in 1998, in the wake of three recent studies of the topic – the British Medical Association's report 'Therapeutic Uses of Cannabis', the House of Lords Select Committee on Science and Technology report: 'Cannabis: The Scientific and Medical Evidence' and the US Institute of Medicine's 'Marijuana and Medicine: Assessing the Science Base' – the government authorized the pharmaceutical company G. W. Pharmaceuticals to 'cultivate, produce, possess and supply cannabis for research purposes'. Since then the company has been pursuing research and running both laboratory and clinical trials. In addition, the Medical Research Council have so far paid out £2.1m for research into the medical use of cannabis, notably into post-operative pain and multiple sclerosis. Perhaps the best indication of the way forward in the UK is in the conclusions of the March 2001 House of Lords report 'Therapeutic Uses Of Cannabis'. This notes an improvement in the government's 'attitude' but regrets the continuing stubbornness of the Medicines Control Agency. This foot-dragging is apparently slowing down research: for instance, were the Medicines Control Agency not to require further extensive toxicological studies on cannabinoids, G. W. Pharmaceuticals claim that they could have a cannabis-based prescription medicine available for patients in 2003. And as the House of Lords adds, the agency are determined to test cannabis as if it were a 'new' medicine, 'though cannabis oil, which contains both CBD [cannabidiol] and THC [tetrahydrocannabinol], has a long history of human use and appeared in the British Pharmacopoeia Codex until 1948'. It also notes that the Medicines Control Agency's objections are based on irrelevant and inaccurate research, and that even if some side-effects might

Cannabis could provide pain relief in a wide range of illnesses – were it legal.

exist, the benefits for a seriously ill patient would far outweigh them. As for the 'recreational use by the back door' argument, the Lords suggest that this 'unsatisfactory situation underlines the need to legalize cannabis preparations for therapeutic use'. With legal and properly controlled medical use it will be easier, not harder, to isolate the recreational users.

The arguments on medical marijuana are likely to continue in any country where governments refuse to address the situation other than with the current pigheaded determination to suppress all useful debate. And even, when as recently in Britain the authorities, however reluctantly and belatedly, decided to downgrade possession of cannabis to a non-arrestable offence the question of medical uses remained off-limits. Those who hoped that the government's new line would include cannabis as medicine were sorely disappointed. The reality, whether it be in the medical or recreational change, will lie in public opinion. Nothing has changed as regards cannabis since the Sixties, when the first agitations for its legalization were heard. Then, the agitators were too small a number to need any proper attention. Thirty years on the demographic has changed: and with it so too, even at snail's pace, have Establishment attitudes. Time, as ever, will tell.

Marijuana and medicine – the science

It is worth quoting the opinions of America's National Academy of Sciences' Institute of Medicine, published in its March 1999 report, 'Marijuana and Medicine: Assessing the Science Base'. The Institute, acknowledged as the 'gold standard of American medicine', recognized the drug's wide range of therapeutic uses, urged that it should be made available to patients and called for research into developing cannabis-based drugs. It accepted the dangers of smoking cannabis, but also noted that some patients could not wait perhaps a decade for a government-permitted substitute.

In addition, the Institute recommended making smoked cannabis medically available, under limited circumstances, until new drugs become available. It was unimpressed by the suggestion that permitting medical cannabis would lead to legalizing recreational use. That 'question is beyond the issues normally considered for medical uses of drugs, and should not be a factor in evaluating the therapeutic potential of marijuana or cannabinoids'. Like the supposedly 'caring' references to smoking, this was a delaying tactic.

It concluded: 'The accumulated data suggest a variety of indications, particularly for pain relief, anti-emesis, and appetite stimulation. For patients, such as those with AIDS or those undergoing chemotherapy, who suffer simultaneously from severe pain, nausea, and appetite loss, cannabinoid drugs might thus offer broad spectrum relief not found in any other single medication. The data are weaker for muscle spasticity, but moderately promising. The least promising categories are movement disorders, epilepsy, and glaucoma. Animal data are moderately supportive of a potential for cannabinoids in the treatment of movement disorders and might eventually yield stronger encouragement'.

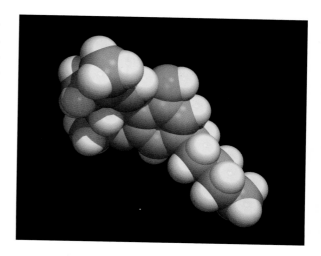

Molecular graphic of tetrahydrocannabinol (THC), a psychoactive drug derived from the hemp plant and the active ingredient of cannabis. THC has the formula $C_{21}.H_{30}.O_2$. The atoms are shown as spheres and are colour-coded: carbon (red), hydrogen (yellow) and oxygen (green).

For the many conditions in which cannabis, legal or otherwise, can benefit patients see pages 202–219. That they may appear to echo those of the pre-prohibition medical use of the drug will surely come as no surprise.

The road to a legal synthetic cannabis

Despite its dead-set rejection of legalized medical cannabis, the US government has, quite paradoxically, made serious efforts to create a synthetic cannabis product that could be given to selected patients. The latest attempt to create a government-approved 'medical marijuana' is known as Marinol (dronabinol), properly referred to as delta-9-tetrahydrocannabinol (THC).

But first a little history. The first such attempt came with the founding in 1969 of the ostensibly secret National Institute on Drug Abuse's 'pot farm', funded and run by the University of Mississippi. Here regular crops of low-grade cannabis were harvested and shipped off to the Research Triangle Institute in North Carolina, where the dried leaves were rolled at a cost of $2 per joint. The joints were stored and frozen, pending delivery. (Although a THC pill was developed during the 1970s, it was seen as both erratic and unpredictable, and the medical establishment accepted that these 'official' joints were what patients needed.) As Dr Monroe Wall of the Research Triangle Institute told a 1978 meeting of the National Cancer Institute, the THC cigarette 'is now highly standardized and is a reliable and reproducible method of administering the drug'.

The problems came with demand. As more and more cancer patients heard that this illegal drug could in fact help them (especially in dealing with chemotherapy-related nausea and lowered appetites), they demanded that their doctors prescribe it. (Californian doctors alone estimated that they would have an immediate take-up of around one million cigarettes.) By 1980, pressure had mounted on the government to make these 'legal joints' more available.

The simple solution would surely be to expand the 'pot farm'. But it was apparently unthinkable for the authorities and was rejected outright. What was needed was a 'proper' synthetic substitute, produced not in the fields but in the labs of the great, profit-making pharmaceutical companies. The first such synthetic cannabis, Nabilone (active ingredient hexahydro-cannabinol) appeared in 1978. It was manufactured by Eli Lilly under the trade name Cesamet. Tests were run on both dogs and humans. Despite the firm's optimism, Nabilone failed: the dogs began to have convulsions; then they died. Nabilone was forgotten.

What took its place was dronabinol sold in capsule form as Marinol by Roxane Laboratories. The drug had never been meant for human use, but with Nabilone out of the picture, it was the only alternative. In October 1980, the National Cancer Institute began distributing Marinol free of charge to 20,000 patients at 800 hospitals in the US.

Marinol is federally recognized as an appetite stimulant and anti-nausea/vomiting (anti-emetic) agent. Dronabinol has a complicated effect on the body's central nervous system, but in basic terms it interferes with the neural impulses associated with nausea and stimulates the appetite. It is available only through special prescription to treat people suffering from chemotherapy- or radiotherapy-related nausea and to treat those suffering from AIDS-related loss of appetite.

Marinol was in high demand, even if patients were still calling for smokeable, 'natural' cannabis. A series of reports underlined their points of view; smokeable cannabis was proving consistently safer and more effective than synthetic THC. It didn't matter: the government rejected the studies.

Despite government backing, and despite the business projections that talked of up to $70m per year from the cancer market and a further $1bn from those with HIV, the drug has yet to take off. First year (1987) profits reached $1.5m but over time the best annual sales have never topped $3m.

Synthetic versus organic THC

Comparisons between synthetic and organic (that is smoked) THC may have some bearing. Whilst Marinol advertising warns those taking its capsules to avoid smoking cannabis in case of an overdose, such a concept is innately paradoxical. Marinol is concentrated THC, 99 per cent pure; the average marijuana joint, even of today's extra-strong varieties, rarely tops 15 per cent, and is more likely 5–10 per cent. Take too many capsules and an overdose, at least to the extent of involuntary unconsciousness, is indeed possible; people may have become higher than they may have desired, but no-one has ever overdosed on organic dope.

Marinol comes with a number of side-effects. As smokers know, things happen when they smoke cannabis – apart from the basic intoxication. They can include euphoria, laughter, anxiety, dry mouth, red eyes, sleepiness, clumsiness and a great desire for snacks, better known as 'the munchies'. But hardcore psychiatric problems? No 'medical' has complained yet. Marinol seems less tolerant and what have been cited as 'disturbing psychiatric symptoms' are apparently frequently reported. As listed in the 1985 *Medical Letter,* these have included 'disorientation, depression, paranoia, hallucinations and manic psychosis'. With this in mind Marinol's 1992 product leaflet notes adverse reactions ('amnesia', 'depersonalization', 'hallucination', 'paranoid reaction', 'depression') and adds, under overdosage: 'Patients experiencing depressive, hallucinatory or psychotic reactions should be placed in a quiet area and offered reassurance'. The same product insert notes that the synthetic drug can be habit-forming and that a regular user who stops 'cold turkey' may well face 'withdrawal' of up to four days.

AN A–Z OF MEDICAL USES

The material in this appendix has been drawn from a number of sources, but the primary information is based on that gathered by G. W. Pharmaceuticals, the company currently licensed to research the medical uses of cannabis, and when legislation permits it, to create cannabis-based medicines.

Of all the paradoxes that attend upon cannabis, the situation as regards medical use is perhaps the most absurd, and for those who have been told with increasing frequency that they might benefit from cannabis-based drugs, but are forbidden to do so, both frustrating and in some cases fatal. This section is based on a number of surveys, themselves dependent on many experts, experiments and case histories, all of which have come to the conclusion that to some extent (often substantial) these illnesses might benefit from therapy with cannabis-based drugs.

Some countries, notably and to its credit the UK, have decided that there is something positive and useful to be explored here. Programmes of research and drug development are well advanced. But even the most positive remain hamstrung by the futile and indeed quite irrelevant 'holy grail' (as it has been described) of making sure that in no way might such drugs ever make anyone high. It displays, one might suggest, a sad picture of governmental priorities. So determined are they to ensure that laws against 'recreational' cannabis – laws that may well be foolish and, in any case, are increasingly ignored – are not undermined, that a disproportionate amount of this expensive research is focused simply on extracting the 'good bit' from the drug. Heaven forbid, seems to be the governmental stance, that some terminally ill cancer patient or a person with AIDS might derive some illegal, inpermissable pleasure.

Reading the material, seeing the enormous potential that expert researchers across the world assure us is possible with the agency of cannabis, it is surely not merely a pro-cannabis rant to suggest that there is something deeply perverse about such topsy-turvy priorities. In the event, deprived of governmental support, thousands of ill people, many of whom might well eschew cannabis in its 'recreational' context, are forced to encriminalize themselves. And many have actually been prosecuted. A century or so ago, no such problems existed. Cannabis was an accepted drug, one of the most popular, and efficacious, in the pharmacopoeia. Thanks to modern research we know not only that the pharmacopoeia was right but also how cannabis interacts with the brain (see pages 23–24) and why cannabis is so useful a medicine. None of that has changed. Only government attitudes have altered. Fortunately, they may change again.

This list covers those illnesses that, after wide-ranging research, have been shown as susceptible to cannabis or cannabis-based drugs. This is not to say that cannabis is the only possible treatment – there are, for instance, a number of highly efficacious non-cannabis methods of treating glaucoma – but that it is a possibility.

AIDS wasting syndrome

One of the common (and potentially fatal) side effects of HIV infection is AIDS wasting syndrome or cachexia, defined as the involuntary loss of 10 per cent of body weight or more that is not attributable to other disease processes. Such weight loss provides a gateway for a range of fatal diseases. Given the need to counter this wasting, the appetite-enhancing properties of cannabis make it a vital helper. As any cannabis smoker will tell you, one of the near-guaranteed effects of a few joints is a definite increase in appetite. The 'munchies', as the slang has it, may tend to the creation of such things as melted Mars bars over ice-cream but, whatever the detail, the bigger picture remains: cannabis stimulates the appetite. With that in mind, a number of medical organizations specializing in AIDS research have termed it 'potentially lifesaving medicine'.

The legal situation means that smoking cannabis, however efficacious, is forbidden; instead doctors are permitted to prescribe the 'medical cannabis' drug – oral tetrahydrocannabinol known as Marinol (dronabinol) both as an appetite stimulant and as an anti-emetic (anti-sickness drug). It does work, but many HIV-positive and AIDS patients are less than happy with the drug. Compared with smoked cannabis, they find that it is substantially less effective in performing its appointed tasks. This is mainly to do with Marinol's delayed onset: taken by mouth it can be up to four hours before the effects kick in – far too late for someone who is already about to be sick. Smoked cannabis, on the other hand, is absorbed almost instantly. But either way, the positive psychological effect of weight gain cannot be underestimated. Finally, patients find it is Marinol, rather than cannabis, that actually renders them excessively stoned.

The bottom line seems to be that cannabis' therapeutic potential as an anti-emetic and appetite stimulant both benefits and, in some cases, actually treats many symptoms associated with HIV infection and AIDS. The US Institute of Medicine concluded that 'cannabinoid drugs might offer broad-spectrum relief not found in any other single medication... [for AIDS patients who] suffer simultaneously from severe pain, nausea, and appetite loss'.

Arthritis

Arthritis refers to any one of many inflammatory joint disorders characterized by pain, swelling and limited movement, and involves the inflammation and degeneration of cartilage and bone that make up a joint. The most common forms of arthritis are osteoarthritis and rheumatoid arthritis. Osteoarthritis, the more common of the two, occurs when the cartilage covering the ends of bones in a joint degenerates. It typically strikes the joints that support weight such as the knees, hips and spine. Rheumatoid arthritis is characterized by painful swelling of the smaller joints with the destruction of the tissue around them.

Cannabis is already recognized as an analgesic (painkiller); it is now emerging that it may also have anti-inflammatory properties. So far there have been no tests of the drug's use in humans, but animal experiments show that it does decrease inflammation. A UK research team writing in 1988, stated that 'Our results would suggest that cultivation of cannabis plants rich in CBD [cannabidiol] and other phenolic substances would be useful...for medicinal purposes in the treatment of certain inflammatory disorders'. The hope, as yet still unproven, is that cannabis' anti-inflammatory properties could reduce swelling and improve mobility in some patients with rheumatoid arthritis. [Source: 'Analgesic and Antiinflammatory Activity of Constituents of *Cannabis sativa L.*,' Inflammation 12 (1988): 361. E. Formukong et al.]

Right up to the 1960s people in South America treated rheumatism with hemp leaves and/or the flowertops that were heated in water or alcohol and placed on the painful joints. This form of herbal medicine is still widely used in rural areas of Mexico, Central and South America, and by California Latinos for relief of rheumatic and arthritic pain. It would appear that only legislation prevents the resumption of its use for such problems elsewhere.

Given that it has been known for some time that smoking cannabis a few times a day will have positive painkilling effects on osteoarthritis, it must be assumed that this condition would also be susceptible to a medicinal form of the drug.

Asthma

This breathing disorder is caused by inflammation and swelling of the small airways (bronchioles) in the lungs along with muscular contraction in the bronchiolar walls. The combined effect, along with excess mucus, is shortness of breath and wheezing as the person cannot get enough air into his/her lungs. Western doctors typically treat asthma with 'bronchodilator' drugs that relax and open the bronchioles and/or anti-inflammatory steroid drugs. Cannabis treatment of asthma was common in the nineteenth century in the West, and for many centuries before that in the East. It is now suggested that up to 80 per cent of asthma sufferers could benefit from smoked cannabis or the medical equivalent – oral tetrahydrocannabinol (THC).

In 1994, the Australian National Task Force on Cannabis determined, 'smoked cannabis, and to a lesser extent oral THC, have an acute bronchodilatory effect in both normal persons and persons with asthma'. The House of Lords reports on cannabis 'Cannabis: The Scientific and Medical Evidence' (November 1998) and 'Therapeutic Uses of Cannabis' (March 2001) acknowledged that cannabinoids seemed to work as effectively as conventional asthma drug treatments. Cannabis also has an anti-inflammatory action and it is possible that asthma sufferers who benefit therapeutically from the drug enjoy a combination of cannabis' medicinal properties. Obviously the side-effects of smoking will cause extra problems for asthma sufferers; therefore it has been suggested that the drug should be best administered in either aerosolized inhalers or sublingual (under the tongue) tinctures.

Cough

A cough is a protective reflex response to irritants or infection within the respiratory tract. Cannabis is one of the best natural expectorants to clear the human lungs of smog, dust and the phlegm associated with tobacco use. Cannabis smoke effectively dilates the large airways – the bronchi – to allow more oxygen into the lungs. It is also the best natural dilator of the tiny airways of the lungs, the bronchioles – making cannabis the best overall bronchial dilator for 80 per cent of the population (the remaining 20 per cent sometimes show minor negative reactions). Statistical evidence indicates that people who smoke tobacco cigarettes are usually better off and will live longer if they smoke cannabis moderately, too. Many joggers and marathon runners feel cannabis use cleans their lungs, allowing better endurance. [Source: UCLA Tashkin Studies, 1969–1983; US Costa Rican Studies, 1980–1982; Jamaican Studies 1968–1974]

Crohn's disease

Crohn's disease is a long-term, inflammatory condition of the intestine. It is typically confined to the lower end of the small intestine, but may occur anywhere within the gastrointestinal tract. Inflammation from Crohn's disease can cause ulcers, bleeding and scar formation that may lead to intestinal blockage. As a result, patients suffer intestinal cramps and spasms, nausea and vomiting, loss of appetite and weight, severe diarrhoea and rectal bleeding. Patients suffering from Crohn's disease are usually treated with anti-inflammatory drugs.

There have as yet been no specific studies to assess the possible uses of cannabis as regards Crohn's disease, but a number of anecdotal reports describe benefits. This is not surprising since cannabis has a proven ability to stimulate appetite, alleviate nausea, control spasms and potentially reduce inflammation.

Depression

Although an overused word in everyday language, depression in the clinical sense is defined as feelings of sadness often accompanied by a loss of interest in life as a whole along with reduced energy levels. Given the intangibility of depression, it is harder to make a positive assessment of any potentially useful role for cannabis. There have been a variety of trials, but they all seem to come up with contradictory results: some patients have benefited; others not at all. A 1994 survey of seventy-nine patients found that those who used cannabis reported relief from depression, anxiety, insomnia and physical discomfort, they also experienced fewer hospitalizations.

A 1996 study cited in the 1999 Institute of Medicine report 'Marijuana and Medicine: Assessing the Science Base' found that oral tetrahydrocannabinol (THC, in the form of dronabinol or Marinol) significantly assuaged mood disturbances and loss of appetite in eleven patients with Alzheimer's disease. (Those with Alzheimer's disease often experience mood disorders, notably depression.) But the risk of paranoia, especially among inexperienced users, renders cannabis potentially dangerous for those who cannot 'handle' its effects. Experts therefore suggest that its most promising potential to mitigate symptoms of depression likely lies with those patients who have previous experience with it and who are failing to respond to traditional therapies. [Source: Institute of Medicine report 'Marijuana and Medicine: Assessing the Science Base' (1999)]

Eating disorders

Such disorders are most commonly seen in Western cultures and particularly affect teenagers and young adults. The two main types are anorexia nervosa and bulimia. That cannabis increases the appetite has been known by anyone who has ever smoked it. The sensual pleasures of taste are increased and so more food is consumed. Thus, it would seem a natural counter to those eating disorders in which the appetite suffers. That said, tests on people with anorexia have had mixed results. This may be because the very cravings that the cannabis accentuates similarly intensify the guilt that people with these conditions equate with eating. However, because those with anorexia nervosa don't respond well to standard treatments and often die from their condition, researchers feel that cannabis may still remain an option to patients suffering from this disorder.

Emphysema

Emphysema is a respiratory condition in which there is dilation and destruction of lung tissue, mainly in the small airways in the lungs. It often goes hand in hand with chronic bronchitis and is then known as chronic obstructive pulmonary disease. Characteristic symptoms include cough, wheeze and breathlessness and the condition worsens in cold weather.

Research indicates that light cannabis smoking might be useful for a majority of patients with mild emphysema. It would improve the quality of life for millions of sufferers and extend their lifespans. Cannabis smoking itself will neither exacerbate nor cause emphysema. [Source: Jack Herer *The Emperor Wears No Clothes* quoting: Dr. Donald Tashkin, the US government's leading scientist on marijuana pulmonary research, who told the publication in December, 1989, and again in December 1997, that you cannot get or potentiate emphysema with cannabis smoking.]

Epilepsy

This common disorder of brain function causes patients to suffer from periodic, recurrent seizures triggered by abnormal electrical activity of certain brain cells. These seizures occur in various forms, ranging from mild to severe convulsions with or without a loss of consciousness.

Standard treatment for epilepsy involves anti-convulsant drugs. However, a number of reports acknowledge the potential of cannabis, because of its anti-convulsant properties, as an alternative and possibly preferable treatment. For example, the 1997 US National Institutes of Health Workshop on Utility of Medical Marijuana concluded that cannabinoids hold promise in the treatment of epilepsy. 'Substantial experimental animal literature exists showing that various cannabinoids…have a substantial anticonvulsant effect in the control of various models of epilepsy, especially generalized and partial tonic-clonic seizures'. They added that 'This is an area of potential value, especially for cannabis therapies by other than the smoked route'. However, other researchers have found that cannabis has had no effect whatsoever and that high doses of tetrahydrocannabinol can actually trigger seizures. But some reports stress that although these seizures may be unpleasant, they are substantially less intense than those experienced by users of pharmaceutical treatments.

Glaucoma

This eye disorder results from a blockage in the draining system of the eye, causing a rise in pressure within the eye (intraocular pressure). Glaucoma progressively impairs vision and may lead to permanent blindness. The aim of glaucoma treatment is to reduce the intraocular pressure.

Several human studies demonstrate that inhaled cannabis lowers this pressure in subjects with both normal intraocular pressure and glaucoma. Some researchers have suggested that cannabis could help up to 90 per cent of sufferers. Cannabis' ability to reduce pressure within the eye was first documented in a series of studies by Dr Robert Hepler of the University of California at Los Angeles in 1971. He found that cannabis lowered intraocular pressure for an average of four to five hours with 'no indications of any deleterious effects...on visual function or ocular [eye] structure'. Hepler later documented that long-term users of cannabis failed to have any deterioration of vision or develop tolerance to its effect on intraocular pressure. At least half a dozen additional human studies also explored the effects of tetrahydrocannabinol – the active ingredient in cannabis – and cannabis on this eye pressure, indicating that cannabinoids help preserve the vision of glaucoma patients. The main problem seems to be regarding administration. Smoked cannabis works best, but it has the drug's usual side-effects. Work with animals suggested an eyedrop formulation might be feasible, but the drops did not appear to work in human subjects.

A 1999 Institute of Medicine report also acknowledged cannabis' ability to temporarily lower intraocular pressure, but cautioned against long-term cannabis use because of potential side-effects inherent to lifelong smoking. They determined: 'High intraocular pressure (IOP) is a known risk factor for glaucoma and can, indeed, be reduced by cannabinoids and marijuana. However, the effect is...short lived and...the potential harmful effects of chronic marijuana smoking outweigh its modest benefits in the treatment of glaucoma'.

The IOM report must however be balanced against the findings in 1992 of the American Academy of Ophthalmology which stated that while: 'there is evidence that marijuana (or its components), taken orally or by inhalation can lower intraocular pressure…there are no conclusive studies to date to indicate that marijuana (or its components) can safely and effectively lower intraocular pressure enough to prevent optic nerve damage…The dose of marijuana necessary to produce a clinically relevant effect in the short term appears to produce an unacceptable level of undesirable side effects'. And in 1997, America's National Eye Institute felt much the same way and added that with the development of increasingly efficient eyedrops, cannabis would at best work as a possible additive. Both official bodies, however, expressed their willingness to acknowledge the results of any new research. That research continues.

Head injuries and stroke

Damage to the skull or brain can vary from minor bumps to life-threatening brain damage. Strokes, too, result in damage to the brain due to an interruption in its blood supply – even if it is for just a short time.

To protect stroke and head injury victims from exposure to toxic levels of reactive molecules – called 'free radicals' – that are produced when the brain's blood supply is cut off, doctors often use anti-oxidant chemicals. Another side to this situation is that head injuries and strokes also cause the release of excessive glutamate (a chemical messenger in the brain), often resulting in irreversible damage to brain cells. Research in 1998, for example, by the US National Institute for Mental Health demonstrated that the cannabinoids tetrahydrocannabinol and cannabidiol are potent anti-oxidants in animals. The US Institute of Medicine also praised cannabinoids' medical potential as anti-oxidants in its 1999 report, 'Marijuana and Medicine: Assessing the Science Base'. Cannabidiol is non-psychoactive, fast acting and non-toxic and the scientists found that it protected rat brain cells that had been exposed to toxic levels of glutamate better than standard anti-oxidants such as vitamins C and E. With this in mind researchers hope that the drug could eventually be administered to stroke victims to limit brain damage.

Herpes skin infections

Infection with the herpes simplex virus can cause a variety of skin complaints from cold sores to genital blisters. Cannabis is a topical analgesic, that is a painkiller that can be applied to the skin. Up until 1937, when all prescriptive use of cannabis was banned, cannabis extract was the primary constituent in virtually all corn plasters, mustard plasters, muscle ointments and the herbal pack applied as a poultice to counter fibrosis.

Smoked cannabis will not cure herpes but a cannabis paste (made from 'strong bud' soaked in rubbing alcohol and crushed into a paste) has been seen to speed recovery – by promoting a faster drying and healing of a herpes infection.

High blood pressure

Also known as hypertension, high blood pressure afflicts between 10 and 20 per cent of adults in Western societies. This condition puts a strain on the heart and blood vessels and so greatly increases the risk of stroke and heart disease. Recent research has shown that a naturally occurring cannabinoid in the body – known as anandamide – relaxes blood vessels, thereby reducing blood pressure. But researchers have yet to work out exactly how this chemical works in the body.

The 1998 House of Lords Science and Technology Committee report on medical cannabis acknowledged that smoking cannabis can lower blood pressure, but warns that it may also raise the heart rate in some users. They concluded that the high heart rates might pose a health risk for patients with a history of angina or other cardiovascular disease and recommended that they be excluded from any clinical trials of cannabis-based medicines. While cannabis may potentially be beneficial in reducing blood pressure, specific studies have not been conducted to determine how safely and effectively it controls the condition. Studies on anandamide (a naturally ocurring cannabinoid) and high blood pressure should provide clues as to how cannabis affects blood pressure; however, such studies are still in their initial stages.

Insomnia

Occasional sleeping difficulties are common but a regular inability to fall asleep or stay asleep can lead to the distressing condition insomnia, with its accompanying fatigue. Because cannabis lowers blood pressure, dilates the arteries and reduces body temperature an average of 0.5°C, thereby relieving stress, those who smoke cannabis in the evening usually enjoy a relaxing sleep. And, because those using cannabis achieve a maximum activity of alpha-type brain waves, which indicate a deeper level of relaxation, the cannabis-induced sleeper will achieve a more complete rest. Unlike prescription sleeping pills, cannabis does not exacerbate the effects of alcohol and it is supposed by medical cannabis advocates such as Dr Lester Grinspoon, that 'cannibidiol (one of 60 therapeutic compounds isolated in cannabis) will be the best sleeping medicine and one of the best anti-anxiety drugs with the least toxic side-effects.' [Source: *Guardian* (UK) 18 September 1993]

Migraine

Migraine is a type of severe headache that can last from a few hours to a couple of days. These headaches often recur in susceptible individuals and tend to be accompanied by a sensitivity to light, intolerance to loud noises and nausea or vomiting. Approximately 15–25 per cent of women and 5–10 per cent of men are reported to suffer from migraines.

The effectiveness of cannabis in the treatment of migraine has been recognized for many years; one of its most celebrated supporters was the surgeon Sir William Osler who wrote in his 1913 textbook *The Principles and Practice of Medicine* that it was 'probably the most satisfactory remedy' for migraine.

Recent reports prove Osler and his many contemporary peers, absolutely right. Writing in the journal *Pain (Journal of the Association for the Study of Pain)* the author stated that 'cannabis delivered…in the form of a marijuana cigarette, or "joint", presents the hypothetical potential for quick, effective, parenteral [non-orally administered] treatment of acute migraine'. He added that cannabis was a 'far safer alternative' than many prescription anti-migraine drugs and reported that a large percentage of migraine sufferers fail to respond or cannot tolerate standard therapies.

Accepting that in the case of migraine, 'there is clearly a need for improved migraine medications', the US Institute of Medicine acknowledged that 'marijuana has been proposed numerous times as that possible treatment'.

Movement disorders

Some neurological conditions can result in overly rigid muscles (spasticity), difficulties in balance and coordination (ataxia) and uncontrollable tics (Tourette's syndrome). Such medical disorders have been studied in detail, especially when looking at potential cannabis treatments.

There have been numerous studies both of animals and humans on the use of cannabinoids on neurological and various movement disorders. The results range from anecdotal reports to surveys and clinical trials. Cannabis' active ingredient tetrahydrocannabinol (THC) is reported to have some anti-spasticity, analgesic and anti-tremor actions.

Several single case histories have been reported indicating some benefit of smoked cannabis for problems with muscular contractions and control. But neither smoked cannabis nor oral THC have helped in the treatment of the neurodegenerative diseases of Parkinson's disease or Huntington's chorea that affect walking and other body movements.

A small number of documented case studies suggest that inhaling the smoke from cannabis, which has proven links with those parts of the brain that control movement, can help deal with the rare genetic condition of Tourette's syndrome. Such a disease normally begins in childhood (mainly in boys) and is characterized by sudden spasms – so called 'tics' – that occur especially in the facial muscles, neck, shoulders and extremities, often in conjunction with grunts, shouts and other noises.

In 1999 a German research team successfully treated patients with Tourette's syndrome with tetrahydrocannabinol, reporting substantial improvement of both the vocal and the motor tics associated with the disease. Researchers believe that a naturally occurring cannabinoid – anandamide – interferes with dopamine production in the brain and it is this uncontrolled dopamine production that is responsible for the nervous tics and outbursts. Thus, using anandamide to suppress dopamine production could help minimize the tics.

Multiple sclerosis

Multiple sclerosis (MS) is a disease of the nerves in the brain and spinal cord and is the most common nervous disorder in young adults. The nerves are progressively damaged, causing wide-ranging symptoms affecting sensation, body function, movement and balance. The nerve damage is caused by abnormal immune activity that results in inflammation and destruction of myelin (the protective covering around nerve fibres) in the brain and spinal cord. This demyelination affects the way in which nervous signals travel through the central nervous system. Common symptoms of MS include muscle spasms, numbness and tingling, fatigue, blurred vision, unsteady gait and depression.

Several clinical trials on cannabis and cannabinoids indicate that they help mitigate MS symptoms. A 1981 study by Dr Dennis Petro demonstrated beneficial effects of cannabinoids on symptoms of MS. A study in 1983 on the effects of tetrahydrocannabinol on eight MS patients showed subjective benefits in five patients and measured improvements in motor coordination in two participants. Investigators in a 1989 study on a thirty-year-old MS patient concluded 'cannabinoids may have powerful beneficial effects on both spasticity [extra-rigid muscles] and ataxia [loss of coordination and balance] that warrant further investigation'. These results and the recommendations for further research that accompany them continue to be obtained from a variety of researchers. Further anecdotal evidence suggests that cannabis may also help MS patients who experience bladder dysfunction, a condition that can affect up to 90 per cent of those afflicted with the disease. (Once more we see a repeat of history, as urinary problems were regularly treated with cannabis before the twentieth century.)

A review article published in the journal *Drug and Alcohol Review* in 1999 stated that the distribution of cannabinoid receptors in the brain suggests that they may play a role in movement control. On this basis the authors hypothesized that cannabinoids might modify the autoimmune cause of multiple sclerosis. If so, it is possible that cannabis may both relieve symptoms of MS and retard its progression. Since then there have been a number of tests and statements to bear out this belief and scientists are pursuing this area of research.

In the UK, the 1998 House of Lords Science and Technology Committee endorsed cannabis' ability to mitigate symptoms of MS and stated 'We have seen enough evidence to convince us that a doctor might legitimately want to prescribe cannabis to relieve…the symptoms of multiple sclerosis, and that the criminal law ought not to stand in the way'. Researchers from the US Institute of Medicine and the 1997 National Institutes of Health Workshop on the Medical Utility of Marijuana also endorsed the potential usefulness of cannabinoids in MS, concluding that 'survey results suggest that it would be useful to investigate the therapeutic value of cannabinoids in relieving symptoms associated with MS'. The same researchers added that cannabis' potential to treat spasticity and neuropathic pain (pain resulting from nerve damage) could play an adjunctive role in future treatments for the disease.

All in all, these studies indicate that cannabis may substantially control the symptoms of MS and may also play a role in halting the progression of the disease. Based on the results of animal experiments, it appears that cannabinoids may be valuable in a more fundamental way by altering the root cause of MS rather than by simply treating its symptoms.

Nausea and vomiting

The sensations of needing to throw up and the forceful expulsion of the stomach contents in the act of vomiting are two of the most unpleasant sensations we experience.

Countless studies show that chemotherapy, one of the primary agents used to tackle cancer and latterly AIDS, can produce the unpleasant side-effects of nausea and vomiting. As proved during a lengthy series of tests in the late 1970s and early 1980s, cannabis, especially when smoked, provides excellent prevention against such nausea. To such an extent that Dr Thomas Ungerleider, who headed California's Marijuana for Cancer Research programme from 1979 to 1984, felt able to state that 'Marijuana is the best agent for control of nausea in cancer chemotherapy'. (And, it even works with motion sickness.)

Ingestion via smoke is especially helpful: vomiting may reject the very anti-emetic pill that is aimed at suppressing it; whereas smoke continues to work. The pills also take effect too slowly for immediate relief. Since those early tests were carried out, several new and more sophisticated anti-emetic drugs have been developed that can be administered alongside the chemotherapy; these do seem to prevent nausea in a high percentage of patients. How cannabis compares with these new drugs has yet to be ascertained, but since there are a number of patients who remain beyond the help of the new drugs, it might well be suitable in their cases. There are, as ever, the potential problems that come with smoking, but given the immediate needs of cancer patients, they may be taken as worth facing. A growing number of oncologists recommend cannabis to their patients despite its prohibition.

Pain

This unpleasant sensation is often felt as a consequence of tissue disease or damage. Among the many uses of cannabis in pre-prohibition Western medicine was as an effective analgesic (painkiller). This was its role in the many patent medicines sold at the time (see pages 183–189).

After reviewing a series of trials in 1997, the US Society for Neuroscience concluded that 'substances similar to or derived from marijuana…could benefit more than 97 million Americans who experience some form of pain each year'.

The authors of the 1999 US Institute of Medicine report 'Marijuana as Medicine: Assessing the Science Base' describe three types of pain that may be ameliorated by cannabinoids: somatic (external bodily) pain, visceral (internal) pain, and neuropathic (affecting the nervous system) pain. Researchers appear most interested in examining cannabis' ability to relieve neuropathic pain – pain that results from injury to nerves, peripheral receptors or the central nervous system. In the treatment of neuropathic pain traditional analgesics are at best only marginally effective; and such pain is often resistant to standard opiate-based analgesics. Cannabis appears to be more effective in dealing with this particular type of pain. Cannabis may also offer fewer side-effects than the current range of drugs, which can be addictive or induce stomach ulcers, bleeding and kidney failure.

Researchers are just beginning to understand how cannabis and cannabinoids, which appear to be part of a natural pain-control system (distinct from the endogenous opioid system) function as analgesics. Tetrahydrocannabinol taps circuitry at the base of the brain to modulate pain signals in a fashion similar to morphine and other opiates. According to a leading researcher in the field, Dr Ian Meng, 'These results show that analgesia produced by cannabinoids and opioids involves similar brainstem circuitry and that cannabinoids are indeed centrally acting analgesics with a new mechanism of action'. Institute of Medicine researchers agree that 'the available evidence from animal and human studies indicate that cannabinoids can have a substantial analgesic effect'.

Another potential benefit of smoking cannabis in offering pain relief is that patients can control the size of the dose they take into their bodies as they feel they need it and experience more rapid relief than they can with oral formulations. (Developments in such administration include a nasal spray that would mimic the speed of action of smoked cannabis, but cut out the unwanted side-effects of smoking.)

In the UK, the 1998 House of Lords Science and Technology Committee described cannabis' ability to treat both traditional and neuropathic pain, noting that its analgesic effects justified 'rescheduling' the drug (that is, reclassifying it), so doctors could legally prescribe it. They concluded, 'There is scientific evidence that cannabinoids possess pain-relieving properties, and some clinical evidence to support their medical use in this indication'. Similarly, the British Medical Association concluded, 'The prescription of...THC and other cannabinoids...should be permitted for patients with intractable pain'.

Cannabis may help with the 'phantom limb' pain that is known to afflict those who have had amputations. Also it can ease the pain from nerve damage and severe, uncontrollable muscle spasms that are typical results of spinal-cord illness or injury. Growing evidence indicates that cannabis may ameliorate both pain and spasms in patients suffering from spinal-cord injuries. In these cases, the speed with which smoked cannabis starts to work is one of its main benefits; however, it also appears that there are equally efficient non-cannabis analgesics for these forms of pain.

Schizophrenia

This serious mental disorder affects people so that they lose their sense of reality and an ability to function socially in everyday life. The innate intangibility of schizophrenia makes it hard to provide an accurate assessment of the way cannabis might benefit sufferers. For instance the Australian National Task Force on Cannabis suggests that it is far from helpful, citing anecdotal evidence that 'schizophrenic patients who use cannabis and other drugs experience exacerbations of symptoms, and have a worse clinical course, with more frequent psychotic episodes than those who do not'. However, it does accept that such evidence is only anecdotal. On the other hand in his book *Marihuana: The Forbidden Medicine*, Dr Lester Grinspoon (with James Bakalar) cites a pair of studies that found patients with schizophrenia who used cannabis responded better to the disease than non-users. One study reported that patients who smoked cannabis had 'fewer delusions and, above all, fewer of the so-called negative symptoms, which include apathy, limited speech, and emotional unresponsiveness'. The other study concluded that those who used cannabis had a 'lower rate of hospital admissions than those who used no drugs at all. [Respondents] said that cannabis helped them with anxiety, depression, and insomnia'. Grinspoon also notes that from his own clinical experience, people with schizophrenia who regularly use cannabis generally regard it as helpful.

Recent research on a cannabis-like compound produced naturally by the brain – the endocannabinoid anandamide – has begun to isolate the way in which cannabis might work. It appears that anandamide interferes with the effects of nerve cells that transmit dopamine, a message-carrying brain chemical responsible for stimulating movement. Some scientists believe that uncontrolled dopamine production is responsible for some of the symptoms of schizophrenia. Researchers have definitely found that there are dramatically elevated levels of anandamide in those suffering from the disease. This finding implies that the people with schizophrenia may produce extra anandamide to cope with or mediate excess dopamine production. Thus, it is suggested, that if a drug such as cannabis could stimulate anandamide production it might be more effective than the dopamine-blocking drugs traditionally used to treat schizophrenia.

Tumours

A tumour is a mass of tissue caused by abnormal growth. It can be cancerous (malignant) or non-cancerous (benign). In 1975 researchers at the Medical College of Virginia discovered that cannabis is incredibly successful at reducing many types of tumours, both benign and malignant. Although this research was banned in the US (by the Drugs Enforcement Administration, see page 190), it is now continuing elsewhere.

Most recently, a Spanish research team reported that injections of synthetic tetrahydrocannabinol eradicated malignant brain tumours called gliomas in one-third of treated rats, and prolonged life in another third by as much as six weeks. Team leader Manuel Guzman called the results 'remarkable' and speculated that they 'may provide a new therapeutic approach for the treatment of malignant gliomas'. This was the first convincing study to demonstrate that cannabis-based treatment may combat cancer.

Ulcerative colitis

This inflammatory bowel disease affects the large intestine – the colon – so that it becomes inflamed and ulcerated. Symptoms of the disease include bloody diarrhoea, pain and spasms around the anus, fever, loss of appetite and weight loss. A case history attributes definite relief to the smoking of cannabis. A recent animal study on the effectiveness of dexanabinol (a synthetic drug similar to cannabidiol) in patients with ulcerative colitis showed promising results. Researchers reported that treatment of rats suffering from experimental ulcerative colitis 'significantly reduced the anorexia [loss of appetite] and the colonic inflammation associated with this condition compared with untreated rats'.

HORTICULTURE – GROWING CANNABIS

As should be clear from all that has been written already, cannabis will grow pretty much anywhere, with the possible exceptions of outdoor cultivation in the icy extremities of the two poles. A distinguishing factor in outdoor crops is the amount of sunlight on offer: thus, the finest – in other words most potent – cannabis will be found in some of the hottest countries, such as those of the Middle East or Caribbean.

There are three varieties of cannabis horticulture: outdoors, indoors and what is termed 'guerilla gardening', blending one's crop in otherwise quite inauspicious environments. The latter, however, requires no special techniques. Seeds can simply be strewn in suitably secluded areas, and nature's magic will presumably do the rest. The harvesting, of course, will require a certain amount of discretion. What follows is the simplest possible guide to growing. The Internet offers many more, usually written from an American point of view (and thus citing American products with regard to soil, fertilizer and lighting). These, whilst doubtless admirable, do have a certain professionalism about them and practicality, as well as legality, once more rears its head. For all their invariable claims to simplicity, these guides suggest that even the most casual devotee becomes a full-time horticulturist. But they are there and are easily inspected.

Growing cannabis outdoors

The first requirement is seeds. The simplest way to acquire these is to retain some from a recent purchase of marijuana. One may assume that good (strong) 'grass' will offer similar seeds to a new generation. For those who prefer what one might term 'the psychedelic garden centre', the Internet is full of sites offering all sorts of seeds. Many of these suppliers are based in Amsterdam where, as is generally appreciated, cannabis finds as welcoming a home as anywhere in Europe.

In the wild cannabis seeds do not tend to germinate (that is sprout shoots and roots after lying dormant for a while); nature seems to manage perfectly well and cannabis has been a hugely successful plant for millennia. However, as a solo grower one needs to give the seeds a helping hand. First, soak the weeds overnight in warm (not hot) water. Second, discard the small seeds and the green ones – one wants the fat, round, brown seeds. Then, lastly, get

The literal pot plant. Don't, of course, try this at home.

some good potting compost (heavy, clay soil will not do, one wants rich, black loam) and plant the seeds individually, about 2.5cm (1in) apart and about 0.6cm–1.2cm (¼in–½in) deep. Good containers at this stage are yoghurt pots or something of a similar size – the pots can easily be cut away once the plants have rooted and sprouted (a process that can take anything from five days to a fortnight).

Ideal conditions

Keep the earth moist but avoid over-watering since this will rot the growing seeds. (A sheet of polythene over the pots will hold moisture in and prevent the likelihood of over-watering.) One needs to maintain a temperature of between 18°C and 27°C (64°F and 81°F) and, fortunately, this represents the average temperature of a house in the UK from March to October. Special light, mimicking sunshine, is not necessary because germination does not require direct sunlight, just warmth and moisture.

Planting out

Once the second pair of leaves appears on the tiny plant, the seedlings are ready to be moved to wherever it is they will be grown. Planting is usually done in early spring, although in a temperate climate (where summer takes time to get going) one can delay the process for a month or so. In terms of ideal location, choose a sunny spot: up against the wall of a south-facing garden is much recommended as it provides shelter as well as sun. (Given the illegality of the process, one might also wish to consider the need for a degree of privacy from inquisitive eyes.)

The soil into which the seedlings are transplanted should, as far as possible, resemble that in which they germinated. Attention to such detail will reduce any trauma the transplanting process might cause the tiny plants. (One does not need to be a dedicated hippie to appreciate that this physical move should be done as carefully as possible.) Each seedling should be moved into a hole large enough to take the ball of roots and earth in which it has been growing; and it is important not to cramp the roots. The earth should be fairly loose and a little fertilizer should have been added a few days before planting. Plant the seedlings about 30cm (1ft) apart so as to leave sufficient room for the adult plants to grow and expand without becoming too close together. (The move is further helped by watering the still potted seedlings a day or so prior to transplanting them. This loosens the soil and makes it easier to remove the pots.)

Once the plants are safely in the ground they should be kept moist (but not wet) and given the occasional dose of fertilizer. Cannabis grown in the open air usually matures between four and five months after planting out.

Cultivation of cannabis indoors

The primary difference between growing cannabis outdoors and growing it indoors is the level of control the 'farmer' possesses over the crop. As the briefest glance at the myriad guides available makes clear, growing indoors can be a highly complex undertaking, with sophisticated artificial lighting, tightly controlled temperatures, methods of forcing and regulating growth, encouraging intensity of resin and many other complicated aspects of the process. This is a very long way from the old tradition of half a dozen plants in a window box and plenty of TLC. As smokers are aware, some of the most potent brands of modern cannabis are created under these very artificial conditions; certainly the winners of Amsterdam's annual Cannabis Cup are the products of intense dedication. However, even without this level of care indoor cannabis, with some form of artificial lighting, is generally more potent than that grown in the garden (as far as temperate climates go).

For those who would simply like a few plants, growing in their flat or house, the basic instructions are as those for growing outside. Germination first, followed by planting. Whilst the window box or plant pot is quite acceptable, the increasing sophistication and affordability of light bulbs that produce 'artificial sunshine', and which can, in turn, create infinitely longer 'days', mean that cannabis can be grown quite successfully in an otherwise darkened room or even cupboard.

A 'sea of green'

Although one can space indoor plants as one would those grown outside, a popular method of indoor growing is termed the 'sea of green', a technique, like much modern cannabis growing, that was developed in the Netherlands. This method relies on the theory of harvesting lots of small plants, matured early to get the fastest production of buds (and so flowers) available. Instead of growing a few plants for a longer period of time, in the same space many smaller plants are grown that mature faster and in less time. Thus, less time is required between crops and so one crop can be started whilst another is maturing, and a continuous harvest, year round, can be maintained. For spacing indoors, position four plants per $0.09m^2$ (1sq ft) as a good start for seedlings, after that have just one plant per $0.09m^2$ (1sq ft).

Each group of plants will create a 'green canopy' that traps most of the light at the top level of the plants. Little light will penetrate below this level, since the plants are so close together. The grower is attempting to concentrate on the top of the plant and use the light and space to the best advantage, in as little time as possible. It's not the size of the plant, but the maturity and quality of the product that counts. Twice as many plants grown half as big will fill the growing space twice as fast, so harvests take place almost twice as often. It's a good idea to become skilled at picking early flowering plants and propagate (i.e. the growing of new plants from cuttings taken from existing stock) only those that are of the best quality.

Sexing the plants

Cannabis plants reproduce sexually and so exist as separate male and female plants. The female plants provide the desirable resin content and so it is necessary to separate the sexes to ensure the optimum crop. The male plant is taller, 'weedier' and lighter; it has something that resembles a flower but is in fact a pod that contains the anthers – structures that produce the pollen that fertilizes the female ovules. The female plant is shorter, squatter and darker. Female flowers have one or two short hairs (themselves covered in more, microscopic hairs) appearing at the end of a pod-like structure (properly called the 'bracteole' see page 12).

Sinsemilla

Sinsemilla – meaning literally 'no seeds' in Spanish – and known for its potency is the result of choosing to stop the female plant from pollinating. The plant, of course, remains unaware, and as usual it grows the resin-filled pods that would normally create seeds. These 'false' seed pods then swell with this resin, which is filled with psychoactive THC. Its pistils turn red and orange and withdraw into the pods. Then the plant is harvested. Given the heavier-than-average intensity of THC, sinsemilla makes for a very potent smoke.

Harvesting the crop

Once the male plants have been identified they can all be removed other than those required for 'breeding'. When the seedlings have reached the four-month mark, the majority of the females are normally 'pulled', other than those that are being left to flower and so produce seeds. Tie some string round the stalk of the uprooted plants near the roots and hang them upside down in a warm, dark place where they can spend the next few days drying out. Spread some clean paper underneath to catch any flowers that fall off.

Whilst the drying process is continuing, check those male and female plants that are still growing. When the female flowers are fully ripe, pull up the males and shake them gently over the female plants to fertilize them. (This is not vital: nature, as ever, is quite capable of promoting fertilization unaided. The choice is yours.) The males can then be discarded. The remaining females will soon start to wilt, at which point one pulls them up. They, in turn, with their fertilized seeds are hung up to dry. Again, it is useful to spread paper underneath to catch any falling seeds.

When all the leaves are dry and crumbly, the plants can be refined. Leaves and flowers are separated from stalks and seeds. Stalks can be used for tea, or simply thrown out. Seeds are saved for a new planting whilst flowers and leaves (the smaller are the stronger) are stored for later consumption.

Harvesting the cannabis crop.

Hydroponics

Hydroponics, literally 'water works' is a method of growing plants without soil. The essence of hydroponics is control. The grower can supply the plant with the right amount of oxgen, of water and nutrients and ensure that all these come at the proper concentrations and temperatures that the plant needs, recalibrating them to suit each stage of growth. With this level of control hydroponically grown cannabis is amongst the world's strongest

USEFUL TECHNIQUES

How to roll a joint

The rolling of joints is very much a matter of personal preference – the ratio of weed to tobacco (collectively described here as 'the mix'), the length of the joint, the thickness of the rolling paper and the element of ritual are all matters of individual choice. There follows, however, some simple guidelines which, allied to practice, can help anyone produce a pleasant smoke.

Method

Making the roach: It is worth using scissors to cut a roach, as any irregularities, rather than a nice rectangle, can cause kinks in your Rizla, resulting in a harder-to-roll, uglier joint! It should be noted that the shorter the roach, the smoother the smoke – but the harder it is to roll.

Preparing the mix: With all but the stickiest hashish I prefer to use a commercial coffee bean blender. Care should be taken when grinding weed, as overgrinding will reduce your bids to fine powder. Decent grade weed can easily be prepared with scissors, but for hashish the grinder is unsurpassed, ensuring no 'hot rocks'. Also, the hash is lightly earmed helping it to relase its oils for better mixing with the tobacco/weed.

Rolling: When rolling make sure you have the right amount of mix next to the roach – too much and it will be hard to draw on the joint, too litle and the resulting gap can build up oil and clog it. You should not be able to feel where the roach ends and the mix begins, neither should the two overlap.
1. Start with your Rizla flat with the glue strip face down and nearest to you. Distribute the mix evenly, slightly toploading for a cone joint. Place your roach at one end of the Rizla. (Here it is to the right). 2. Hold the roach between the right thumb and first finger. Dealing with the roach end first, move your left thumb and first finger up and down the joint, rolling slightly between the two until a satisfactory shape has been achieved. 3 Next, roll the glue strip away from you and round the roach. Tuck it in all the way up the joint. (*Slight* outward horizontal pressure can be spplied to help maintain a tight joint.) Only roll the paper around once i.e. when you can see the glue strip through the paper, stop. 4.Now lick through the paper, making sure you wet all the glue. Leave approximately two minutes to dry. Then lightly press down the mix in the open end of the joint and twist shut with the excess rizla. 5. Now, in one motion tear off the excess

flap of paper. I usually hold the spliff vertically, roach up, and tear down but you can do it the opposite way round as shown here. Some people even burn the excess. 6. Et voilà, one back-rolled joint.

Rolling the backroll

A back-rolled joint has one main advantage over a regular joint: less paper, and therefore better taste.

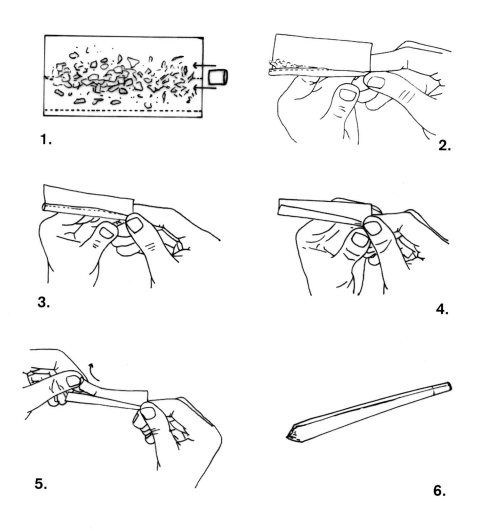

1.

2.

3.

4.

5.

6.

VARIATIONS

While the basic joint, backrolled or otherwise, will suffice for most occasions there are other options on offer. Whether they actually smoke better is debatable. Many are simply down to the number of papers in use, which can be anything from one, to the 'classic' three still preferred by thousands of hash smokers who learned the art back in the Sixties, and right up to a majestic dozen. Of the three illustrated the latter pair are more fancy roach than actual joint, and take far too long for the average smoker to construct. The top one, the 'tulip' is probably better known, being as it is the favoured style of many Amsterdam coffee shops (and hence its name).

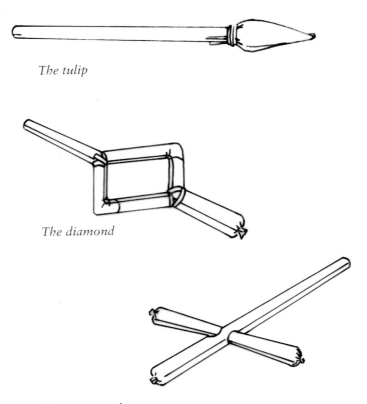

The tulip

The diamond

The cross roads

HOW TO MAKE A BONG

The practice of smoking through a bong was imported from Asia to the West by Vietnam veterans. Today it's a generic term for a Western waterpipe, especially a home-made one. Bongs are useful because they filter out many of cannabis' impurities, such as tar, while leaving the THC, which is non-soluble, intact and undiminished.

This illustration offers the basic parts: the chamber (a container such as a plastic bottle) into which, towards the top, a small air-vent should be pierced; some form of stem or tube which will be inserted into the bottle (a plastic biro tube is adequate), a container for the cannabis, which will be attached to the head of the stem (again, for the simplest version, one can use heavy-duty kitchen foil). The stem must be sealed at its point of entry: chewing gum is feasible, but silicone, as used for DIY, is far more efficient. The container is half filled with water, so that the incoming stem is fully submerged. (Hot water does the best filtering job; cold will cool the smoke.) Cannabis is placed in the foil; the smoker sucks. The cannabis bubbles through the water and down one's throat. Note: when smoking this bong, place the finger over the air-vent while inhaling, keep it there until the bottle is full of smoke. Remove the finger and inhale the chamberful. Each smoker in a group should repeat the process.

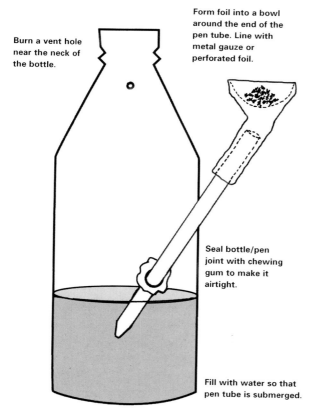

Burn a vent hole near the neck of the bottle.

Form foil into a bowl around the end of the pen tube. Line with metal gauze or perforated foil.

Seal bottle/pen joint with chewing gum to make it airtight.

Fill with water so that pen tube is submerged.

THREE CLASSIC CANNABIS RECIPES

While cooking can offer a variety of pleasures something to expand one's mind is not usually on the menu. Nor, for all its pyschotropic properties, is food what one first considers when thinking about cannabis. Yet cooking with both hashish and marijuana is a time-honoured practice, whether as part of India's religious festivals or as an ingredient in Alice B. Toklas' famous 'brownies', and there are sufficient cookbooks on the market to show that the demand is definitely there. For those who want to explore this particular culinary byway, a list of such books is given on page 239. In the meantime, herewith three 'classic' recipes: for hash brownies, for lassi, and for cannabis ghee, a fundamental ingredient of nearly all cannabis recipes.

WARNING: As anyone who has eaten cannabis is aware, ingesting the drug by mouth means that it takes a good deal longer to feel the effects – it can be up to an hour before one starts to feel high and several more hours before the peak effect finally kicks in – but when they do start, they can be much stronger than those of a joint or two, and will last for many hours. This is based on the way the eaten drug is absorbed: a full stomach slows the process considerably. All of which calls for caution: don't use excessive amounts of cannabis in recipes, and don't eat too much at a sitting. No-one really wants a serving of paranoia with their hashish fudge.

Hash Brownies

These classic 'space cakes' are really simple to make and they taste divine. Don't be tempted to eat too many at once though, they are also very potent if eaten in quantity (see note above).

2–4g (¹⁄14 – ¹⁄7 oz) hashish
115g (4oz) butter, melted
225g (8oz) white sugar
2 eggs, beaten
50g (2oz) self-raising flour
40g (1¹⁄7 oz) unsweetened cocoa powder
¼ teaspoon salt
1 teaspoon vanilla extract (not vanilla essence)
2 tablespoons walnuts, chopped (optional)

1 Preheat the oven to 180°C (350°F)

2 Grease and flour a baking tin about 20cm x 20cm (8in x 8in) in size or use a muffin tin lined with paper cases.

3 In a large bowl, beat together the butter and sugar to form a creamy paste. Add the beaten egg and mix well.

4 Combine the dry ingredients of flour, cocoa and salt in a separate bowl, then stir into the buttery mixture.

5 Now add the vanilla extract and walnuts, if using, and sprinkle in the hash. Give the mixture a good stir.

6 Pour the finished mixture into the baking tin or, if using a muffin tray, pour the mixture into the paper cases in equal measures.

7 Bake in the preheated oven for 25–30 minutes until firm at the edges. (Note: Muffins will cook more quickly than one big tin so check on these after 20–25 minutes.)

8 Cool on a wire rack and then cut into squares; leave the muffins to cool down in their tray.

Something for those munchies – or to bring them on: *plats du jour* **at a cannabis cafe.**

Bhang lassi

This potent drink is time-consuming to prepare but the end result is well worth the effort. You can vary the flavour according to your own tastes, popular alternatives include: vanilla, cinnamon, poppy or sunflower seeds, pistachios and cardamoms.

25g (1oz) marijuana
475ml (16fl oz) water
950ml (32fl oz) warm milk
2 tablespoons blanched and chopped almonds
⅛ teaspoon garam masala
¼ teaspoon ground ginger
½ to 1 teaspoon rosewater
250g (10oz) sugar

1 Boil some water and pour into a clean teapot, cover with the lid.

2 Remove any seeds or twigs from the marijuana and then add it to the teapot and replace the lid.

3 Let this infusion steep for about 7 minutes. Then, strain the marijuana infusion through some muslin cloth into a bowl and save this 'water'.

4 Next, take the marijuana leaves and flowers in your hands and squeeze them, over the bowl of 'water' to extract any remaining liquid.

5 Place the squeezed-out leaves and flowers in a mortar, add a little of the warm milk and slowly but firmly grind them together.

6 Again, pick up the marijuana mixture in your hands and squeeze out as much of the residual milk as possible into a clean bowl nearby. Add the milk from the mortar to this, too.

7 Repeat steps 5 and 6, four or five times, until you have used about 120ml (4floz) milk. By now, the marijuana will have become a pulpy mass.

8 Add the chopped almonds and some more warm milk to the pulpy marijuana and grind in the mortar until it resembles a fine paste.

9 Squeeze this paste by hand and collect any liquid as before. Repeat a few more times until all that is left are some fibres and nut meal. Discard these.

10 Combine all the different liquids that have been collected, including the water the marijuana was first infused in, and add to a new bowl containing the garam masala, dried ginger and rosewater.

11 Add the sugar to taste along with the remaining milk. Chill and serve.

Cannabis ghee

When cooking with cannabis it's best to extract as much of the active ingredient – tetrahydrocannabinol (THC) – as possible and 'store' it within a fat, such as butter or oil. The best such storage medium is ghee (an Indian version of clarified butter), which can be found in most Asian supermarkets or the specialist food section of large, standard supermarkets. Cannabis ghee can be substituted for butter in any recipe. In general, aim for a ratio of 25g (1oz) cannabis to 450g (1lb) ghee, e.g.:

90g (3½ oz) ghee
(⅛ oz) cannabis (if using resin, warm gently in a metal bowl and crumble into a fine powder or use a very fine grater; if using leaf/buds, then dry gently first before grinding to a fine powder.)

WARNING: Be careful when dealing with ghee as it's exceptionally hot when liquefied.

1 Prepare the cannabis so that it's in powdered (or crumbled) form.
2 Measure out the correct amount of ghee for the supply of cannabis you have and put the ghee in a saucepan. Place the saucepan on a gentle heat to melt the ghee.
3 Once the ghee has melted, lower the heat and sprinkle in the cannabis and stir gently. Leave the saucepan on a gentle heat and keep giving the mixture an occasional stir to make sure that all the THC is extracted – this usually takes about an hour to happen.
5 When the ghee is cooked, sieve the mixture through a clean muslin cloth into a pan or bowl and leave to cool.

Some cannabis cookbooks

The Art and Science of Cooking With Cannabis: The Most Effective Methods of Preparing Food & Drink With Marijuana, Hashish & Hash Oil by Adam Gottlieb. Ronin Pub., 1993. Paperback.
Gourmet Cannabis Cookery; The High Art of Marijuana Cuisine by Dan D. Lyon. Loompanics Unlimited, 1999. Paperback.
Aunt Mary Jane's Baking With Pot by Mary Jane, Peter Gorman. High Times Press, 2000. Paperback.

A GLOSSARY OF CANNABIS

The vocabulary of cannabis is unsurprisingly substantial, whether in its standard terms or in the vast and ever-evolving range of slang coined by its users. This glossary has a little of both: the primary section outlines some of the major terms associated with the drug; the list that follows after gives samples from the lexicon of nicknames that have been created for it.

bhang n. [mid-19C+] the dried leaves of the cannabis plant, with the flowering tops removed when it is carefully prepared. The leaves are exposed to sun and dew alternately (thus they both wilt and dry) and once cured are pressed and stored. It is smoked or taken in a drink or, when combined with other ingredients, as a sweetmeat. The term, loosely translated as 'hemp', probably comes from the Sansrkit *bhanga* 'breaking'; however, the explorer and Orientalist Sir Richard Burton preferred the Coptic nibanj, a preparation of hemp. Of this *Hobson-Jobson*, the dictionary of the Raj, notes: 'here it is easy to recognize the Homeric Nepenthe' – the drug of forgetfulness.'). Bhang is the term in most Indian languages; one also finds the Persian equivalent *bang* and the Arabic *banj* and *benj*.

A bong, from Thai *baung* literally a 'cylindrical wooden tube.'

bong n. [1970s+] a kind of bowl-shaped water-pipe used for smoking marijuana (the specifics vary according to the maker); thus (Aus.) bongineering, bongology, the construction of such pipes. From Thai *baung*, literally a 'cylindrical wooden tube'. The bong was imported from the East to the US, and thence to the West, by Vietnam veterans who had first encountered this form of pipe – then most commonly made of a bamboo tube – for smoking hashish, marijuana or opium.

bud n. [1980s+] 1. the nickname for marijuana. Other names include Indonesian bud, crystal bud, mud-bud (homegrown), budlies and budulars. Budiqette is the ritual that attends on smoking. 2. the flowering heads of the female cannabis plant in which the majority of THC (tetrahydrocannabinol) is concentrated.

cannabis n. [mid-16C+] 1. common hemp. 2. *Cannabis sativa, Cannabis indica, Cannabis ruderalis*: any of three varieties of the hemp plant which are smoked or eaten for their intoxicating and/or hallucinogenic properties. The word comes from the Greek *kannabis* and Latin *cannabis*, both meaning hemp. Deeper origins may be seen in Indo-European and Semitic languages, which are found in Europe and the Middle East, where the Sanskrit roots 'an' and 'ang' recur in a variety of 'cannabis' terms. Linguists have also stated that the notional prehistoric German, Teutonic, would offer *khanipiz* or *khanapiz*.

A dried flowering head of high-strength 'skunk' cannabis, grown in Europe under lights.

charas n. [mid-19C+] a variety of potent hashish (and today generic for hashish in India). The term comes originally from the Persian and meant 'a leather bag for pressing hemp dust'.

chillum n. [1950s+] (originally West Indian) a funnel-shaped pipe, traditionally made of terracotta, used for smoking cannabis. From Hindi *chilam*, the bowl of a *hugga* or *hookah* (literally 'round casket') pipe that contains the tobacco and balls of charcoal. In India *chillam* also means 'a pipeful', which is asked for in the same way as one might request 'another glass' of alcohol.

ganja n. [mid-19C+] 1. a preparation of the female flowering tops of the hemp plant (to which the intoxicating resin clings). The word comes from Hindi *ganjha*, dried hemp. The tops are put in heaps and trodden or manually rolled; they are then allowed to dry (and wilt) in the sun, are rolled again, dried again, until the whole mass is of the right consistency and sufficient resin has been pressed out of the tops to make the mass stick together. 2. In the West Indies, notably Jamaica, a highly resinous form of marijuana prepared from the flowering tops and leaves of selected plants and usually smoked. The term was presumably imported to the Caribbean by indentured Indian labourers.

hashish n. [late 16C+] the concentrated resin of the cannabis plant, smoked for its intoxicating or hallucinogenic property. From Arabic: *hashish*, dry herb, hay, the dry leaves of hemp powdered, the intoxicant thence prepared.

Hashish names: Afghan (af); Black Pak; black rock; brown; chitral; commersh; double zero; finger; gold seal; Leb; Nep; rocky; temple ball.

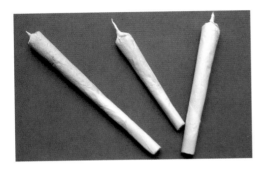

joint n. [1930s+] a hand-rolled cigarette composed of cannabis and tobacco; a cigarette composed of marijuana. The cannabis/tobacco mixture usually has a small cardboard filter. The original joint, coined circa 1920, was an opium pipe, but the cannabis use represents the same image: the 'joining' of the drug and the medium with which it is smoked. The word has also been used to refer to the hypodermic syringe used for injecting heroin or cocaine.

As most people encounter it: a trio of joints – the best-known slang for 'cannabis cigarettes' and the way in which most people first encounter it.

marijuana n. [late 19C+] a preparation of the hemp plant – based on the dried leaves, flowering tops and stems of the cannabis plant – used as an intoxicating and hallucinogenic drug. The origin of the term is debatable: the popular root is the jocular use of the name 'Mary Jane'; other suggestions veer between the Mexican *mariguano* or Panamanian *managuango*, both of which mean intoxicant. It should be noted that here again, one can see the Sanskrit 'an'/'ang' root, linking it to cannabis itself.

resin n. the separated resin, whether crude or purified, obtained from the cannabis plant. It is seen as the dried brown or black resinous secretion of the flowering tops of the cannabis plant. Resin is the basis of hashish and is obtained by threshing herbal material against a wall, rubbing herbal material between the palms of the hands or against a rubber sheeting, crushing dried herbal material to a powder that is later kneaded or immersing the plant material in boiling water and then removing the resin from the surface.

The raw material: three lumps of cannabis resin or hashish.

roach n. [1930s+] 1. marijuana. 2. a marijuana cigarette. 3. the remaining unsmoked portion of a marijuana or hashish cigarette. The term is an abbreviation of 'cockroach'. It is linked, presumably, to the popular Mexican song 'La Cucaracha', with its lyrics, '*La cucaracha, la cucaracha, / Ya no puede caminar; / Porque no tiene, porque le falta / Marijuana que fumar.*' [loosely translated: 'The cockroach can't walk any more because he has no marijuana to smoke.']

sensimillia n. [1980s+] (abbreviated to. sense, sensi, sess) From the Spanish for 'seedless'. A variety of extremely potent marijuana; it has no seeds because it is kept away from male pollen during the blooming process; instead, these female marijuana plants make more tetra-hydrocannabinol (THC), thus intensifying the potency of the effects.

A flowering head of a female marijuana (*Cannabis sativa*) plant. The resin that makes for the drug's potency can be seen gleaming on the leaf.

shotgun v., n. [1960s+] 1. v. to blow cannabis smoke into someone else's mouth by reversing the cigarette inside one's own mouth and blowing; the other person places their open lips near the stream of smoke and inhales for as long as they can; thus shot-gunning, the act of doing this; 2. n. the act of thus transferring smoke. 3. n. a type of pipe used for smoking marijuana

THC abbr. [1940s+] (-)3,4-trans-delta-l- tetrahydrocannabinol, the only one of the sixty cannabinoids present in the cannabis plant that is both highly psychoactive and present in large amounts, usually 1–5 per cent of the plant by weight. In short it is the ingredient that makes those who consume cannabis 'high'. Recent research has discovered nerve receptors in the brain that are stimulated by THC. This suggests that the body produces its own version of the substance. The receptors are found mainly in the cerebral cortex, which governs higher thinking and in the hippocampus, which is a locus of memory.

Glossary of common nicknames for cannabis

A-bomb
Acapulco gold
Acapulco red
ace
African
African black
airplane
Alice B. Toklas
angel drink
angel dust
Angola
ashes
astroturf
atom bomb
atshitshi
Aunt Mary
Baby
baby bhang
bad seed
bad shit
bale
bam
bambalacha
bamber
bammies
bammy
bash
beat
belyando spruce
benny mason
birdwood
bitchweed
black bart
black ganja
black gold
black gungeon
black gungi
black gunion
black mo
blend
block
blonde
blowing smoke
blue de hue
blue moons
blue sky blond
bo
bobo
bohd

boo
boo-boo bama
boogie
boom
bottleneck
brand X
brick
broccoli
brownie
buddha sticks
bullion
bumbud
bundle
bush
butter
butter flower
Cabbage
Cam
Cambodian red
Cambodian trip
Canadian black
canamo
canappa
candy blunt
catnip
cavite all star
cavvy
cess
charge
cheeb
cheeo
cheever
chiba
Chicago black
chira/chicharra
chronic
chunky
co
cochornis
coli/collie
colom
Colombian
Colombian red
Colorado cocktail
Columbus black
commercial
commersh
compellance weed
Congo bush

corn
cosa
crazy weed
cryp
cryptonite
crystal bud
culican
Dacca
dagga
dak
da kine
dank
dank nugs
dawamesk
dew
diablito
diambista
dimba
ding
dinkie dow
dirt grass
ditch
ditchweed
djamba
do-do
domestic
dona juanita
don jem
Don Juan
donk
doobage
doradilla
d.p.
draf
draf weed
drag weed
Durban poison
durog
durong
duros
dust
Endo
esra
Fine stuff
finger lid
fir
fire
flower
four-twenty

frios
fry daddy
fu
fuel
fumo
Gage
gangster
ganja
gash
geeba
geek
gimmie
gizzy
goblet of jam
gold
golden leaf
gold star
gong
good giggles
good stuff
goody-goody
goof
grass
grata
greefo
green
greenbud
greenery
green goddess
greenhouse
greens
green stuff
green tea
greeny
greeter
grief
griff
groceries
gunge
gungeon
gunjeh
gunny
Ha-ha
haircut
happy grass
Hawaiian
hay
hemp
herb

hocus-pocus
holy herb/weed
homegrown
homestone
houdini
hydro
Indian hay
Indo
Indonesian bud
i-shence
Jabooby
jane
jarpot
jay smoke
Jim Jones
johnson
jolly green
joy
joy hemp
joy smoke
joy weed
juanita
Juan Valdez
Kaffir tobacco
kali/cooly
kali mist
kaya
k.b.
Kentucky blue
key
k.g.b.
kill
killer
killer weed
kiwi green
kumba
La
lace
lah
lakbay diva
lambsbread
laughing grass
laughing weed
leaf
leno
liesca
lima
limbo
little smoke
l.l.
loaf
loc

loco
locoweed
loho
long green
love boat
lovelies
love weed
lubage
lucy
lumber
Lumbo
Machinery
macon
magic smoke
maharishee
mah jong
majat
Malawi grass
Manhattan silver/white
marigold
marihoochie
mariweegee
mary
mary and johnny
mary ann
mary jane
mary warner
mary weaver
meg/meggie/meggs
meth
Mexican brown
Mexican bush
Mexican green
Mexican red
mezz
miggle
m.j.
mo
modams
mohasky
monte
montezuma gold
mooca
moota
moragrifa
mota
mother
mother nature
Mr Mason
mu
mud-bud

mule
Nalga de angel
Nam black
New York City
silver
Nixon
noble weed
northern lights
nugs
nuke
O.j.
olly
Pakalolo
Panama cut
parsley
pat
pocket rocket
pod
pot
p.r.
pretendica
primo
Queen Ann's lace
Ragweed
railroad weed
rainy day woman
rama
rangoon
rasta weed
reefer
righteous bush
rooibaard
root
rope
rosa marie
rose mane
roulie
Salt and pepper
Santa Marta gold
sassafras
scissors
seeds
sen
sensimilla
sess
shake
sheeba
siddi
silver pearl
skunk
sleng teng
snop

soul
spear
speed boat
splay
spliff
square mackerel
squirrel
stickies
stink weed
stop
straw
sucker weed
sugar weed
super bio
superskunk
sweet Lucy
Taima
takkouri
tea
Texas tea
tex-mex
Thai (stick)
thing
thirteen
thumb
tical
timber
tree of knowledge
trees
trom
turbo
turnip greens
Viking
vitamin T
Wac/wack
wana
weedhead
weed tea
whacky baccy
wheat
white-haired lady
white widow
wisdom-weed
X/x-ing
Yeh
yellow submarine
yen pop
yerba
yesca
Zacatecas purple
zambi
zoom

CHRONOLOGY

6000BC Cannabis seeds are used for food in China.

4000BC Textiles made of hemp are used in China.

2737BC In China, in the world's first medical text, or pharmacopoeia, *Pen-Ts'ao Ching* by Shen Nung, cannabis is referred to as a 'superior' herb.

1500BC Cannabis-smoking Scythians sweep through Europe and Asia, settling and inventing the scythe.

1200–800BC The Hindu sacred text *Atharvaveda* ('the Science of Charms') cites cannabis as 'Sacred Grass', and lists it amongst the five sacred plants of India. It is used medicinally and ritually as an offering to Shiva.

700–300BC Scythian tribes leave cannabis seeds as offerings in royal tombs.

700–600BC The Zorastrian *Zend-Avesta*, an ancient Persian religious text refers to bhang as Zoroaster's 'good narcotic'.

circa 500BC Gautama Buddha is said to have survived on a daily diet of a single hempseed.

500BC The Scythians introduce hemp into Northern Europe.

450BC The Greek historian Herodotus, writing in *The Histories*, tells of the Scythians of Central Asia throwing hemp onto heated stones under canvas: 'as it burns, it smokes like incense and the smell of it makes them drunk'.

AD45 St Mark establishes the Ethiopian Coptic Church. The Copts claim that marijuana as a sacrament has a lineage descending from the Jewish sect, the Essenes, who are considered to be responsible for the Dead Sea Scrolls.

70 Roman Emperor Nero's surgeon, Dioscorides names the plant *Cannabis sativa*. He praises cannabis for making 'the stoutest cords' and for its medicinal properties.

170 Roman physician Galen (the most influential physician of the next half-millennium), alludes to the psychoactivity of cannabis seed confections.

400 Hemp cultivation is recorded for the first time in England.

512 The first botanical drawing of cannabis appears in the codex 'Constantinopolitanus', a contemporary materia medica.

500–600 The Jewish Talmud mentions the euphoriant properties of cannabis.

800 Muhammed, founder of Islam, allows cannabis but forbids the use of alcohol.

1000 The English word 'hempe' is first listed in a dictionary as a translation of the Latin *cannabum*.

1090–1256 During this period, in Khorasan, Persia, Hassan-i Sabah, the 'Old Man of the Mountain', recruits followers to commit assassinations. Legends develop around these warriors' supposed use of hashish. They lead to some of the earliest written tales of the discovery of cannabis' inebriating powers and the supposed use of hashish.

1100–1125 Hashish smoking develops throughout the Middle East.

1150 Europe's first paper mill is established under Muslim management. Hemp is the primary ingredient in the paper-making process and it remains so for the next 850 years.

1155–1221 The Persian legend of the Sufi master Sheik Haidar's personal discovery of cannabis is originated and spreads across the Middle East. Although ultimately specious, it helps spread the plant's mythology.

1200–1300 Arab traders bring cannabis to the Mozambique coast of Africa.

circa 1250 The oldest monograph on hashish, *Zahr al-'arish fi tahrim al-hashish*, is written. It has since been lost.

1271–1295 The Italian traveller Marco Polo includes the story of Hassan-i Sabah and his hashish-taking 'assassins' in his best-selling 'Journeys'.

1379 In Egypt, Emir Soudon Sheikhouni prohibits cannabis consumption amongst the poor, destroys the crops, and has offenders' teeth pulled out.

1484 Pope Innocent VIII singles out cannabis as an unholy sacrament of the Satanic Mass.

1526 The first recorded use of hashish in Afghanistan.

1545–1555 Invading Spanish conquistadors bring cannabis cultivation to South America.

circa 1550 The epic poem, *Benk u Bode*, by the poet Mohammed Ebn Soleiman Foruli of Baghdad, deals allegorically with a dialectical battle between wine and hashish.

1619 The British colony of Virginia makes hemp cultivation mandatory; most of the newly founded colonies follow suit.

1621 Robert Burton's book *The Anatomy of Melancholy* claims cannabis is a suitable treatment for depression.

1753 *Cannabis sativa* classified by Swedish botanist Carolus Linnaeus.

1783 The French biologist Jean Baptiste de Lamarck classifies another species of cannabis – *Cannabis indica*.

1798 After invading Egypt Napoleon bans his troops from buying and using cannabis. The prohibition fails and some even take samples back to France.

1809 Antoine Sylvestre de Sacy, a leading Arabist, reveals the linked etymology of the words 'assassin' and 'hashishin'.

1839 The homeopathy journal *American Provers' Union* publishes the first of many reports on the effects of cannabis.

1840 Medicinal preparations with a cannabis base are available in America.

1841 Psychologist and 'inventor' of modern psychopharmacology and psychotimimetic drug treatment, Jacques-Joseph Moreau de Tours documents physical and mental benefits of cannabis after experimenting with a variety of animals and then human mental patients.

1841 In his essay 'On the Preparation of the Indian Hemp or Ganja' the Irish physician Dr William O'Shaughnessy introduces cannabis to Western science. It is the first of hundreds of future medical studies extolling the drug's efficacy as a medicine.

1843 The 'Club des Hashichins', ('Hashish Eater's Club'), whose bohemian membership includes the writers Gautier, Balzac and Baudelaire, is founded.

1854 US writer Bayard Taylor publishes his essay 'Visions of Hashish'.

1856 The colonial British government begins taxing India's trade in ganja and charas.

1857 US writer and drug experimenter Fitzhugh Ludlow publishes *The Hasheesh Eater*.

1857 Smith Brothers of Edinburgh start to market a highly active extract of *Cannabis indica* for use as a basis for innumerable tinctures.

1860 First governmental commission study of cannabis and hashish conducted by Ohio State Medical Society. It catalogues the conditions for which cannabis is beneficial, which includes neuralgia, mania, asthma, muscular spasms, epilepsy, uterine haemorrhage, alcohol withdrawal and loss of appetite, amongst many others.

1868 The Emir of Egypt makes the possession of cannabis a capital offence.

1870 Worried about cannabis use among Indian workers, South Africa passes a law forbidding the smoking, use or possession of hemp by Indians.

1870 Cannabis is listed in the *US Pharmacopeia* as a medicine for treating various ailments.

1876 Hashish is served freely at the American Centennial Exposition.

1877 The Sultan of Turkey makes cannabis illegal, to little effect.

1890 Sir Russell Reynolds, Queen Victoria's personal physician, prescribes cannabis for menstrual cramps. He claims in the first issue of *The Lancet* medical journal that cannabis 'when pure and administered carefully, is one of the most valuable medicines we possess'.

1890 The Greek Department of Interior prohibits the import, cultivation and use of hashish. Neighbouring Turkey follows suit.

1894–1896 The Report of the Indian Hemp Drugs Comission, running to over three thousand pages in seven volumes, is published. This inquiry, commissioned by the British government, concludes: 'There is no evidence of any weight regarding the mental and moral injuries from the moderate use of these drugs....Regular, moderate use of ganja or bhang produces the same effects as moderate and regular doses of whiskey.'

1895 Supporters of the Mexican rebel Pancho Villa celebrate marijuana use in their song 'La Cucaracha', which tells how one of Villa's men goes looking for his '*marijuana por fumar*'.

1910 Anti-marijuna campaigners play the race card as the right-wing press (under newspaper tycoon William Randolph Hearst) attacks the influence on whites of African-American 'reefer' use in the jazz clubs of New Orleans. At the same time Mexicans are reported to be smoking cannabis in Texas. Both groups are portrayed as frenzied beasts under the influence of the drug.

1911 South Africa bans cannabis.

1912 The Hague Convention for the Suppression of Opium and Other Drugs is drawn up, requiring parties to confine to medical and legitimate purposes the manufacture, sale and use of opium, heroin, morphine and cocaine; cannabis is not included, but a move towards its control is posited.

1912 'Essay on Hasheesh' by Victor Rolson is published.

1915–1927 Cannabis begins to be prohibited for nonmedical use in the US, especially in south-western states: California (1915), Texas (1919), Louisiana (1924), and New York (1927).

1923 The South African delegate to the League of Nations claims mine workers are not as productive after using *dagga* (cannabis) and calls for international controls. The UK insists on further research before any controls are imposed.

1924 At the second International Opiates Conference, the Egyptian delegate calls for and obtains international controls on cannabis (erroneously classified as a 'narcotic').

1925 The 'Panama Canal Zone Report' is conducted due to the level of cannabis use by soldiers in the area and concludes that there is no evidence that cannabis use is habit-forming or deleterious. The report recommends that no action be taken to prevent the use or sale of cannabis.

1928 In the UK, the Dangerous Drugs Act (1925) becomes law and cannabis is made illegal in Britain.

1930 Henry Ford makes an experimental automobile out of hemp, using hemp paint and hemp fuel.

1931 The Federal Bureau of Narcotics is formed with Harry J. Anslinger at its head. By now 29 US states have banned non-prescription cannabis.

1937 The Marijuana Tax Act is passed in the US. Cannabis is outlawed by Federal law.

1941 Cannabis is dropped from the *US Pharmacopeia*.

1943 Colonel J. M. Phalen, editor of the *Military Surgeon*, declares that: 'The smoking of the leaves, flowers, and seeds of *Cannabis sativa* is no more harmful than the smoking of tobacco...It is hoped that no witch hunt will be instituted in the military service over a problem that does not exist'.

1944 The New York Mayor's LaGuardia Report 'The Marijuana problem in the City of New York' concludes that smoking marijuana does not lead to addiction in the medical sense of the word, that juvenile delinquency is not associated with marijuana smoking and that the publicity concerning the catastrophic effects of marijuana smoking in New York is unfounded. Anslinger responds by denouncing LaGuardia and threatens doctors with prison sentences if they dare carry out independent research on cannabis.

1948 Anslinger now declares that using cannabis causes the user to become peaceful and pacifistic. He also claims that the Communists would use cannabis to weaken the American's will to fight.

1951 According to United Nations estimates, there are approximately 200 million marijuana users in the world, the major centres being India, Egypt, North Africa, Mexico, and the United States.

1952 The first cannabis arrest in the UK is made at the Number 11 Club in Soho, London.

1961 UN Treaty 406 Single Convention on Narcotic Drugs seeks to outlaw cannabis use and cannabis cultivation worldwide and to eradicate cannabis smoking entirely within 30 years.

1962 President Kennedy (a user of cannabis for pain relief) sacks Anslinger.

1962 The first hashish (rather than *kif*) is made in Morocco.

1964 In the US, the first 'head shop' for the sale of cannabis-related goods is opened by the Thelin brothers in San Francisco.

1964 Cannabis' active ingredient tetrahydracannabinol, THC for short, is first isolated.

1966 The folk singer Donovan becomes the first celebrity hippy to fall foul of the law.

1967 UK police raid the Beatles and the Rolling Stones in a series of high-profile cannabis-related arrests.

1967 The UK legalization campaign group SOMA publishes a petition in the *Times*; it urges legalization of cannabis. The Beatles and many well-known figures sign it. Some 3000 people hold a 'smoke-in' in Hyde Park.

1967 Abbie Hoffman and the Yippies mail out 3000 joints to addresses chosen at random from the New York City phonebook. They offer the recipients the chance to discover what all the fuss is about, but remind them that they are now criminals for possessing cannabis. The mail-out, secretly funded by Jimi Hendrix, attracts huge publicity.

1967 'Release', the first UK drug advice centre, is founded.

1968 In the UK, a Home Office select committee, chaired by Baroness Wootton, looks at the 'cannabis question'. Its report, delivered in 1969, concludes that cannabis is no more harmful than tobacco or alcohol, and recommends that the penalties for all marijuana offences be reduced. Delivered in 1969 it is immediately rejected by the government.

1970 In Canada the LeDain Report recommends that serious consideration be given to the legalization of personal possession of marijuana. It finds that cannabis use increases self-confidence, feelings of creativity and sensual awareness, facilitates concentration and self-acceptance, reduces tension, hostility and aggression and may produce psychological but not physical dependence. The report recommends that possession laws be repealed and notes that the debate on the non-medical use of cannabis 'has all too often been based on hearsay, myth and ill-informed opinion about the effects of the drug.'

1970 R. Keith Stroup founds NORML the 'National Organisation for Reform of Marijuana Laws' in the United States.

1971 The UK's Misuse of Drugs Act lists cannabis as a Class B drug (along with amphetamine and codeine) and bans its medical use. The Act prescribes a maximum five years' imprisonment for possession.

1972 In the Netherlands, the Baan Commission presents a report to the Dutch Minister of Health suggesting that cannabis trade below 0.25kg ought to be considered as a misdemeanour only. In the US, the Nixon-appointed Shafer Commission urged the use of cannabis be relegalized, but their recommendation was ignored. President Nixon says 'I am against legalising marijuana'.

1973 The US Shafer Commission declares that personal use of marijuana should be decriminalized as should casual distribution of small amounts for no or insignificant renumeration.

1973   Oregon becomes the first US state to take steps towards the legalization of cannabis.

1973 Nepal bans cannabis shops and export of charas (hand-rolled hash).

1973 The Afghan government makes hashish production and sales illegal.

1975 In the US, the FDA establishes a 'Compassionate Use' programme for medical marijuana.
1976   The Netherlands adopt a tolerant attitude to cannabis and many coffee shops and youth centres are allowed to sell it.

1978 New Mexico becomes the first US state to make cannabis available for medical use.

1980 Paul McCartney spends ten days in prison in Japan for the possession of cannabis.

1980s Morocco becomes one of, if not the largest, hashish-producing and exporting nations.

1988 In Washington, DEA Judge Francis Young states that 'Marijuana in its natural form is one of the safest therapeutically active substances known to man'. He recommends that medical use of marijuana should be allowed, for certain life- or sense-threatening illnesses. The DEA administrator rejects the ruling. The US Senate adds $2.6 billion to federal anti-drug efforts.

1988   A United Nations' Convention against illicit traffic in narcotic and psychotropic substances continues to include cannabis.

1990   The discovery of THC cannabinoid receptors in the human brain is reported in the science journal *Nature*.

1992   The Frankfurt Charter is signed by 17 European cities agreeing to tolerate social use of cannabis.

1992   The UK government issues licences to grow cannabis for industrial uses or scientific research.

1995   The Henrion Commission Report, the official French State Commission in charge of drug policy supports decriminalization of cannabis and calls for a two-year trial period of regulated retail trade in cannabis. The French government rejects these proposals.

1998   Italy decriminalizes possession of drugs and permits small-scale cultivation of cannabis for own use.

1998   Belgium officially decriminalizes cannabis, making it impossible to be prosecuted for personal consumption.

1998   The British House of Lords rules that, based upon the evidence presented for them, the government should make cannabis available to the sick without further delay, but that they are against legalization for recreational use. Jack Straw, Home Secretary, rejects the Report.

2001   The UK government announces its intention to move cannabis from class B to class C, making possession a non-arrestable offence.

FURTHER READING

Searching on the Internet for the word 'cannabis' gives one 689,000 hits; 'hashish' an added 89,000 and 'marijuana' a daunting 1.28 million. Many will of course be irelevant, but the resources for cannabis research and information as offered by the Net are virtually illimitable. With that in mind, one can offer but the tiniest subset. These have helped in the compilation of this book. They all contain a great deal of information on site, plus a wide range of links.

Probably without rival for the researcher is the Schaffer Library of Drug Policy at http://mir.drugtext.org/druglibrary/schaffer/. This offers information on specific drugs (as well as cannabis, it deals with all 'recreational' drugs) plus wide-ranging sections such as: Major Studies of Drugs and Drug Policy; Basic Information on the War on Drugs; US Government Publications Related to Drug Policy; Historical Research on drugs and drug policy; The Drug Legalization Debate – Opinions, arguments, and debate manuals; Miscellaneous Statements on Drug Policy and Media Articles related to drug policy. It has a vast selection of texts, many quite rare, that can be read online.

Other sources include:
http://www.druglibrary.org/ (The Drug Reform Coordination Network)
This offers links to all major online research centres.
http://www.drugscope.org.uk/library. This is effectively an electronic card index of the library of Drugscope UK, Britain's primary drug research centre. One can visit this Library, and read its books and journals, but the website is only useful for reference.
http://www.lindesmith.org/, now the Drug Policy Alliance, offers a large and diverse online library of full-text drug and drug policy-related documents.
http://www.ccguide.org.uk/index.html (the UK Cannabis Campaigners Guide)
http://www.erowid.org/ The Vaults of Erowid, another drug resource centre: as well sections dealing with plants and drugs, freedom and law, mind and spirit and arts and sciences, it features an extensive Bibliography.

Books

Many of the most important books, essays and articles that deal with cannabis, whether as to its history, its horticulture, its properties or the international laws established to suppress it, are available online. For those who prefer the printed text, here are some of the more interesting books on the subject. Like so much else on this topic, this is a tiny example – and most of these books will have their own large bibliographies.

Abel, Ernest L. Marijuana, *The First 12000 Years*. New York: Plenum, 1980.
Andrews, George, and Vinkenoog, Simon, eds. *The Book of Grass: An Anthology of Indian Hemp*. New York: Grove Press, 1968.
Barrett, Leonard E. *The Rastafarians*. Boston: Beacon Press, 1977.
Berke, Joseph, and Hernton, Calvin C. *The Cannabis Experience: An Interpretive Study of the Effects of Marijuana and Hashish*. London: Peter Owen, 1974.

Bonnie, Richard H., and Whitebread, Charles H. *The Marihuana Conviction: A History of Marihuana Prohibition in the United States*. Charlottesville: Virginia University Press, 1974.

Brecher, Edward M., and the editors of Consumer Reports. *Licit and Illicit Drugs*. Boston: Little, Brown, 1972.

Cherniak, Laurence. *The Great Books of Hashish*. Vol. 1 of 9 vols. Berkeley, California: And/Or Press, 1979.

Cohen, Sidney. *The Therapeutic Potential of Marijuana*. New York: Plenum, 1976.

Clarke, Robert Connell *Hashish!* Red Eye Press, 1998.

Davenport-Hines, Richard. *The Pursuit of Oblivion*. London, Weidenfeld & Nicolson, 2000.

De Ropp, Robert S. *Drugs and the Mind*. New York: St. Martin's Press, 1957. Revised edition, Delta Books, 1976.

Frank, Mel, and Rosenthal, Ed. *Marijuana Grower's Guide* (Deluxe Edition). Berkeley, California: And/Or Press, 1978.

Gottlieb, Adam. *Cooking With Cannabis*. Berkeley, Cal.: And/Or Press, 1978.

Grinspoon, Lester, MD. *Marijuana, the Forbidden Medicine* (revised and expanded edition). New Haven, Connecticut: Yale University Press. 1997.

Grinspoon, Lester. *Marihuana Reconsidered*. Quick American Archives, 1994.

Herer, Jack. *The Emperor Wears No Clothes* Quick American Archives, 1996.

Inglis, Brian. *The Forbidden Game: A Social History of Drugs*. New York: Scribners, 1975.

King, Jason. *The Cannabible* Ten Speed Press, 2001.

LeDain Commission. 'A Report of the Commission of Inquiry into the Non-Medical Use of Drugs'. Ottawa: Information Canada, 1974.

Ludlow, Fitzhugh *The Hasheesh Eater: Being Passages from the Life of a Pythagoreun*. New York: Harper and Bros., 1857.

Margolis, Jack S., and Clorfene, Richard. *A Child's Garden of Grass: The Official Handbook for Marijuana Users*. North Hollywood, California: Contact Books, 1969. Reprinted, New York: Pocket Books, 1970. Revised edition, New York: Pocket Books, 1975.

Mayor's *Committee on Marihuana*. 'The Marihuana Problem in the City of New York'. Lancaster, Pa.: Jacques Cattell Press, 1944.

Mechoulam, Raphael ed. *Marijuana: Chemistry, Pharmacology, Metabolism and Clinical Effects*. New York: Academic Press, 1973.

Mezzrow, Milton, and Wolfe, Bernard. *Really the Blues*. New York: Random House, 1946

Mikuriya, Tod H., ed. 'Marijuana: Medical Papers, 1839–1972'. Oakland, California: Medi-Comp Press, 1973

Pollan, Michael. *The Botany of Desire*. New York: Random House, 2001

Rosenthal, Franz. *The Herb: Hashish versus Medieval Muslim Society*. Leiden: E. J. Brill, 1971.

Schofield, Michael. *The Strange Case of Pot*. Baltimore: Penguin Books, 1971.

Sloman, Larry. *Reefer Madness: The History of Marijuana in America*. New York: Bobbs-Merrill, 1979.

Solomon, David, ed. *The Marihuana Papers*. New York: Bobbs-Merrill, 1966.

Watts, Alan W. *The Joyous Cosmology: Adventures in the Chemistry of Consciousness*. New York: Random House, 1965.

Weil, Andrew T. *The Natural Mind: A New Way of Looking at Drugs and the Higher Consciousness*. Boston: Houghton Mifflin, 1972.

INDEX

Acknowledgements

The author /publishers would like to thank
Lucien Green, Gabriel Green, Craig at the Royal
Botannical Gardens Library at Kew.

Captions p.1 An Albanian child plays amongst the family's crop of cannabis. p.2 A marijuana farmer holds buds from his crop, California USA, 1982. p.4 A police helicopter carries a bunch of confiscated marijuana at the end of a rope after a police raid on a pot grower in Mendocino county, California, 1993. pp. 8–9 A Kirlian photograph of a leaf of the hemp plant (*Cannabis sativa*), showing the electromagnetic discharge around the edges. pp.32–33 'Manners and Customs', one of four drawings depicting the manufacture and use of narcotics, by an Amritsar artist, circa 1870. pp.76–77 *Smoking Hashish*. Emile Bernard (1868–1941) Musee D'Orsay. pp.132–133 Lies, damned lies, and (erroneous) statistics: Harry Anslinger pushes through the Marijuana Tax Act, 1937. pp.172–173 Pots of cannabis-based preparations to be used in India's Ayurvedic medicine.

Picture Library Credits 1 STR/Reuters; 2 Roger Ressmeyer/Corbis; 4 Phil Schermeister/Corbis; 6 Mike Bluestone/Science Photo Library; 9 Garion Hutchings/Science Photo Library; 11 Rex Features; 15 John Augustus Atkinson/Stapleton Collection/ Bridgeman Art Library; 16 Romeo Ranoco/Reuters; 18–19 Bettmann/Corbis; 21 Henry Diltz/Corbis; 23 Pascal Goetgheluck/Science Photo Library; 27 Bettmann/Corbis; 30 Redferns; 32–33 British Library/Bridgeman Art Library; 35 Andes Press Agency; 37 Ancient Art and Architecture Collection; 38–39 Bettmann/Corbis; 40 Rex Features; 44 Lindsay Hebberd/Corbis; 47 Mike Meaner; 49 Ancient Art and Architecture Collection; 50 British Library/ Bridgeman Art Library; 53 David Browne/Parachute Pictures; 54 Jeffrey L. Rotman/Corbis; 59 Mary Evans Picture Library; 63 Peter Johnson/Corbis; 66–67 Daniel Lainé/Corbis; 70 Owen Franken/ Corbis; 74 Rex Features; 76–77 Giraudon/ Bridgeman Art Library; 79 Michael Maslan Historic Photographs/Corbis; 85 National Library of Medicine/Science Photo Library; 90 JFB/The Art Archive; 92 Horace Vernet/Hermitage Museum/Scala; 95 Mary Evans Picture Library; 98–99, 102 Jean-Loup Charmet/Bridgeman Art Library; 105 Mary Evans Picture Library; 106, 111, 117 Hulton|Archive; 119 *Illustrated Police News*; 122–123 (Main image) The Kobal Collection/ Universal (Clockwise from top left) The Kobal Collection, The Kobal Collection/20th Century Fox , The Kobal Collection/20th Century Fox, The Kobal Collection/Paramount; 124 Michael Ochs/Redferns; 125 Bettmann/Corbis; 126–127 Bojan Brecel/Still Pictures; 128 Rex Features; 130 Herb Green/Redferns; 132–133 Harry J. Anslinger Collection/Historical Collection and Labor Archives; 138 Rex Features; 143 Hulton|Archive; 144 Rex Features; 146–147 (All images) The Advertising Archive; 148 Bettmann/Corbis; 151 Rex Features; 152 Bettmann/Corbis; 157 Rex Features; 159 Timepix/Rex Features; 160, 162–163, 166 Rex Features; 168–169 Furry Freak Brothers/Rip Off Press Inc.; 171 Peter Morgan/Reuters; 172 Dinodia Picture Agency; 175, 176 David Hoffman Photo Library; 179 The Wellcome Trust Medical Photographic Library; 183 The Advertising Archive; 187 Mary Evans Picture Library; 193, 194 Rex Features; 197 Prof. K. Seddon & Dr. T. Evans, Queen's University Belfast/Science Photo Library; 200–201, 202 Rex Features; 203 David Hoffman Photo Library; 204 (top) David Hoffman Photo Library; (bottom) Medipics; 205 David Hoffman Photo Library; 227 Science Photo Library; 231 Cristina Pedrazzini/Science Photo Library; 237 Rex Features

First published in the United States in 2002 by
Thunder's Mouth Press
An imprint of Avalon Publishing Group
Incorporated
161 William Street, 16th Floor
New York, NY 10038

Text © Jonathon Green 2002
Illustrations on pages 12, 227–229 © Lotte
Oldfield 2002
The moral right of the author has been asserted

Layout: Ghost. Designer: Philip Delamore.
Commissioning editor: Kate Oldfield. Copy
editor: Nikki Simms. Indexer: Derek Copson

A CIP catalogue record for this book is available.

ISBN 1 56025 476 9

Colour reproduction at Classic Scan Pte Ltd,
Singapore
Printed and bound at Phoenix Offset Ltd, Hong
Kong

2 4 6 8 10 9 7 5 3 1